Cross-Dressing
in Chinese Opera

Cross-Dressing
in Chinese Opera

Siu Leung Li

香港大學出版社
HONG KONG UNIVERSITY PRESS

Hong Kong University Press
14/F Hing Wai Centre
7 Tin Wan Praya Road
Aberdeen
Hong Kong

© Hong Kong University Press 2003, 2006

Hardback edition first published 2003
Paperback edition first published 2006

ISBN-13: 978-962-209-832-9
ISBN-10: 962-209-832-0

Secure On-line Ordering
http://www.hkupress.org

British Library Cataloguing-in-Publication Data
A catalogue record for this book is available
from the British Library.

Printed and bound by Liang Yu Printing Factory Ltd., in Hong Kong, China

CONTENTS

ILLUSTRATIONS

ACKNOWLEDGEMENTS

Special thanks to Stephen Ching-kiu Chan for his great advice for the right move at critical moments; Professor Meaghan Morris for reading part of the manuscript and her continuous encouragement; all my dear colleagues in the Department of Cultural Studies at Lingnan University, for breathing into the workplace with a quality I shall call "Mozartian simplicity": perfect harmony and clear form interwoven in sincerity with a touch of optimistic naïveté. A special thank-you to my teachers at the University of Massachusetts Amherst for my intellectual direction: Professors David Lenson, Ch'ing-mao Cheng, Sarah Lawall, Elizabeth Petroff and William Naff. I am grateful to the Chinese opera performing artists in Beijing, Shanghai and Hangzhou who kindly shared with me their ideas. I am most indebted to Ms Yang Fengyi and Mr Wen Ruhua for their precious time and generous firsthand materials. Thanks to Professor David Der-wei Wong for bringing my attention to the art of Mr Wen. Sincere thanks to Professors Bell Yung, K. Y. Wong, Yu Siu-wah and Michael McClellan for their support and comments on the "Liang-Zhu" chapter at various stages of its development. I thank Brown University for the Joukowsky Postdoctoral Fellowship in Comparative Literature and East-Asian Studies from 1996-98, the Division of Humanities at the Hong Kong University of Science and Technology for two Direct Allocation grants in 1996 and 1999. Thanks to Camilla Lai and especially Chan Shek for providing excellent research assistance. A big thank-you to Yung Sai-shing, Chan Sau-yan and Wong Wang-chi for their consistent intellectual support in all these (post-) colonial years of living anxiously and likely to be, in the near future, dangerously.

INTRODUCTION

The history of Chinese opera can, among many possible characterizations, be instructively described as a series of narrative fragments of "gender trouble." In the beginning (of its textual history), Chinese theatre was to a significant extent constituted in and through gender b(l)ending. The enchantment of the figure of the "male *dan*" [*nandan/qiandan*] — female impersonator — remains a stubborn residual element in the cultural imagination in some layers of contemporary Chinese societies. The various kinds of queer possibilities in the social and cultural locality of Chinese opera, epitomized in its commanding tradition of cross-dressing, have yet to be examined in depth. Viewing the various dramatic and performance texts and practices as signs of historical processes and drawing on "those gestures or analytical models which dramatise incoherencies in the allegedly stable relations between chromosomal sex, gender and sexual desire" (Jagose 3), the present study investigates Chinese opera in terms of the highly mediated representations of gender and sexuality embodied in the prevalent practice of theatrical cross-dressing presented in a variety of discourses, texts and artifacts from the eighth century to the present time. An attention to the ideological and cultural complexities of theatrical transvestism throughout history underlies this interrogation. This research employs an interdisciplinary approach to address the prominent configurations of cross-dressing and pertinent issues in classical Chinese drama and today's regional operas, placing them in a larger intercultural context of (trans)gender, theatre, and literary studies. This study draws on contemporary cultural theory as well as traditional historical scholarship.

Cross-dressing has had a unique significance in Chinese opera from the time of the Yuan Dynasty (1271–1368) — the period scholars generally cite as the "golden age" in the history of Chinese theatre. Female players at this time played a leading role on stage, often cross-dressing to play male roles. Later, in the Ming (1368–1644) and Qing (1644–1911) periods, both private troupes maintained by the gentry and public theatres prominently featured cross-dressing. Private troupes were predominantly female theatres composed of girl actresses performing in the most elegant Kunqu style, and theatre historians have attributed an important role in the development of the performance of this opera to these young women.

The prevalence of the boy actor/boy actress in the public theatre, which was monopolized by men during the mid- to the late Qing period saw the fetishization of this cross-gendered body into an object of composite desires and taboos. In the modern era, although all-female troupes gradually emerged in the public theatre from the last years of the nineteenth century on, the climax of the sexually ambiguous figure of the male *dan* as a cultural obsession occurred in the golden age of Beijing opera, the 1920s to the 30s, culminating in the body of the ultimate icon Mei Lanfang (1894–1961). In the People's Republic of China, male cross-dressing is at the brink of extinction under the state's cultural policy of discontinuing male *dan* training at Chinese opera schools, while female cross-dressing has survived and developed in a relatively more benign climate than its male counterpart.

The complexity of ideological operations and subversive resistance coded in gender play in Chinese opera is the pressing issue to be examined here. My research goes beyond "the historians' favored position of judging and evaluating theatre history from the text" and embraces investigations of the stage performance itself, i.e., "the very impermanence and fleeting transitoriness of the supercharged experiential moments" which "create problems for historians" (Ferris,

Acting Women x). The significance of this characteristic of *performing*, I believe, goes even further in problematizing relations of power. It is this unstable process that makes the theatre a cultural practice highly dangerous to the powered hierarchy and a possible transforming agency in society for the disempowered. Chinese opera has always been policed and co-opted by rulers through regulation, censorship, prohibition and imposed silence (to borrow Foucault's terms), because it embodies disruptive social immediacy and occupies sociocultural locations embedded among the common people throughout history.[1]

Focusing on the indeterminacy of cross-dressing as a destabilizing force, the present study begins by offering a revisionist narrative of a history of Chinese theatre in transvestism, with special reference to the participation of female players in the cultural (re)production and subversion of gender differences in various historical periods. Recent cultural criticism has pointed out that the patriarchy

> has lately been dislodged from the status of a transhistorical and unitary phenomenon which was accorded it by varieties of essentialist feminism — the ongoing (and by no means conclusive) attempts to combine class and gender analysis have dismantled it into a historically and culturally variable, complex and even contradictory amalgam of institutions and attitudes.
>
> (Loomba 1)

If this is the case, then it is time to begin a revisionist history of the potential resistance of Chinese female players as agents in negotiating patriarchal containment and male ideological authority in performance, with special attention given to the historical and cultural specificities of Chinese theatre in various periods. If feminist and gender criticism is understood to be "based in very precise political struggles and practices and remains inseparable from them," if it is important *not* to "homogenize, colonialize, and neutralize the specificities of struggles" (Alice Jardine 15), it is my intention to locate the specificities of the history of women in theatre in imperial China. An awareness of cultural differences is vital in cultural studies today, which are inescapably "inter"; at the same time we also dance on the common ground of "gender-conscious analyses" across cultures "when the culture in question uses gender as a major organizing principle, in social organization, in *mentalités*, or as is most usual, both" (Malti-Douglas 6). Through a comparison with the experience of women in European theatre, I shall try to particularize the experience of women in Chinese theatre. Discourses on the female performer and the female theatrical tradition in Chinese theatre will be reread to locate points of tension in this cultural production relating to the definition of feminine and masculine difference, and struggles over gender definitions and hierarchies.

Early modern English drama copiously produced plays built upon cross-dressing as a structural device, specifically that of heroines in male disguise.[2] Looking at the extant works of classical Chinese drama, the Ming Dynasty writer Xu Wei (1521–1593) appears to have pioneered the use of cross-dressed heroines in his famous twin plays of *Ci Mulan tifu congjun* [Maid Mulan joins the army in her father's stead] and *Nü zhuangyuan cihuang de feng* [The female top graduate declines a she-phoenix and gets a he-phoenix].The former play portrays a military woman and the latter a gentry woman. Written in the mid-sixteenth century, both plays were dramatizations of existing tales and the story of Hua Mulan had been especially popular, thanks to the household narrative poem "Mulan ci" [The ballad of Mulan], which dates back to the sixth or seventh century. A mainland Chinese critic believes that Xu "inspired" writers in the late Ming and early Qing period to produce a series of cross-dressing plays (Ye Changhai, *Quxue yu xijuxue* 87). It is notable that many of the authors of these works were female writers from the Jiangnan area.[3] Equally significant is the predominance of plots involving female cross-dressing.[4] The only exception is the play *Chen Zigao gaizhuang nanhou ji* [Chen Zigao disguises as a male queen] by the late-Ming playwright and drama theorist Wang Jide (?–1623), who was a student of Xu Wei. With its plot concerning male cross-dressing, the play is unique in the extant works of classical Chinese drama, and opens up a site for the free contention of power for transgender and queer reading. The female cross-dressing dramas form a category of their own that interlocks with issues surrounding the (self-)representation of women and feminine writing. These plays, either written by men to glorify the ability of women, or written by women aspiring to become men via the imaginary of the cross-dressed heroine, largely resulted in upholding and perpetuating the existing male-dominated power hierarchy. Dorothy Ko rightly argues that

> [i]nstead of challenging the ideology of separate spheres by mixing and redefining gender roles, these heroines encouraged their female readers to aspire to be more like men.
>
> (140)

She further points out that prominent woman writers in seventeenth century China were "[r]evered as honorary men in real life" (139). We can interpret the gender condition during this period in China as one of the existence of a single ideal sex — the male — that the secondary sex aspires to transform into. This kind of textual representation does not disturb the premisses of the patriarchal gender system. In the negotiation between containment and subversion, the early new historicist view of authoritarian closure has long been engaged by a more dialectical view attending to social agency, and Ko is quick to point out that these woman writers through their "temporary transgressions of gender boundaries . . . had begun to blur the centuries-old boundary between inner and outer and between the male and female spheres" (141–2).

The interactive negotiation between subversion and containment is my central concern in investigating Chinese opera's three most celebrated figures — the concubine, the woman warrior and the "Butterfly Lovers" and their related dramatic and performance texts in connection to transvestism. These texts are interrogated as fields of contention of desire, power and queer identities. These figures have been reappropriated not just on the Chinese operatic stage in modern times, but also in the process of the globalization of media culture. Concubine Yu of the Hegemon King and Hua Mulan the woman warrior have been capitalized by transnational cinema (*Farewell My Concubine* [1993]; *Mulan* [1998]), whereas the Butterfly Lovers have been implicated in the queer web of subtexts of the "M. Butterfly" imbroglio.

The complexities of gender politics in representing resistance and containment must be situated in the contemporary social-cultural context in order to be effectively decoded. While Hua Mulan, the woman warrior disguised as a man happily returns to the social position demarcated for her by Confucianism at the end of the day, thereby suggesting little room for transformation, perhaps a greater threat is posed to the patriarchy via the bodies of the other military heroines more prevalent on today's Chinese opera stage. Women who do not take up gender disguise yet are potentially more threatening as "virtual cross-dressers" in their resplendent costumes of masculine armor.

If we assert that the (at times double and triple) cross-dressed players on the Chinese opera stage are conflicting figures taking to task any claim to an authentic or stable gender identity, I find this destabilization no better represented than in the ubiquitous "Zhongdu Xiu Yuan drama mural" — incontrovertibly the ultimate artifact bequeathed us from the classical Chinese theatre of the fourteenth century. This wall painting is seen in the form of photographs or illustrations of various sizes and quality in any number of books and journals concerning Chinese theatre, published in many languages. The wall painting has inspired numerous studies by scholars across cultures and disciplines over the past few decades. These narratives (ranging from historical through anthropological to feminist) and the visual renditions of the mural are re-scrutinized to illustrate a moment of crisis in gender representation in the context of Chinese opera — the studies present conspicuously contradictory interpretations of the mural precisely because they have uniformly presumed the stability of gender representation.

All in all, from the historical practice of cross-dressing through representations in performance, text, and artifact, gender crisscrossing in Chinese opera has inevitably generated the subversive notion of gender as performance, and thereby disrupted the stable order of binary gender. Alisa Solomon argues that "the mutability of human identity promised by theater, and figured by the norm of transvestism, is precisely what makes theater the queerest art, perennially subject to railing by those with a stake in promoting the 'natural order' of the status quo" (*Re-dressing the Canon* 2). Rereading classical Chinese theories on acting the other sex in relation to the categories of *zhen* [real] and *jia* [fictional] reveals that femininity and masculinity are notions constituted in performance, not essential qualities defined as real or fake given by nature.

The male construction of and obsession with the ideal feminine in Chinese drama, as literature, and theatre, as a performing art, are unique critical issues to be addressed. This specific case of the gendering of genre — discoursing Chinese opera in feminine tropes — will be investigated in the context of power contention between the binary poles of Kunju opera and Beijing opera, "prettiness-eroticism" [*se*] and "artistry" [*yi*], the orthodox and the unconventional, the exquisite and the vulgar, the elitist and the popular. The cross-dressing practice prevalent on stage, combined with the obsession with prettiness-eroticism and artistry in traditional theatre aesthetics, have engendered the subversive feminine embodied most poignantly in the male *dan* in Beijing opera, and has rendered Chinese theatre an unstable site of ideological contestation subsuming a simultaneous perpetuation and dismantling of bipolar gender notions and social-political hierarchies. The male *dan,* this most obsessed and obsessive body in Chinese opera is now passing into extinction in the appearance of "the last female impersonator in Beijing opera." The significance of the male *dan* lies in both the performance aesthetics and the gender politics of this special theatrical configuration of the boundary-crossing (fe)male body. The present critique situates its last object of study in context by swinging back to the discourse of sexuality and theatrical cross-dressing in modern China, which is the subject of discussion in the prologue.

In maneuvering queer theory's fluid formulations of gender and sexuality and the cultural tactic of using "queer as a verb," I hope that it "may hold transformative potential" (Louise Allen 20) — that critical reflections on traditional culture can be made to speak to the concerns of today's ideological resistance to political hegemony and cultural dominants, through the unveiling of polyvalent meanings of gendering and gendered differences that are constructed, reproduced, dismantled, and contested in that particular site of Chinese culture — Chinese opera.

NOTE ON TRANSLATION AND ROMANIZATION

Unless otherwise indicated, all translations are my own. I have generally followed the pinyin system for transliteration of Chinese names and words, but for names of Chinese authors from Hong Kong and Taiwan, I have followed the transliteration systems used in these places. Other exceptions are cases in which the Wade-Giles system was originally used in a quotation, and those terms, such as "Confucius" and "Tao," that are already familiar to English readers.

The textual instability produced in *translating* culture is inevitable in intercultural studies such as the present one. The problem is more seriously exposed when highly cultural-specific terms and concepts are involved. I would like to clarify, as much as possible, several Chinese terms that are used throughout the present work.

We are told that Confucius once said, "If something has to be put first, it is, perhaps, the rectification of names . . . When names are not correct, what is said will not sound reasonable; when what is said does not sound reasonable, affairs will not culminate in success. . ." (*Analects* 118). If what Confucius calls "rectification of names" [*zhengming*] has its validity and advantages in reality, Japanese theatres seem to have attained this in Western discourse. *Noh* and *kabuki*, for instance, have established themselves in English as "Noh theatre" and "Kabuki theatre," they are not referred to as some kind of "opera." Whereas the traditional Chinese theatrical genre of *xiqu* (very literally, *xi* means "play/drama" and *qu* "songs/music"), whose name has posed great problems in its translation, has not been able to "rectify" its name in an alien discursive practice. Therefore, I shall briefly define my use of the terms "[Chinese] drama," "[Chinese] theatre," "[Chinese] opera," and "[Chinese] music drama" which are used in various contexts to *represent* the Chinese term *xiqu*. "Chinese drama" is used when the emphasis is literary, while the term "drama" is used as the standard "equivalent" of *xiju* on related occasions (literally *ju* means "drama"; the two characters *xi* and *ju* are often used interchangeably). "Chinese theatre" leans more on the stage, performance, and the spectator-player interaction in the performing location. I use the term "Chinese opera" to refer to the whole tradition of the practice of musical theatre in China, as well as to denote the various regional traditional theatres in performance today, as commonly adopted by ethnomusicologists (e.g., Bell Yung; Chan Sau Yan; Rulan Chao Pian). In addition I have employed "Chinese music drama" to translate *xiqu* only in book and article titles in order to render a more literal translation (this has nothing to do with the Wagnerian notion of *musikdrama*).

It is necessary to note the delicate difference between the two similar and often interchangeable terms *kunqu* and *kunju*, since this form of Chinese opera is a major reference throughout this study. Kunqu is a specific style of singing and music that prevailed from the mid-sixteenth century to the nineteenth century. The music theatre that performs in Kunqu is nowadays called Kunju (for further explanations, see Wu Junda 3–6; see also Wang Shoutai, ["Xulun"] 1). Although Beijing opera has been the best known in the West of the some 350 regional theatrical forms in mainland China today (*Zhongguo dai baike quanshu: xiqu, quji* 1), Kunju opera has remained the most revered form in China. It traces its heritage back to the classical dramatic genre of *chuanqi* [literally "marvelous tales"] in the Ming Dynasty, and is esteemed for its classical elegance and perfection in musical expression, stylized acting, dancing and movement. The uniqueness of this form lies in its convention of simultaneous singing and dancing. Due to its appropriation by the literati for three hundred years and its long career of domination in the history of Chinese theatre, Kunqu became the forebearer and foundation of many subsequent forms of Chinese theatre. The training of Beijing opera performers is very much based on the tradition of Kunju opera, and a considerable portion of the repertoire of Beijing opera is either directly taken or adapted from that of Kunju opera (see Lu Eting for a performance history, Hu and Liu for a comprehensive history; for a brief English explication of Kunqu, see Scott, Introduction; for an explanation of the music of Kunqu as well as Beijing opera, see Liang Mingyue). The term Kunju is a modern usage; in classical dramatic criticism, Kunqu refers to both the musical style and the theatre itself. I shall in general use the term Kunju opera, except in translating classical sources where the term Kunqu was used in the original, and when making historically specific references to this theatrical genre.

The highly culturally specific and multivalent Chinese term *se* renders any translation problematic and contingent. For this, I shall adopt either "prettiness-eroticism" or simply "prettiness," depending on the context of utterance. I provide further explanation in the "Gendering Genre: The Dialectic of Prettiness-Eroticism and Artistry" section of chapter 8.

PROLOGUE

ONE

LU XUN'S STRAIGHT WORDS AND
THE QUEER WORLD OF CHINESE OPERA

Lu Xun, Transvestism, Chinese Opera

Lu Xun (1881–1936), arguably the best known modern Chinese writer in his own country as well as in the West, once drew an analogy between theatre and politics by way of a critique of the cultural practice of the female impersonator in Chinese opera.[1] In a short article entitled "Zui yishu de guojia" [The most artistic country] (March 30, 1933), Lu Xun gives a scathing criticism of the hypocrisy and deception in the politics of Republican China. According to him, the Republican government and the corrupt politicians participating in the game of power had hitherto been reluctant to give real democracy to the Chinese people. Interestingly, he opens this mordant article with something that not only has no immediate connection with sociopolitical criticism, but is also seemingly antic — cross-dressing; or perhaps more accurately, transvestism — as Lu Xun obviously implies an inevitable circulation of sexual and erotic energy in a culture which, according to his own unique interpretation, is remarkable for its artistry in cross-dressing:

> Our country China's greatest, most eternal and universal "art" is man playing woman. The worthiness of this art lies in the fact that it is entrancing on both sides; or we can call it "the middle path"! What men see is "playing woman"; what women see is "man

playing." On the surface it is neutral; in the inside it is of course all
the same still a man. However, were it not for the disguise, could it
still be an art?

(503)

The focus of the present cultural project is not Lu Xun or his
ideas about Chinese opera. Nor is my critical focus the artistic revival
and aesthetic celebration of a traditional heritage presumably endowed
with essentially given greatness.[2] Instead, I find that Lu Xun's brief
passage betrays the politics of Chinese opera as a cultural practice: his
appropriation of transvestism as a trope in his pungent political protest
coincidentally yet appropriately reproduces significant cultural
assumptions concerning power as the object of struggle at the
intersecting site of cross-dressing, gender construction, and homo/
hetero-eroticism in relation to theatre in a culture where theatre has
historically been both an integral cultural product, and one of the most
unstable cultural products. Lu Xun's essay is therefore a fitting and
revealing starting point for my critique which aims at offering an
alternative kind of cultural history structured as an investigation of
traditional Chinese theatre and drama in terms of the highly mediated
representations of cross-dressing, gender, and erotic desire in various
discourses in the imperial past, as well as modern times.

Using a rhetorical device that can be related to *xing* in traditional
Chinese poetics — i.e., "to begin by mentioning something else to
elicit what is intended to be sung about,"[3] Lu Xun begins by talking
about transvestism, which leads immediately to the political critique
which is his real concern. Two lines further down, he writes:

> . . . this Republic has been suffering from the lack of maintenance
> in these years. Even [the color of] its signboard has totally peeled
> off, just like the rouge on the *huadan*'s face.

(503)

Lu Xun uses the Chinese opera role-type (*hangdang*) of *huadan*
(the "witty young female," a sub-category of the *dan* — the female
role-type)[4] as a simile to embellish his sociopolitical rhetoric. In this
context, the transvestism he refers to is obviously the male cross-dressing

tradition on the Chinese stage. We can also see that Lu Xun is unmistakably biased against traditional Chinese theatre as a cultural form: why should the facial makeup of the *dan* player — who is inevitably a male transvestite[5] as contextualized in Lu Xun's assertion of "China's greatest, most eternal and universal 'art' is man playing woman" — be necessarily and always in a state of "peeling off," as is presumed in his lines? Contrary to Lu Xun's appropriation, the cultural signification of the figure of the *dan* has more often been an obsession with intense feminine prettiness that is also associated with a heightened sensuality.

Renowned for his relentless attacks on the evils of old Chinese culture, Lu Xun seldom talked about Chinese opera and it seems that he had never held a high opinion of it. When he did mention Chinese opera, it was often in a negative context, as is the case in point: male cross-dressing and its ultimate iconic representation on the stage (i.e., the *dan*) is linked with corruption in politics and age-old sociopolitical evils lurking in the shadow of a false democracy. Mei Lanfang, generally acknowledged to be the greatest Beijing opera *dan* performer of this century,[6] a *female impersonator*, who was also a catalyst for Bertolt Brecht's influential theory of *Verfremdungseffekt*[7] — is harshly criticized by Lu Xun in a two-part essay "Lüelun Mei Lanfang ji qita" [Brief comments on Mei Lanfang and other topics] (1934), in which Mei is censured as an artist distanced from the masses. Lu Xun also remarks in the same essay that the artistic conventions of traditional Chinese drama are superficial (637–41).

Lu Xun, extolled in 1940 by Mao Zedong as "a chief commander of the revolution of culture in China, a great literary writer, a great thinker, and a great revolutionary" and thus apotheosized in the cultural and academic discourses in the Mainland,[8] was also arbitrarily misread as having expressed enlightened ideas about Chinese opera, as exemplified by Huang Shang's 1953 article "Lu Xun xiansheng dui xiqu de yixie yijian" [Mr Lu Xun's comments on Chinese music drama]. Recently however, some scholars in mainland China have voiced different opinions, revising the orthodox perspective and criticizing Lu Xun for his negative views on Mei Lanfang and his disparaging criticism of Chinese opera as a cultural heritage.[9] While everything Lu

Xun said, including his criticism of Chinese opera, was apotheosized as infallible in mainland China, the renowned Japanese sinologist Yoshikawa Kōjirō criticized Lu Xun's views on Chinese theatrical transvestism as impudent in a 1956 article:[10]

> I think more should have been said about the criticisms on Mei Lanfang's artistry. His marvelous acting embraces the essence of the artful [*sizen denai*][11] in the expression of an old man of sixty disguising as a woman and speaking in an exact female voice. Once Lu Xun's criticism of this was rather rude: "Our country China's greatest, most eternal and universal 'art' . . . ."

("Bai Ranhō so no ta" 598)

Immediately following these critical remarks, Yoshikawa quotes the same passage that I analyzed at the beginning of this chapter. Although Yoshikawa comments on this passage out of its political context, his comments expose Lu Xun's biased criticism of theatrical transvestism and Chinese opera.

The change in the interpretation and re-evaluation of Lu Xun's criticism of Chinese opera and Mei Lanfang indicated the opening up of some layers of intellectual space in post-Mao China. As a result there has been an audacious reaffirmation, perhaps excessive at times, of the value of the same traditional musical theatre that was banned as a "feudal evil" for some ten years during the so-called Great Proletarian Cultural Revolution (1966–1976).

Cross-Dressing and the Circulation of the Sexual and the Erotic

One of the assumptions underlying Lu Xun's brief statement is betrayed by his automatic consignment of the traditional Chinese stage to the domain of male cross-dressing. An uncritical and unconscious notion of *the* tradition of Chinese theatre as *essentially* a *male* transvestite theatre has been unknowingly inscribed in quite a few minds. This misleading impression was created, to a great extent, by the legitimation of Beijing opera as "the national theatre" in recent times — in Taiwan however, this regional opera is still often referred to as *guoju*, i.e., theatre of the country. Beijing opera, one among the more than three hundred traditional operatic forms existing in China today, has dominated the Chinese stage for more than a hundred years and it is still regarded as the leading form among all regional operas.[12] It was exclusively a male theatre until the last decade of the nineteenth century when its stage gradually accommodated female performers who had been excluded from the public theatre for about two centuries. In line with this recent perception of "the male transvestite Chinese theatre" held by many people (Chinese and non-Chinese alike), the male cross-dressing practice has forever been foregrounded, signifying the ideology of a male theatre and the patriarchy that produced it. Therefore, we find that the passage by Lu Xun which grew out of this specific cultural context and expresses in various ways its ideological assumptions, has already taken for granted male transvestism as a norm on the traditional Chinese stage, thereby rendering invisible the parallel existence, long history and strong presence of female theatrical performers, including female cross-dressers, who first came into prominence simultaneously with the maturity of Chinese theatre in the thirteenth century. In fact, male performers occupy only the margins in the theatrical records of that time.

This female intervention in the theatre inevitably renders the contention of gender paradigms on the Chinese stage a much more complex cultural signification than conventionally envisioned. Although the public stage was monopolized by men in the eighteenth and nineteenth centuries, female performers thrived in the private theatre until at least the latter part of the eighteenth century. One must also not overlook the fact that the actress emerged again as a disruptive force in a male-centered cultural formation in twentieth century China, with one of the prominent examples being the success and popularity, since the mid-1920s, of the (almost) all-female regional opera Yueju from Zhejiang province.

By exposing the average impression of "male cross-dressing as the essential Chinese theatrical tradition" as a partial misconception, I do not mean that the historical *fact* (however fluid its discursive constitution would be) of the female presence on the Chinese stage has been intentionally neglected or totally suppressed by scholars and others concerned. On the contrary, this is a historical fragment that has constituted a part of the existing academic discourse on traditional Chinese theatre. From theatre history to literary history, the history of sex workers to the history of women, the "actress" has been an integral piece among the various objects of the historical narrativization used to validate a patriarchal ideology. The urgent issue is that an ideological repression of female agency is often reinforced by male-centered representations of women performers in the conventional construction of the history of Chinese theatre. The female tradition has to be recharacterized and reinvented in ways different from the conventional writing of literary-cultural history.

Lu Xun's comments also interestingly point to another issue that deserves critical attention in a cultural approach to Chinese opera; that is, the engendering of the spectacle and the spectatorial gaze, and the circulation of the sexual and the homo/hetero-erotic in a multiple crisscrossing within and across the binary hierarchies of man/woman, sex/gender, (male) gaze/(female) object, erotic desire/object of desire — all subsumed within a heterosexual matrix. The sexual ideology implied in Lu Xun's passage is that heterosexuality is the only *normal* sexuality and that women and men's sexual relations with other women/ men in the theatre (it so happens that the one he refers to is characterized by cross-dressing) are read in the matrix of compulsory heterosexuality: "What men see is 'playing woman'; what women see is 'man playing'" in his words. The multiple crisscrossing possibilities of non-heterosexual gender and sexual positions are erased: with the male spectator seeing "the *man* playing woman" and the female spectator seeing "the *woman* played by man" (homosexual); the male and female spectator each sees both man and woman in the player's body (bisexual), or even sees beyond sexual dimorphism and envision a "third sex, third gender" (Herdt). This heterosexist assumption, commonly shared by various peoples and cultures, is so prevalent that in the Anglo-American critical discourse it also underpins some radical critiques of gender and sexuality by prominent critics of early-modern English theatre, which, similar to Beijing opera before the twentieth century, was distinguished by its solely male transvestite theatrical practice.[13] An intervention from a "third category" perspective is required for an effective critique of theatrical cross-dressing and the circulation of the sexual and the erotic in traditional Chinese theatre, which in imperial times was constituted as a site of rival sexual ideologies that constantly put orthodoxies into question. Chinese opera must not be domesticated by the heterosexual binarism of modern times. Lu Xun's sexual ideology toward same sex desire was already a far cry from that of imperial times. Suffice it to say that the present study is undertaken with an awareness of the Foucauldian critique that "homosexuality" as a form of identity is a modern European invention (*The History of Sexuality*), and that China in imperial times had relatively open and tolerant attitudes toward male and female same sex love (Van Gulik, *Sexual Life in Ancient China*; Xiaomingxiong; Hinsch).

Transvestism in Lu Xun's essay is also juxtaposed with political anomaly. However, Lu Xun does not in any way imply any causal relation between the two, while the traditional discourse on *renyao* (human prodigy/human monster) does.[14] The decline of a dynasty, corruption in the court and the bureaucracy, or natural disasters were attributed in the imperial past to the appearance of deviants, a category which included people who disguised themselves as the other sex, or had hermaphroditic sexual features and were non-classifiable as either female or male within a rigid heterosexual binary structure. Nevertheless, the analogical juxtaposition between transvestism and sociopolitical crises appends Lu Xun's remarks to the discourse of the "human prodigy" in imperial China as another utterance of gender anxiety in modern times. Hidden in Lu Xun's words is the assumption of a focal center, a stabilizing (hetero)sexual identity as a frame of reference for the production of steady meaning in a world operating on gendered binary systems. Therefore to him, as well as many others, "in the inside it is of course all the same still a man."

A radical rereading of this short article of Lu Xun's is most instructive in the context of cultural criticism in relation to sociocultural discourses in mainland China today. The opening of China after the death of Mao Zedong in 1976 and its rapid economic reforms (in contrast to its die-hard reluctance in political reform) has enabled a variety of critical voices and fractured the once relatively monolithic socialist country into multivalent sites of ideological contestations.

Former forbidden zones have been transgressed and transformed into unstable and incoherent "twilight zones." From the public realm of power politics to the private realm of sexuality, the sociopolitical planes have been ruptured and spaces opened up for critiques. Among the telltale signs of this are the numerous publications on sexuality, gender, women, eunuchs, etc. The Chinese translation of Robert Hans van Gulik's *Sexual Life in Ancient China* (1961) came out in 1990,[15] that of *Erotic Colour Prints of the Ming Period, with an Essay on Chinese Sex Life from the Han to the Ch'ing Dynasty, B.C. 206-A.D. 1644* (1951) in 1992;[16] new cultural histories of sexuality in imperial China have been written, critiques of sexual oppression past and present are flourishing, a dictionary of "Chinese sexology" has been compiled (*Zhonghua xingxue cidian* [A Chinese sexology dictionary] [1993]), histories of prostitutes and of women as well as literary histories of women writers published in the early decades of the twentieth century have been reprinted . . .

But in this proliferation of discourse on sexuality and gender in the Mainland, which was incited and empowered (again!) by Euro-American culture,[17] is ironically inscribed, among other things, the binary logic of heterosexism and the rigid hierarchy of the natural and the deviant. In a voluminous work published in 1993 by Liu Dalin, probably the most outspoken mainland Chinese scholar on sex culture, a kind of normative-patriarchal-homophobic-heterosexist ideology recurs in his otherwise liberal historicizing of sex in ancient China.[18] For instance, after an account of people's attitudes toward human prodigies in imperial times, he comments:

> . . . as for cross-dressing, nowadays society in ordinary circumstances does not criticize women dressing in men's clothes. However, men's fondness for women's clothes in daily life is an abnormal sexual psychology (it is called "transvestism"). Rectification and treatment are necessary.

> (Liu Dalin *Zhongguo gudai xingwenhua* 1: 302)

On another occasion, he calls the practice of cross-dressing among male prostitutes in the Southern Song Dynasty (1127–1279) "extremely abnormal":

These male prostitutes wore women's clothes, applied cosmetics, addressed each other as women. This is a kind of extremely abnormal social phenomenon.

(2: 632)

This unreflective attitude toward sexualities not classifiable by the heterosexual paradigm is prevalent in today's writings on sex in mainland China. The desire to be liberated from the extreme asceticism implanted by the Chinese Communist Party's rule is contained in a deep-rooted heterosexism, resulting in contradictions and self-canceling operations in this discourse that set out to resist oppression, yet is still far from emancipating.

Another recent critical work on China's sexual culture, *Zhongguo Xingwenhua* [The sex culture of China] published in 1994, again reproduces the heterosexist binary logic. Posing as a critique of Chinese sexual ideologies with examples drawn from both the past and the current social reality in China, and staking out a self-proclaimed confrontational position against sexual oppressions and taboos at a time when "the waves of great cultural reflection is overwhelming an open China that is under reform" (Zheng Sili 5), the writer appropriates Lu Xun's oft-quoted commentary on theatrical transvestism, removes it from its larger sociopolitical context, and asserts:

In Chinese society, "sexual displacement" is a kind of commonly seen psychological *anomaly*. . . . in ancient drama there were often women dressing as men or men dressing as women due to the *restrictions* of theatrical conventions, resulting in the tendency of gender displacement in performers of certain role-types (mainly the young male and the young female role-types). From this, the *anomalous* aesthetic psychology in society was reinforced. Lu Xun had criticized this *unhealthy* social practice and psychology. He said that a major characteristic of Chinese drama was men playing women and women playing men, which could gratify men as well as women for the reason that men saw "women playing" while women saw "men playing," thus pleasing everybody. In fact, this kind of psychology aptly reveals the *sickness* of Chinese society.

(360; emphasis added)

The normative agenda underpinning this work turns it into an accomplice of the ideology it seeks to challenge. Unreflectively contained in hierarchical binary thinking, the writer, in representing the production of "sexual displacement" in traditional Chinese theatre and citing Lu Xun's words, at once prescribes and legitimizes what is asserted to be "normal, natural and healthy," while simultaneously rejecting what is relegated to the position of "abnormal, anomalous and sick." The work's critical posture of tracing the genealogy of Chinese sexual culture and questioning sexual oppressions in Chinese society past and present paradoxically reinscribes a dominant and dominating heterosexist ideology. The stage practice of cross-dressing, which bends the heterosexual binary genders of male and female, is also seen as an abnormal "restriction," implying a normative assumption that a performer playing her/his gender is "natural and free of restrictions." This is exactly in line with the Party's policy on cross-dressing in Chinese opera as set down since the 1950s (see the chapter "The Last Female Impersonator" for a detailed discussion). The removal of Lu Xun's remark on theatrical transvestism from its incisive political context results in an ahistorical reading and a reduction of the scope of the interpretative and critical possibilities opened up by a remark interlocking the fields of theatre, gender and politics.

In addition, Lu Xun's focus was also a one-way male cross-dressing — "men playing women" and the grave misappropriation of this focus onto a two-way cross-dressing — "men playing women" and "women playing men" — is a consequential misreading that could mislead the critique of gender and sexuality in Chinese culture, for it is the anxiety of male homoeroticism, not lesbianism,[19] that underlies Lu Xun's passage. And it was mostly male homoerotic desire and the anxiety it generated that had created multiple and multivalent discourses on desire and the ambiguously gendered body. The overly and overtly visible gay and ambiguous bodies in official histories, notation books [biji], fiction and drama have made possible the reconstruction of "a male homosexual tradition in China" (Hinsch) in contemporary research. In fact, a collection of 52 stories (historical, literary, and legendary) of male homosexuality had already appeared by the early seventeenth century. Entitled *Duanxiu pian* [The cut sleeve compendium], it was compiled by Wuxia Ameng and adorned with the compiler's comments. In modern times, the first edition of Xiaomingxiong's compilation *Zhongguo tongxingai shilu* [History of homosexuality in China] (1984) was a pioneering work.

Contrary to the widespread accounts of male homosexuality, references to lesbianism in traditional sources are rare; so much so that Bret Hinsch can only give a six-page account of lesbianism in imperial China in his book, and because of his "failure" to give an equal treatment, he offers an apology (7).

It was due to the specific historical-cultural constructions of sexualities in imperial China which placed so much weight on male homosexual and homosocial desires, that the notion of the male transvestite theatre was given a pre-eminent position in theatrical discourse. It was not an accident, nor was it merely the influence of the dominant male cross-dressing practice in Beijing opera that caused Lu Xun to show a blindness by failing to mention (suppressing) female cross-dressing and/or a two-way cross-dressing while privileging male transvestism in traditional theatre as "the greatest artistic achievement in China."

The ideological assumptions about gender that I have delineated with reference to Lu Xun's brief passage are not unique to one person, but are shared and/or contradicted to different degrees by people in specific historical moments in one culture, e.g., Chinese, and cross-culturally for instance, Chinese and English, as drawn on in the present study. These commonly held assumptions are not to be taken for granted and I have already hinted at some of the questions that will be raised in the context of the present critique: How far are these assumptions sanctioned and/or contended in various specific historical moments in the history of Chinese opera? If monolithic, unitary and linear concepts in cultural analysis are highly questionable, then what do the complexities and contradictions in the construction and reproduction of gender relations tell us about Chinese opera, not merely as a literary-aesthetic form, but as an institution participating in, and helping to create, the struggle of power in culture and society in various historical moments? Putting the issue in a broader perspective, what are the differences in cultural meanings, if any, between China (with the late imperial period as a special focus) and the West (with Greek drama as its beginning and early-modern English theatre as a contrasting example) in terms of the agency of the players and the effects of cross-dressing in the construction and contestation of gender categories and power hierarchies? What can the similarities and differences in the discourse of gender in Chinese opera with reference to the early modern English stage tell us about gender politics past and present in the Chinese location? These are some of the issues to be addressed in the following chapters, which are meant to investigate, interrogate and intervene, rather than provide definitive answers.

HISTORY

TWO

A THEATRE OF CROSS-DRESSING:
A REVISIONIST HISTORY

In the Beginning Was Men-Dressing-As-Women

Beginning with classical Greece, theatre in Europe was characterized by the absence of women and the silence of their voices (Case). European theatre has been criticized as male-generated, with one-sided male cross-dressing, and for excluding women from the stage for two thousand years (Ferris, *Acting Women*). It was not until the seventeenth century that actresses were gradually accepted on the stage, yet they were often commodified as objects of desire for the pleasure of the male audience. After all the reason for putting women on the stage to begin with, as well as for dressing actresses in men's clothes in English theatre at the end of the seventeenth century was, as a critic puts it, simply that "conventionally attractive female bodies sell tickets" (Straub 128).

Owners of Chinese opera troupes in the late nineteenth century who unconventionally put young women on the public stage that had been monopolized for several centuries[1] by men obviously shared this conventional realization that the female body as a medium of exchange would yield high returns in the theatre business.

Women in Europe never had an active role in theatrical representation which, from a materialist feminist perspective, "conspired from the beginning to detach women as a gender class from their material base and to create them instead as a transcendent myth used to serve the male ideology cultural practices perpetuated" (Dolan 96). The long-term displacement of the female on the stage, the cultural and social construction of "femininity" in masculine terms, the dissymmetry between men playing women and women playing men, the longstanding prejudice that women were lesser performers who merely played themselves rather than creating roles — these aspects of a male-dominated theatre led to the feminist critique of "the notion of woman as a sign, a symbolic object manipulated and controlled artistically by male playwrights and male actors" (Ferris, *Acting Women* xi). Women, as theatrical signs, are constructed as passive and subject to the manipulation of men, the active users of signs (28–30). A rigorous rethinking, from the perspective of gender studies, of the extent to which these aspects have been discernible in traditional Chinese theatre and their specific modes of operation in this Asian cultural context will expand our cross-cultural understanding of theatres that feature cross-dressing as a major performance practice.

Among various European theatres, the English stage seems to have been more entangled in "male" obsessions. In early modern Europe, when actresses had already been seen on stage on the continent, in Spain, Italy and France, for instance, the stage in England was still restricted to men. It was not until the second half of the seventeenth century, after the restoration of Charles II (reign 1660–1685), that women performers were admitted on stage. Stephen Orgel, in proposing that "the male public theatre represents a uniquely English solution to the universal European disapproval of actresses" ("Nobody's Perfect" 7–8), cites the theatres of Spain, Italy and France to illustrate that continental European public theatre did not restrict the stage to men (8–9). This was not because gender ideology on the continent was very different from that of England, but rather that attempts made to curb the appearance of women on stage were not successful. In Spain, for instance, Isabel of Bourbon in 1644 (coincidentally the same year that the Manchus established the Qing Dynasty, during which the public stage was monopolized by men) issued a decree that

> no unmarried woman or widow was allowed to appear on stage, and no gentleman was permitted to visit an actress more than twice.

> Similar legislation had been passed before, and was to be reenacted later, to little effect. Equally unsuccessful were the numerous attempts made, first to prevent actresses wearing masculine dress at all and then to restrict it to above waist level.
>
> (McKendrick, *Woman and Society* 34–5)

Orgel also suggests that to the Spanish authorities, "the spectacle of the transvestite boys was found even more disturbing than that of theatrical women," so much so in fact, that the 1596 ban on actresses was rescinded four years later ("Nobody's Perfect" 8). Once permitted on stage, however, the spectacle of women cross-dressing as men also became disturbing to Spanish authorities. Here it is not just a question of the male exclusion of females in theatrical production but also the problem of the anxiety and crisis of gender categories which are in no other contexts as stringently put to question as in cross-dressing. As Majorie Garber states: "transvestism is a space of possibility structuring and confounding culture: the disruptive element that intervenes, not just a category crisis of male and female but the crisis of category itself" (17). In the Chinese cultural context as we shall see, this is nowhere more prominently embodied than in the sign of the "human prodigy" and its derivative discourse.

Meanwhile, in early modern English theatre, the body of the "boy actor," "boy actress," or "play-boy"[2] became a theatrical fetish, constituting an ultimate sign of the concomitance of theatre and male cross-dressing in a specific historical moment in Europe. In imperial China, boy and girl troupes had a long history, prospering in the private theatre under the literati from the sixteenth to the eighteenth century, with the girl players being more popular. Yet the teenage boy actor re-emerged in the public theatre as a fetish reaching its height in early nineteenth century Beijing. Its consummation is embodied in a famous remark made by a theatre connoisseur in 1842:

> Each of the four Hui opera troupes has its unique excellence . . . . The Four-Happiness Troupe is famous for its Kunqu. . . . The Three-Rejoice Troupe is renowned for its new, full-length plays. . . . The Peace-Spring Troupe is distinguished for its acrobatics. . . . The Spring-Stage Troupe is celebrated for its *boy actors.*
>
> (*Menghua suobu* 352; emphasis added)

Clearly, at this time boy actors had become the essential symbol of one of the four leading troupes in Beijing.[3] The boy actors were figured as *flowers*, affectedly dainty, priceless, and in a subordinate position to be sheltered by the powerful. The author of *Menghua suobu* [Trivial records of reverie] continues: "These flowers of wonder and youthfulness deserve protection and affection from dedicated persons with the fortune of a hundred thousand golden bells" (352). Invented by the literati in an activity of spectatorial gaze they called "ranking flowers" (as best exemplified by Chen Sen's novel *Pinhua baojian* [Precious mirror of ranking flowers], written in the mid-nineteenth century) and textualized in a genre of writing concerning stage players aptly designated "manual of flowers" [*huapu*], these boy actors' bodies were fetishized as the ultimate figure of the feminine constructed by men — the actual women were displaced.

The rise of the great female impersonators in Beijing opera in the early decades of the twentieth century saw another peak in the fetishization of the female image constituted in the body of the transvestite actor, which generated a "fantasy of exchange *between* men *about* women" (Phelan 158; original emphasis). This climax of theatrical transvestism in Beijing opera emerged in and characterized a period (circa 1917–1937) designated as the height of this theatre in an "official" theatre history recently published in mainland China (*Zhongguo Jingju shi* 2: 1–212). The history states that "the robust prosperity of various performance schools of the *dan* role-type was the *most distinguished* accomplishment of this period" (104; emphasis added).

The history of the female absence/presence and the construction of women as a sign in Chinese theatre initially looks similar to that of Europe. The first record of play-acting is found in the biography of the ancient comic entertainer You Meng of the Spring and Autumn Period (770–476 B.C.E.). Scripted by the great historian Sima Qian (c. 145-c. 90 B.C.E.), it is the story of a *male* player celebrated for his impeccable impersonation of another man (*juan* 126, 10: 3201). The male player not only constitutes the beginning of playacting in the textual history of China, but extant historical records also tell us that male transvestism in theatrical acts again came before female cross-dressing. The earliest recorded instance of female cross-dressing is found in the eighth century in the time of the Tang emperor Suzong (reign 756–763) (Tseng 41), when actresses played the role of the male officer in a theatrical act known as *canjun xi* ["The military counselor"].[4] Male transvestism in theatricals appeared several hundred years before that instance of female cross-dressing. Quoting Yang Yongxiu (1488–1559) of the Ming period, the Qing scholar Jiao Xun (1763–1820) mentions that the practice of *zhuangdan* (literally "counterfeit woman-parts") among players could have begun in the Western Han Dynasty (206 B.C.E.–24 C.E.) (91). But Yang's words have yet to be proven accurate (Tseng 32–3; see also below). The Ming critic Hu Yinglin (1551–1602) suggests that the use of rouge and powder by eunuchs in the Han court was the beginning of female impersonation in subsequent ages (1b). Finally, an official historical source provides reliable evidence that male transvestism in a theatrical act appeared at the latest in the third century when the corrupt Wei emperor Feidi (reign 240–254) made two young entertainers who were his favorites playact *Liaodong yaofu* [The devil woman of Liaodong] for his voluptuous entertainment (quoted in Wang Guowei *Song Yuan* 8).

Masking Gender

"Drama" in its "full sense" — as defined by Wang Guowei (1877–1927) — can also be traced back to an incident of male transvestism in Chinese history. In his *Song Yuan xiqu kao* [Study of Song and Yuan drama] (1912), a pioneering work which initiated and established the status of the study of drama in modern Chinese literary scholarship, Wang defines *xiju* [drama] as an art form that "must combine language, action and singing to perform a story so that the meaning of drama is fully realized" (44). He argues that "the combination of singing and dance to perform a story" first came into existence in the sixth century during the Northern Qi Dynasty (550–577) and cites two examples: the theatrical acts of *Daimian* ["The mask"] or *Damian* ["The big face"] and *Tayaoniang* ["The stomping-swaying wife"] (10). It is noteworthy that both of these theatrical acts, to which the inception of "true drama" in China is attributed, were "produced in and as a gendered matrix of relations" (to borrow an expression from Judith Butler) and had already intertwined with the politics of gender.

"The Mask"/"The Big Face" is an act of the reassertion of masculine power in the performance of gender. It is recorded in Cui Linqin's *Jiaofang ji* [An account of the Music Academy], dated to the latter half of the eighth century:

> "The Big Face" — originated in Northern Qi. Changgong, Prince Lan Ling, was *brave and heroic yet born with a face that looked like a woman's.* Disappointed by this appearance that was not fierce enough to intimidate his enemies, Prince Lan Ling made a wooden mask to wear on the battlefield. The incident was thus made into this play; it was also set to music and songs.
>
> (17; emphasis added)[5]

This pioneering theatrical act in the history of Chinese theatre is instructive from the perspective of the present study. Embodied in the referent (Prince Lan Ling the man) is the incongruence within the sign of the masculine gender, i.e., the mismatch between the "essential" masculine signified in the inside, a valiant warrior — the character of a person, and the "ostensible" feminine signifier on the outside, a woman's face — the look of a person. This dislocation in a bipolar mimetic notion of gender is the source of gender anxiety that gives rise to an act of *masking* — an act of theatricality to rectify the dislocation of gender. Thus, the gender notions of masculinity and femininity, which are themselves cultural constructions, always have to be put into *performance* in order to naturalize the underlying incoherences and to restabilize the paradigm of two genders that is itself also built upon a mimetic structural relation. To align all his inner and outer masculine gender attributes, Prince Lan Ling has to wear a mask to *perform* his masculinity. Furthermore, the historical Prince Lan Ling was already staging a theatrical to demonstrate and reinstate masculine power when he wore the mask on the battlefield in *real life*. Hence the *theatrical act* of "The Mask"/"The Big Face" was a double-theatricalization moving in two directions: it was the performance of a performance of gender and a self-referential theatrical act of acting as *masking* (in a figurative sense), i.e., the disguise of identity. In retrospect, this very early theatrical act in Chinese cultural history subtly points to the theatricality of life itself.

Also recorded in Cui Lingqin's *An Account of the Music Academy*, "The Stomping-Swaying Wife" was a comic dramatic sketch in which the character of the wife had originally been played by a man during its performance in Northern Qi times when it was created:

> A certain man named Su of Northern Qi had a red nose. Although he held no official post, he called himself by the official title of Palace Attendant. Whenever he was drunk he beat up his wife. The wife in turn would complain to the neighbors of her plight. Their contemporaries made fun of them [in a theatrical act]: *a man wearing woman's clothes* walks slowly onto the scene, singing while walking. At each refrain, others join in, "Where do you come from, swaying as you walk? What grieves you, swaying woman?" Because the wife sings as she walks, she is known as the "stomping-singing" wife. Because she complains, the word "grieve" is used. When her husband appears, the two engage in an imitation of a fight *to arouse laughter and amuse the spectators.*[6]
>
> (18; emphasis added)[7]

Cui adds that in his era the character of the wife is performed by women ("now it is women acting it"). He comments negatively on this contemporary enacting of "The Stomping-Swaying Wife" (which had altered several old conventions in addition to the replacement of the actor by an actress), saying that "the old significance [of this theatrical act] has all been lost". The original transvestite effect served as a source of comic invention in this cultural context (coincidentally similar to the effect of cross-dressing in classical Greek comedies) though this was obviously lost in the later practice of putting a woman in the role of the wife. In this earliest traceable instance of a Chinese theatrical act that fits Wang's definition of a full sense of drama, women are a parodic representation invented by men for the purpose of arousing laughter and providing amusement at the expense of women — the battered woman as a burlesque representation "dressed" in transvestism. In the beginning, male transvestism in Chinese theatricals was a travesty of the female gender and a misogynist mockery, and this "legacy" too, has lasted. To give an example drawn from today's regional operas, the Kunju opera *zhezixi* [select-scene play] "*Yangdu*" [Lamb belly soup] retains the performing tradition of casting a *chou* actor — the comic role-type that is male-gendered and mostly played by men — to play the character of Mother Zhang who is mistakenly poisoned to death by her villainous son Zhang the Donkey. Zhang originally intends to frame the virtuous widow Dou'e with the murder of her mother-in-law.[8] This supposedly tragic scene is enacted in a comic manner by the *chou* actor's travesty acting of a woman. By the late Ming period, an amateur actor called Ding Jizhi was noted for his excellence in playing Mother Zhang. Yu Huai describes Ding's stage impersonation of Mother Zhang as "the best for a generation" (5019).[9] This tradition in Kunju and Beijing operas of having the *chou* actor cross-dress to play old female characters in comic situations reveals certain underpinning gender ideologies that have endured for ages. "The Stomping-Swaying Wife" is analogous to what feminist gender critics have called the "misogynist drag" that "mak[es] fun of the socially subservient class by parodying it" (Solomon, "It's Never Too Late to Switch" 145). In this ancient Chinese theatrical act, the object of misogynist mockery through transvestism is the subservient women, a battered wife, encompassed in the Confucian patriarchy. In general, the "origin" of Chinese theatre is seemingly similar to that of the European theatre in that both were *generated by males*. However, this does not set up "Chinese theatre" as a parallel of "Western theatre." Each of these theatres has its own complexities.

Transvestite Theatre and Chinese Opera

In his 1979 work *Dressing Up: Transvestism and Drag: The History of an Obsession*, Peter Ackroyd describes Japanese Noh theatre and Chinese opera in terms of male transvestism. The specific genre of "Chinese opera" he draws on, judging from his description, is in fact Beijing opera. He observes Chinese opera from an interesting perspective and offers inspiring insights, but also misrepresents this theatrical tradition in several ways:

> The tradition of male cross-dressing on stage, in both of these countries [China and Japan], is a long and consistent one. And here we can trace an old and by now familiar pattern: the drama which employs transvestites has its origins in sacred and festive rituals, and these rituals generally involve the myths of fertility. Japanese Noh drama, for example, derives from *dengaku*, a folk-dance associated with rice planting and harvesting. Chinese Opera, although fixed in its most recent forms only a century ago, has its origin in the song and dance patterns of ancient Chinese religious festivities.
>
> In Chinese operatic performances, the female impersonators, the *tan* [*dan*], follow prescribed and highly stylized techniques for the enactment of female roles. A number of fixed gestures are used, and the impersonator wears a female mask corresponding to the kind of woman he is portraying: *chingyi*, an elegant lady, *huatan*, a lower-class woman, or *taomatan*, an Amazon or militant. The performer here is, as Leonard Pronko asserts in *Theatre East and West*, "the master of a complex and extremely rarefied art", an art of images and symbols that denies naturalistic conditions and, therefore, the limitations of native sexuality.
>
> (94–5)

Ackroyd's last comment contextualizes Chinese opera in terms of sexuality and points to a significant aspect of Chinese opera: the fact that its transvestism, acted in highly stylized conventions, transgresses "natural" categories of sexuality.

An examination of primary sources reveals that writings about men playing women in Chinese theatre were often permeated with sexuality and eroticism. This practice culminated in a series of writings on transvestite actors which began in the late eighteenth century, with the famed *Yanlan xiaopu* [Manual of orchids] by An'le Shanqiao (1786) being the most representative work. The origin of this cultural practice of male cross-dressing seems to be interwoven with the sexual and the erotic, as evidenced by the earliest references to theatrical transvestism examined above.

But Chinese opera is also in some respects misrepresented in Ackroyd's passage, beginning with the question of whether male theatrical transvestism originated from sacred and festive rituals in

Chinese theatre. Obviously Ackroyd made his statement about Chinese opera by speculation, without the means of access to primary sources. Despite this drawback, however he may have come rather close to the "real" historical situation. As mentioned above, the Ming scholar Yang Yongxiu (as quoted by Jiao Xun writing some three hundred years later) said that the practice of female impersonation had begun in the Western Han Dynasty:

> In the "Book of State Sacrifice and Worship" from *History of Han*, it is recorded that male entertainers disguised themselves as female players. This is the beginning of female impersonation in subsequent ages . . . .

(Jiao 91)

If these words could be proven to be historically accurate beyond doubt, Chinese male cross-dressing could convincingly be established as originating from ancient rituals. However, Tseng Yung-i, a leading Chinese drama scholar from Taiwan, points out that there is no record of "male entertainers disguised as female players" in the "Book of State Sacrifice and Worship" from the *History of Han* [*Hanshu*] (33). The thesis therefore requires further historical investigation before it can be accepted as fact, not to mention Ackroyd's extrapolation of an "old and by now familiar pattern." Even the question of whether or not Chinese theatre had its origins in ritual and shamanism is far from being definitively answered. Although some scholars have argued for this, several different theses have been put forward to account for the inception of Chinese theatre.[10] An eclectic thesis of multiple origins has also been argued by the mainland Chinese scholar Zheng Chuanyin (*Zhongguo xiqu* 44–69).

Secondly, as I shall analyze in detail below, female cross-dressing has a tradition as "long and consistent" as male cross-dressing in the history of Chinese theatre. In fact the first full-fledged Chinese theatre (in the thirteenth century) was distinguished by female cross-dressing, not male transvestism.

Lastly, a factual inaccuracy: in Beijing opera as well as other regional operas, the *dan* performer does not wear a mask. Although the various vivid and contrasting patterns of painted faces [*goulian*] are a distinguishing feature in Chinese opera, masks are rarely used (there are any number of often colorful publications in various languages on these painted faces). In today's standard repertoire of Beijing opera, one can cite only the "partial" mask, covering only part of the face worn by the arhats in the very popular "military plays" *The Eighteen Arhats Fight the Monkey King* [*Shiba luohan dou Wukong*] and *The Eighteen Arhats Capture the Roc* [*Shiba luohan shou dapeng*].[11]

Ackroyd and other Western writers and scholars who write on gender and sexuality often make references to male cross-dressing in Chinese opera.[12] In fact, how could they fail to, given its prominence as a tradition in Chinese theatre? Some of these Western references, though only in passing and not central to the core work which they serve as illustrations, do include inaccuracies that contribute to the myth-making and stereotyping of cultures of the Other as well as misrepresenting the "alien object" in ways that indigenous researchers would not be as likely to, although they could of course commit other errors. For instance, while it is correct to say that Mei Lanfang was "regarded as the greatest female impersonator in living memory" and "the idol of China," Roger Baker's assertion that female impersonators in China "have always been greatly admired by the public" and "were always praised, revered and well known" (155–6) is, from my perspective, more than merely a misperception of historical facts.[13] It is a misreading and simplification of the highly complex cultural production of the Chinese "male *dan*" — an oxymoron that aptly signifies this sexually ambiguous body's embodiment of the culture's politics of class (discrimination), sexuality (complex), gender (perplexity), and the obsession with sensual artistic glamor (see chapters 8 and 9 for further discussion).

In his historical narration of drag, Baker's idea of the "Oriental" theatrical female impersonation — the Japanese *onnagata* and the Chinese *dan* — is an imaginary invention of an idealistic oppositional Other to the West in his critique of Western culture: "their work bears no resemblance to female impersonation as we have experienced it in the West" (149). I do not have the expertise on Japanese Kabuki and Noh to comment on *onnagata*; however, the Chinese *dan* at least, has on this occasion been literally rendered a *pure* Other ("no resemblance") in a Western discourse that takes no account of the Other's history. Many other representational problems appear around gender and culture, in addition to many Orientalist representations of Asian cultures invented by Sinologists or Japanologists.

In addition to a textual-historical origin engendered by men, the rise of Beijing opera to its maturity in the last quarter of the nineteenth century[14] and its dominance in the subsequent one hundred years have rendered an excessively high profile to the tradition of male transvestism in Chinese opera. This historical circumstance has easily misled many people to simplify the picture and inscribe Chinese opera/theatre in the persona of Beijing opera as, predominantly, a male transvestite theatre.

The enormous success of David Henry Hwang's celebrated Broadway hit *M. Butterfly* (1989), the winner of three Tony Awards, and Chen Kaige's Palme d'Or winning film *Farewell My Concubine* (1993)[15], further reinforced the impression of Chinese opera as a male transvestite theatre throughout the 1990s.

Moreover, in terms of the literary-dramatic canon, Chinese drama has been, not surprisingly, almost exclusively male: female playwrights in particular, and women writers in general, being largely neglected by conventional Chinese (literary) history until recent times. These factors contributed to the formation of a discourse of male-originated and male-dominated dramatic-theatrical tradition in Chinese cultural history. But it is also at this point of our discussion that we encounter the first contradictions and signs of the possibility of multiplicity of discourse about "Chinese theatre" through the female dominance and the insignificance of male cross-dressing on the stage of Yuan *zaju* [literally "variety drama"] and the prevalence of girl players in the Ming-Qing private theatre.

The Female Presence on the Yuan Stage

The first fully developed Chinese theatre to emerge in the Yuan Dynasty favored female players and female cross-dressing. Subsequently women were confined to, yet still prospered in, the private performance context in the Ming and Qing periods when the public stage was appropriated and monopolized by men. The tradition of female players and female cross-dressing gradually declined in the nineteenth century, but returned to play a significant role at the beginning of the twentieth century, as demonstrated by the re-emergence of actresses on the public stage and the triumphant revival of the Zhejiang Yueju opera in our times.

It is by no means a new observation to note that female players prospered in the Yuan period and that there were many female private troupes during Ming-Qing times, in fact to appropriate some sprightly words, "there is some absurdity in so bald a pronouncement of the obvious" (Greenblatt 1). After all, scholars in the field cannot have failed to realize that there *have* been actresses in Chinese theatre. Many studies of Chinese drama bring up the female theatrical tradition in detail or in passing, and in various contexts. Chinese opera theatregoers and fans are obviously aware of the female Yueju opera that is arguably the most successful regional opera today, at a time when the most representative regional opera, Beijing opera, is waning and the most prestigious, Kunju opera, is literally dying, with their male transvestite traditions almost eradicated in contemporary China. However, knowledge of some historical facts is merely a passive state of knowledge, and the historical "truth" of whether there was a female presence in, or dominance of, traditional theatre is not the cardinal issue here. What is immediately relevant is how knowledge is represented in the dominant cultural discourse. This "female theatrical tradition" already constitutes a part of the representation of Chinese theatre history, which in turn is produced in, and produces, Chinese cultural history. Yet this tradition has always been relegated to the position of an optional attachment to a male-centered theatre history, and this is what requires further reflection and interrogation in order to expose the politics played out in this cultural discourse.

It is clear that the role of female players in various theatre histories has been downplayed to a subordinate position and survives in conventional discourse only *in* and *as* the shadow of the *male* (transvestite) theatrical tradition. In general, the present fragments of "histories" of this female tradition in Chinese theatre have thus far been *paradoxically* written by men and constructed from ancient textual gleanings which were also authored by men. More ironically, one may even argue that this "female tradition" — the organization and ownership of female troupes, training of female players, theorization of the art of (female) acting, etc. — has been mostly shaped by the hands of the patriarchy since the inception of the first full-fledged Chinese theatre in the thirteenth century. A re-presentation of female players in terms of empowerment and resistance is required in order to expose the ideological slippage of signification in the kind of patriarchal writing that strives to subsume the feminine Other within a model of history that always assumes a masculine position in a "natural" posture. In the process of relocating the cultural-historical specificities of the representation of female players in Chinese theatre history, I shall make references to its European counterpart to situate my critique on a wider horizon.

The first theatre of the West — Greek drama — was accompanied by an apparently unquestioned stage convention of cross-dressed male players;[16] and it is not certain whether women spectators were admitted into the theatre.[17] The Romans, successors to the Greeks, maintained the tradition and in their pantomimes, which claimed to present Greek tragedies (which the Greeks would not have been able to recognize), the Roman stage was reserved for male players. Women performers were found only in troupes of traveling players who performed street mime (Harris 10–3). In ancient Rome, pantomime actors were the great stars of the theatre, able even to come into imperial favor. It is not surprising that entertainers/performers also commonly became male favorites of emperors and powerful ministers in imperial China,[18] pointing to a complex cultural manifestation of the structuring of gender relations in terms of power and the modalities of erotic desire.

The rise of women's presence in the theatre seems to have often caused patriarchal anxieties. Pope Sextus V issued an edict in 1588 banning the appearance of women on stage just as actresses were gaining importance in the *commedia dell'arte*, and in the papal states of eighteenth century Rome, a religious ban on actresses was enforced. As Goethe wrote in 1788,

> The ancients, at least in the best periods for art and morality, did not permit women on the stage. Their plays were organized in such a way that either women could be more or less dispensed with, or

else female roles were played by an actor who had prepared himself especially for them. This is still the case in modern Rome and in the rest of the papal states . . . "(48)

Goethe obviously greatly admired the Roman theatrical tradition, however from a feminist perspective, his words are aimed at maintaining male dominance of theatrical creation and ingenuity.

In medieval Europe, female players were extremely rare, and the two or three examples of women performing in mystery plays have been repeatedly cited. The incident in 1468 in which the daughter of Dediet the glazier at Metz played St Catherine of Siena is frequently quoted in medieval studies.[19] However, these rare examples of female stage appearance cut both ways, indicating the apparent *rarity* with which women performed on stage in the medieval period, rather than indicating that women had a part of any significance in making their own theatrical image. It has been suggested that the main reason that women seldom appeared in the mysteries was "more probably because the organizations responsible for presenting the plays were *male*" (Harris 150; emphasis added). The validity of this suggestion is backed up by the record indicating that the patron of the 1468 St Catherine, was a woman, Dame Catherine Baudoiche (Muir, "Saint Play" 142).

The marginalization of women in this male-generated Western theatrical tradition is further revealed by a staging of mysteries in Metz fifteen years later. In 1484 a barber's son was chosen to play St Barbara by the citizens of Metz, although the earlier female player's performance as St Catherine was reported to have been overwhelmingly successful. The cross-dressed male player was equally successful, "being very good-looking, 'like a beautiful girl,' and playing the role 'so discreetly and devoutly' that several people cried with compassion" (Harris 150). Here we see yet another theatrical reproduction of "femininity" by a male alone in the absence of the female. In Europe — from the all-male Greek theatre through the middle ages' restrictions of women on stage, through early modern England's insistence on male actors until the mid-seventeenth century, and the Italian papal states' religious bans on actresses in the late eighteenth century — male theatrical power seems to have been born together with theatre itself and to have reasserted itself throughout history in the form of a transvestite theatre that continued to exclude women from the stage.

In another space and time named "Cathay" by medieval Arabs and Europeans, the "first" theatre appeared much later than in Europe. One and a half millennia after the glittering culture of ancient Athens faded out, thirteenth century Khan-balik (i.e., Beijing) under the Mongol ruler Kublai Khan (reign 1264–1294) became a center of power. The empire's cultural grandeur awed the Venetian traveler Marco Polo (1254–1324) and its unprecedented military power petrified Europe. The first full-fledged Chinese theatre, Yuan *zaju*,[20] appeared at this historical juncture, when *man*'s power was at its highest magnitude, a period designated as the *alien-ruled* Yuan Dynasty in the political history written by Han Chinese. Interestingly enough, in contradiction to this male dominance in political power, the Yuan stage saw the ascendancy of female players over male players — a circumstance sharply different from the situation of women on stage in medieval Europe. The Yuan theatre featured women who not only played their own gender, but also, very frequently, male roles. In stark contrast to the classical Greek theatre and Chinese theatres in later eras, especially the Qing period, the Yuan theatre was also open to audiences of both men and women.

Zhao Shanlin, in his distinguished study *Zhongguo xiqu guanzhong xue* [A study of the audience of Chinese music drama] (1990), stretches a Yuan imperial edict prohibiting performances in public places a bit far as one of the examples in his account of the "feudal" oppression of the female audience in Chinese theatrical history (98). In my opinion, however, the case in point is not the exclusion of women from theatrical events, but the fear of "the mixing of men and women" and of massive gatherings of people. The edict states these reasons for the prohibition:

> . . . gathering crowds of people, blocking streets and markets, mixing men and women — all these not only incite fights and quarrels, but also instigate other trouble . . . .

> (Wang, *Yuan Ming Qing* 5)[21]

Of course women were also to be prohibited as potentially disrupting the established order; but the object of prohibition was not the female audience but public performances which gathered crowds

— it was the activity itself that was banned. In this Yuan edict the presence of women is not singled out as a problem, rather it is the public mingling of, and interaction between, men and women that appears to constitute a problem threatening the stability of a hierarchical social order. The persistence of this obsessive fear on the part of the ruling power is seen in the recurrence of similar prohibitions throughout the history of imperial China, especially in the edicts of the Qing Dynasty. Particularly notable is the fact that in most cases the same words *nan'nü xianghun* [male and female mixing together] are used.[22]

The separation between men and women in the theatre is one of the signs indicating an anxiety arising from the recognition of the potential instability of a binarism that was the foundation of the whole social order. The most relevant manifestation of this binary order in the present critical context being the constitutive cosmological forces of *yin* [female/darkness/passivity] and *yang* [male/brightness/activity], each defined and given specific roles within a hierarchical Confucian social order. The separation of men and women was more strictly reinforced after the Yuan era, as evident in the repeated assertion of the immorality of the public mingling of the sexes. In addition, although there were various imperial edicts prohibiting theatrical activities during the Yuan period, none were aimed *solely* at excluding a female audience. It was in other periods before, and especially after Yuan, that a number of edicts specifically prohibiting women audiences and performers were issued.[23] It is ironic that a very early ban on women players in imperial China was initiated by a woman, the *Jiu Tang shu* [Old Tang history] records that in 661, "the Queen [of Emperor Gaozong] requested a ban on women acting in the empire and her request was granted" (Liu Shu 1: 82).

During the Yuan period much more attention and importance was accorded to actresses than actors. This can be constructed thanks to the great number of related materials extant — the literati left much information relating to the theatre in their writings. Scholar and high official Hu Zhiyu's (1227–1293) works dedicated to female players are some of the most quoted materials in classical Chinese drama studies. His works include studies of dramatic theory and criticism (Ye Changhai *Zhongguo xijuxue shigao* 36–8), acting (Xia Xieshi 34–5), and the history of theatrical troupes (Zhang Faying 86–7). Hu's "*Zeng Songshi xu*" [Preface for Miss Song], in which he gives profuse praise to an actress, is an excellent illustration of the privileged status of actresses in the Yuan theatre. In this essay Hu first praises Yuan *zaju* theatre as an art form able to encompass themes from political to social criticism, and provide a means to deeply express a full range of human experiences. He then praises Miss Song for her excellence in expressing all aspects of life and human emotions through her theatrical art:

> There is not a single thing that cannot be captured in terms of its emotion and exhaustively described in terms of its form [in *zaju* drama]. Being a woman but enacting the deeds of millions of people, and at the same time entertaining the ear and the eye, relaxing the heart and mind: this is something for which ancient female entertainers are beyond comparison. I see it in Miss Song that she fully embodies all these.

(8: 57)

In the first sentence of the quoted passage, Hu in effect elevates drama, together with the actress's art as its medium of expression, to the level of the ultimate expressive power of *shi,* the highest poetic genre. His use of the same high critical language used in poetry criticism reinforces this elevation. Operating within and against the existing sociocultural hierarchy, Hu is speaking against established institutional values for two discriminated Others: the theatre, a literary form traditionally regarded as morally degrading and artistically low and not worthy of attention by the literati, and actresses, a class of people often associated with prostitution and occupying one of the lowest ranks in society. That Hu, a scholar-official of repute in Chinese society, included several pieces dedicated to actresses and actors among the high literary writings in his collected works, reveals a system of values more relaxed and flexible than the orthodox Confucianism of the time.

Female players are also prominent in many other scholars' writings, including those of another noteworthy source, Hu's friend Wang Yun (1227–1304). Wang, a high official like Hu, wrote poetry and prose for the actresses Zhu Lian Xiu and Cao Jin Xiu.[24] Zhu was a famous Yuan theatre actress much admired by Hu and was acclaimed as pre-eminent in performing *zaju* in her brief biographical entries in two important historical sources: Xia Tingzhi's *Qinglou ji* [The green bower collection] (19) and Tao Zongyi's (1316–1403) *Chuogeng lu* [Records after ceasing to plow] (566; *juan* 20).[25] These and other similar textual sources have been the key elements in the construction of a picture of the Yuan theatre in performance. A recent study has also made extensive use of archaeological methods and historical relics (e.g., paintings on silk, murals, sculpture on bricks) to argue for the dominance of female actresses/entertainers, often cross-dressed, in the Song and Yuan periods (Liao 288–91).

Among the various historical and archeological sources on the theatre of Yuan, the text that has most affected the reconstruction of a female dominated Yuan stage is the above-mentioned *Green Bower Collection,* also the most substantial source for our knowledge of actresses in the Yuan Dynasty. In this work, the author Xia Tingzhi, a writer of dramatic lyrics,[26] gives accounts of and names some 120 female players, and also mentions more than 30 actors along with about 50 playwrights, writers of dramatic lyrics, poets, well-known scholars and celebrities. In an essay entitled "Qinglou ji zhi" [On *The Green Bower Collection*] which is attached to an important Ming edition of the work, Xia says that he wants to "let people in later times know that during this time of prosperity and peace, there are talented female players who are all the rage at the time" (8).

The achievements and popularity of female players in this period are certain, but it is important to bear in mind that there *were* male players active on stage as well — the most obvious evidence being that Xia himself briefly mentions about 30 actors, some of whom were married to the actresses he describes. Xia also goes on to say, immediately after the lines quoted above, that he intends to write another work to record the performers who play the male leading role-type in Yuan theatre, namely the *moni* (8). Judging from the context, the performers that Xia refers to were evidently male. However, this work was either never written or has been lost.

The possibility that Xia never wrote this work on male players further hints at the prosperity and predominance of female players. At the same time, it is important not to overlook the fact that *The Green*

Bower Collection is a work written *especially* to record female players. We should not take this vital piece of evidence hastily and attribute *absolute* dominance to women in the theatre of Yuan. In his *A History of Chinese Drama* (1976), probably the most comprehensive English account of Chinese drama from the earliest times to the 1960s with attention also given to aspects of performance, William Dolby cautions that the impression of the predominance of female players in Yuan theatre "may be colored by the wealth of biographical material there is about some actresses, and the paucity of it concerning actors" (*History* 61). However, he immediately goes on to describe *The Green Bower Collection* as "a collection of biographies of singing girls and actresses" (61), leaving out the male players mentioned in the work and thus reinforcing the kind of *mis*-impression he had previously cautioned readers against.

Whose Throat Was It?

In Wayne Koestenbaum's queer reflections on European opera, the opera queen's throat is closed. The queen, i.e., the gay opera fan, is silent, for "no sound 'comes out' of the queen's throat (the queen is reduced to the closet by his passion for opera)" (45). In Chinese opera, the *piaoyou* [literally "ticket-fan," an aficionado] is, more often than not, vocal regardless of his or her skillfulness in the art. Listening to Chinese opera — queerly — the issues in focus are often "whose throat it is" and the kinds of aesthetics of performance that are incited and formulated. The crisscrossing of the two pairs of binaries of male/female throat and male/female voice has rendered the various gender representations of Chinese opera fluid as a result of the mismatching of essential and visible/audible gender attributes — oftentimes we do know the true gender of the performer. However, in the re-examination of Yuan theatre, a debate centers around the radical argument that it was the female throat that did all the singing, that the leading performer-singers in Yuan theatre were *exclusively* female.[27]

    A little explanation of the formal features of Yuan *zaju* drama is necessary and will be helpful before I continue to examine this issue.

In this music theatre, and as inherited in today's Chinese operas, performers and all dramatis personae were classified into various role-types, which are divided — first and foremost — along gender lines, with other categories that include class, station, age, etc. The two predominant general types being the female [*dan*] and the male [*mo*]. In Yuan theatre, only the leading role was given singing parts throughout the whole play. Each play was, very uniquely, written as either a female role-type script [*danben*] or a male role-type script [*moben*]; and all supporting roles had only spoken lines. But here we must differentiate carefully between the dramatic character and the role-type. A leading role-type performer was occasionally assigned to play more than one character in different acts of the same play. Therefore in certain plays (very limited in number in the extant corpus) there is more than one *dramatic character* singing, but it is always the same *role-type* performer playing these various characters and doing the singing. This aspect of Yuan theatre has been misinterpreted by many people, including Arthur Waley, who inaccurately states that "almost invariably only one *character,* either the hero or the heroine, sang" (89; emphasis added).[28]

Therefore if the suggestion made by some scholars that only female players sang in Yuan theatre is correct, it means that at the least all *leading* male roles, if not *all* male roles, were played by women cross-dressing as men; and that women were the only leading performers in this theatre, playing both the *dan* and *mo*. If the assertion that "Yuan theatre was sung *only* by females" could be proved beyond doubt, it would be rather unsettling evidence for today's cultural concern about patriarchal hegemony. However, additional textual research and historical scholarship[29] have revealed that it is likely that men also played the leading male role in the Yuan theatre, and this is generally accepted by scholars. But gender issues concerning the (leading) performers/singers on the Yuan stage are still far from closure.

Before further addressing these issues, I would like to suggest that the answer to the question of which sex sang the leading roles in Yuan theatre has in fact been already provided by the author of *The Green Bower Collection* — a writer with firsthand experience of Yuan theatre who could and did make direct factual statements about it. Scholars have been well aware of his commendations of three actresses "excellent

in playing both the female and male role-types" [*dan mo shuangquan*]
(28–9, 39), and of two good at playing emperors (22–3) — clear
evidence that women cross-dressed as men on the Yuan stage. But in
his essay "On *The Green Bower Collection*" Xia also says that "the
female role-type script is played by woman . . . the male role-type
script is played by man" (7) — thus indicating that there were also
men playing men. This piece of direct historical evidence has not been
quoted, for one reason or another, in the debate concerning this issue.
Putting these pieces of evidence together it is quite certain that in the
conventions of Yuan theatre there were female players who, apart from
playing the leading female role, also cross-dressed to play the leading
male role, and equally certain that there were also men who played the
leading male role.

With regard to the role of female performers, Yuan theatre may
well serve as a counter-example to the male-generated theatre of the
West. While Western "classical acting practice reveals the construction
of the fictional gender created by the patriarchy . . . suppressing actual
women and replacing them with the masks of patriarchal production"
(Case 318), Chinese theatre first matured as a theatre mixing women
and men on the stage and female players who also often cross-dressed
as men were prevalent on stage. Although the dramatic texts were
exclusively the creations of male playwrights,[30] Yuan acting practice
gave women the power to represent both genders on stage. Female
players not only occupied a more prominent position as leading
performers, they also held the power to represent the other gender
and, so far as we know at present, superceded men in this domain of
representational power in the practice of acting. In the beginning of
the first Chinese theatre there were women dressing as men.

But this is not to represent in simple and naïve terms Yuan theatre
and its society as the opposite of patriarchal structures, or as a
progressive and radical cultural production. After all, the theatre and
its performers, both male and female, were regulated by the patriarchy
and relegated to one of the lowest social categories, associated with
prostitutes, throughout the history of imperial China. In fact, the
institution of *yuehu* [music entertainers] was first established in the
Northern Wei period (386–534) to contain the wives of criminals. This

inferior social category of music entertainers (consisting mostly of women) constituted what were almost slavery, conflating the identity of entertainer and prostitute under the regulation of the government.[31] The institutionalization of entertainers as a social category was first and foremost part of the patriarchy's oppression of women. So many female household members of political criminals were classified as music entertainers in the early Ming period that high officials criticized this act of the emperor in their memorials to the throne (Zhang Faying 4). Many actresses were courtesans, mistresses, or concubines in the Yuan, Ming, and Qing periods. Women playwrights did not emerge until the turn of the seventeenth century and they have just begun to receive some attention from literary historians.[32] A figure with the literary stature of Aphra Behn (1640–1689) has yet to be reconstructed in the history of Chinese drama.[33] Furthermore, one major reason for the rise of female players was obviously the commodification of the female body as a feminine erotic spectacle for the consumption of the male spectator in a male-centered society. Early in the southern Song period (1127–1279), Wang Zhuo criticized his contemporaries for favoring female entertainers:

> The ancients became famous for their skills in singing; there was no differentiation between men and women. . . . Nowadays people are only fond of female entertainers, regardless of their artistic standard. Scholars also advocate a pretty and gentle style in writing lyrics . . . .
>
> (111)

His comments are significant in yet another way, as a criticism of the feminization of poetic writing. This gendering of genre is a major aspect of the issue of women, the feminine, and Chinese theatre that I shall return to in the penultimate chapter.

Meanwhile, the presence of female players *on* the Yuan stage functioned as more than acting. One of the theatrical practices of Yuan theatre was the display of the "offstage" actresses further back on the stage in order to attract the audience and customers for prostitutes[34] (Zhang Faying 78; Liao 292). Physically present on the stage but temporarily outside the play-world (since they were not acting in the play at the moment), these actresses were constituted in both the realms of the real, and the juxtaposed fictional play-world in the same physical space of the stage, deictically as a feminine spectacle subordinated to the spectatorial male gaze, and as sexual commodities to be selected by the consumer. Undoubtedly Yuan theatre was very much operating in the confines of a patriarchal structure.

However, the significant point about this theatre in terms of women is that the performing convention began with the presence of actual women on the stage and some representation of the experience of women in the theatre. The southern drama *Huanmen zidi cuo lishen* [The wrong career of an official's son] is a good example of a play representing the experience of people in and connected to the theatre. It is the story of an actress who leads a traveling family troupe and her romance with a young scholar who betrays his class and "lowers" himself to join the actors' profession, hence the ironic "wrong career" of the title.

According to Case, the division between the public (the property of men) and the private life (the confinement of women) in classical Greek culture privileged the public life in the classical plays and histories and rendered private life relatively invisible, resulting in the suppression of actual women in the classical world and the male invention of a representation of the gender "Woman" (Case 318). This binary division of public/private was enforced in China with the fall of the alien Yuan rule and the restoration of orthodox Confucian sexual ideologies during the last two imperial dynasties. One result being the development of male transvestism in the public theatre, which reached a peak in the nineteenth century and later experienced its greatest height in the early decades of the twentieth century.

Yuan Theatre: The Other and the Alien

The Other is not just theatre itself; the Other was also the "origin" of Chinese theatre.[35]

Yuan theatre was a cultural space open to possibilities which became deviant exceptions in the theatres of subsequent periods of late imperial China; for instance, female players on the public stage, the dominance of female players, the mixing of female and male players on stage, the cross-gender casting frequently practiced by female players, and the presence of a female audience. These differences between the Yuan theatre and later theatres must derive from a set of historical-cultural codes in Yuan society which deviated from the traditional mores of Han-Chinese. Again in sharp contrast to Ming and Qing times, there was no edict specifically banning female entertainers in the Yuan period. Ironically, in two Yuan government legal documents we find an imperial edict of 1278 forbidding officials and rich and powerful people from forcing actresses into marriage in order to protect the female entertainers under the administration of the government Office of Music [*jiaofang*][36] from exploitation. It seems obvious that it was because the regular administration of the Office of Music was being severely impeded that the Office's director sent the memorial to the emperor that led to the imperial edict.

The alien rule of the Mongols, whose intrusion into Han-Chinese culture had at least partially and temporarily suspended the constraint of orthodox Confucian values, was perhaps fundamental to the emergence of these exceptional theatrical phenomena as well as to the rise of the first drama in China. Yoshikawa Kōjirō, for instance, attributes the vitality and vivacity of Yuan drama to the destruction of traditional Chinese views by Mongolian rule. He also describes the first years of Yuan society as a period divorced from tradition and permeated with freshness and liveliness (*Yuan zaju yanjiu* 223).[37] The ideology of the binary-oppositional and divided spheres for men and women, seen in the enforcement of the strict separation of male and female troupes in Ming and Qing China, was notably absent in the Yuan theatre.

Thus Chinese theatre emerged in a cultural climate that was already *alien* and *Other* to the Han-Chinese system. This Otherness contributed to the formulation of a Chinese theatre whose essential performing conventions became taboo in later theatres when orthodox Confucian ethical values were restored. In fact, the maturation of the first Chinese theatre was a result of the cultural intrusion of an Other. This mature theatre generated various boundary-crossing performance practices many of which were later suppressed as deviant after the restoration of Confucian values. The inferior status of the genre of musical theatre in literary history and of stage players as a social class throughout Chinese history is an embodiment of the anxiety of a normative society toward the deviant and transgressive Other.[38] Chinese theatre is not merely one among the many theatres in world history that have been policed and censored as a transgressive Other by normative structures of society; it differs in that it was in fact, *generated* in a location of cultural Otherness and then *relocated* in the traditional Confucian system.

The Girl Actress in the Ming-Qing Private Theatre

In European theatre, it was not until the late medieval period that women gradually disrupted the monopoly of men on the stage. In southern France, the specific cultural and social circumstances of the position of women — the previous existence of female troubadours (*trobaritz*), women's noble birth and control of fiefdoms and their ability to inherit land, the importance and popularity of women in *commedia dell'arte* in Italy and France — enabled a break of the male theatrical monopoly in the sixteenth century (Ferris, *Acting Women* 36–8). In England during the Queen Anne era (1695–1706) between one-third and one-half of the new plays staged in London were authored by six women playwrights.[39] Between 1640 and 1740, more than a hundred plays were written by some thirty women with social positions ranging from a duchess to a servant (Pearson xi). Women not only appeared on stage after the Restoration, but also gained importance in dramatic creation. Furthermore, female cross-dressing became more visible in European societies in the late sixteenth century, becoming prominent in the subsequent two hundred years before being lost in the nineteenth century, the practice being by far strongest in the Netherlands, England and Germany (Dekker & Pol 2).

In the theatre of the same time, in addition to playing female roles, women also played men's roles. According to John Harold Wilson's *All the King's Ladies* (1958) on the London stage, from its reopening in 1660 to 1700, 89 plays out of some 375 first productions had one or more roles for actresses in male clothes (73). He also comments that, "In at least fourteen more plays we know that women were assigned to don breeches and play parts *originally written for men*, not for female impersonators. At least three plays were 'acted all by women,' who *took both the male and female roles*. In addition there were many revivals of older plays with breeches parts *originally played by boys*" (73; emphasis added). The male anxiety underlying this account (although written in the mid-twentieth century) is revealing. The repeated stress on women *dis*placing and *re*placing men, i.e., taking up man's *role* — both his theatrical profession and gender identity, points to a potential inversion of the hierarchy in theatre. This inversion culminated in the eighteenth century with the female cross-dresser functioning as an invert,[40] embodied in her perversely visible body, as exemplified by theatrical female cross-dressers like Charlotte Chark — a popular performer in the 1730s who specialized in breeches roles, who was disowned by her father, the playwright and actor Colley Cibber, for being a cross-dresser on and off stage.[41]

While women in European theatre were emerging on stage from the early modern period, female performers in late imperial China lost ground to male players from the seventeenth to the nineteenth century. Female cross-dressing in Chinese society experienced the same reverse development compared to Europe. The fashion of women cross-dressing as men prevailed for a time in the Tang Dynasty (618–907) among the nobles and the gentry class (Huang Shilong 122–3) and in Song times, emperors' concubines, ladies in waiting and female servants in high officials' households still kept this custom (Dai 162).[42] An existing group of wall paintings in Shanxi province, dated to the Yuan period, shows representations of ladies in waiting dressed in male costume (Liao 230). In the Ming and Qing periods, when the Confucian sexual ideology of division of men and women was more seriously and determinedly carried out, this domestic cross-dressing was still practiced among some gentry women and courtesans. However the courtesans, for instance Liu Rushi cited by Dorothy Ko, "the freest to negotiate and even to violate gender norms and roles," ironically cross-dressed herself not as an "androgynous *person*" but an "androgynous *woman*" (279; original emphasis). The androgynous body in this case only reaffirmed, but not blurred, the male/female gender binary. In the meantime, female performers vanished from the public stage, and the presence of actual women on the stage in Chinese theatre experienced multidimensional changes after the Yuan period as well.

First, we can conclude that there was a general backlash against women because the ideology of separate spheres for women and men was rigorously enforced in society. In the theatre we see the male monopoly of the public stage and the restriction of female players in the private theatre. Although female players were composed of professional actresses [*zhuanye nüling*], courtesan-entertainers [*changjianyou*], and private singing-girls [*sijia geji* or *nüyue*], their performance context was restricted to the private realm. Female players never went on stage in public locations such as temples and market places (Lu Eting 155). Second, the prohibition on mixing male and female players in any performance context was also reinforced in the Ming-Qing theatre. Third, to a great extent it was due to the great fashion among the scholar-gentry class and the aristocracy of keeping private troupes (either all girls or all boys) that a specific genre in the performance history of Chinese theatre, the "female musical troupes" [*nüyue*], a kind of female troupe [*nüxi*][43] constituted solely of teenage girls, emerged and (unintentionally) exerted significant influence in the stage history of imperial China.

The first Ming emperor, Taizu (reign 1368–1398), launched a fierce attempt to eradicate the alien and "barbaric" cultural influence of the Mongols in the early years of the Ming Dynasty. The emperor "decried with disgust the moral turpitude of his subjects with their traditions corrupted by the intermingling of Mongol customs," traditions which included style of dress, use of personal names, ways of greeting as well as the marriage system and relations among family members; he "utterly detested the Mongols' levirate marriage system and the practice of a stepson's marrying his father's lesser wife if she became a widow" (T'ien 2). Van Gulik argues that after the alien rule of Yuan, Ming society saw an excessive return to Confucian principles and "developed an exaggerated veneration for the national heritage" (*Sexual Life in Ancient China* 264). When it came to the power relation between women and men in society the oppressive effect of this return to the native in reaction to the so-called "barbaric" alien ways was ultimately the enforcement of the confinement of women to the private household headed, of course, by men. Van Gulik writes that:

> Patronized by the government, the Confucianist principles began to work through to the daily life of the people. The separation of the sexes and the seclusion of women began now to be practised in earnest.
>
> (264)

Van Gulik also argues that Han Chinese men first came to be fully aware of the "value" of the segregation of women and the necessity of enforcing it under an alien rule:

> Thus the Chinese found themselves confronted with all the problems that face an occupied nation. . . . One of their first worries was how to prevent their womenfolk from being importuned by the conquerors. Householders, having Mongol soldiers billeted on them, tried to keep their women as much as possible confined to their own apartments, and now began to appreciate more the Confucianist rules for the seclusion of women. One suspects that it was during this period that the germs of Chinese prudery came into existence, and the beginnings of their tendency to keep their sexual life a secret from all outsiders.
>
> (245–6)

Again women were turned into an Other — the object of desire — in the struggle for mastery between men. Having his right to the total ownership of his women infringed by another man represented a complete defeat and conquest of one man by another, and as a consequence of this male anxiety, women were confined to the household. The next step, that of secluding women from the public theatre, should not surprise us at all. But in the Yuan period women were not yet strictly confined to the private sphere. After all, the Yuan Dynasty was an alien rule that in many ways opposed, and challenged the Confucian Chinese tradition, regardless of the extent to which the Mongols had become Sinologized. As mentioned earlier, Yuan imperial edicts did not specifically prohibit women's participation in theatre, although they do betray an anxiety at the mixing of men and women in the public sphere.

In one of the two moralistic treatises, "Table of Merits and Demerits" [*gongguo ge*], which were edited by Ming scholars in the sixteenth century (Van Gulik 246) but in terms of style and content "point to the Yuan period," we find a merit-deducting entry related to the present issue:

> Not keeping men and women separate in one's household – 3 [three merits to be deducted]

> (250)

The fear of mixing the two sexes not only appeared in government edicts, but also found expression in moralist writings such as these treatises used by the master of the house. It was with the re-emergence of Neo-Confucianism under such conservative return to "Chinese" culture in Ming China that women (as well as sexuality) were tightly confined to the private sphere. The separation of men and women was not only enforced between the public and the private realm, but also within the private household. So on the one hand, female players disappeared from the public stage; while on the other, girl actresses in domestic troupes were secluded from the males in the household. The girl troupe of the Ming scholar-official Qian Dai, which we know about from the notation book *Bimeng xu* [Records of dreams], was put solely under the strict supervision of senior handmaids and two female teachers (3242–3), and one of the house rules was that no boy servants were allowed backstage when the girl players were performing. When a boy servant was found peeking at the girls from another room while Qian was entertaining a distinguished guest with his girl troupe the boy servant was beaten up and expelled from the household (3242).

Another anecdote, recorded in the notation book *Lüyuan conghua* [Collected chats of Lüyuan] by the Qing writer Qian Yong, reveals how the idea of separating girl actresses from boy actors was still in force in the eighteenth century. The scholar-official Wang Wenzhi was famous for having five remarkable girl actresses in his domestic troupe. When they came of age, he married off three and gave the remaining two away to another scholar-official, Bi Huafan, who also kept a female troupe. Bi discovered right away that the two were actually males disguised as females, although Wang had had their feet bound and their hair was worn in the style of women (men in the Qing era shaved their foreheads and wore a short plait behind their head). Bi released them from their female disguises with a smile and made them his boy servants (based on the account in Zhang Faying 182–3). Through this anecdote, we see that troupes mixing girls and boys were never ideologically accepted. The need for Wang to *secretly* disguise two boys as girls, even to the extent of having their feet bound in order to render them the ultimate fetish for male desire, points to a specific gender ideology underpinning theatrical practices. Paradoxically however, in this case the urge to separate the two sexes in order to make a clear distinction between them resulted in a crossing of the two genders.

An oppression necessarily incites what it strives to oppress: as a result of a strict division between men and women on stage, the necessity of transvestism and the resultant fetishization of the actor's body radically problematized gender and sexuality rather than creating stabilized boundaries. The stage practice of separating female and male players after Yuan times arose more from gender ideologies than from formal theatrical considerations such as that suggested by Wang Guowei: "After the Song-Yuan period, men were able to disguise themselves for the female role and women for the male role. Therefore, there was no mixing of male and female players in performance" (*Guju* 199). It is curious logic to say that since either women or men can technically take up each other's roles on the stage there is no more need for the other sex. I would say that it was because of a patriarchal ideology of secluding women that women were totally prohibited from playing on the public stage (either as themselves or men), and that men and women were not allowed to appear together on stage in the private theatre and thus could not play their respective genders. As a consequence of these prohibitions performances mixing women and men vanished after the Yuan Dynasty and cross-dressing became compulsory.[44]

Because of the strict separation of male and female players, Chinese theatre had necessarily become a cross-dressed theatre. But unlike, for instance, the English Renaissance stage, which was a strictly *male* transvestite theatre, the division and polarization of the performers' gender in the Ming-Qing theatres simultaneously engendered two oppositional forms of cross-dressed theatre existing parallel to each other, and thereby generated even more multivalent structures of gender representation.

Now let us look at how the history of the female troupes is represented in major research works on the topic. The members of "domestic troupes" [jiaban] were mainly concubines, handmaids, or boy servants owned by the master of the house. The master/slave relationship seems omnipresent in history, with women always included in the latter term. The whole phenomenon of domestic troupes was in fact mostly one of "girl troupes." Hu Ji and Liu Zhizhong in their *Kunju fazhanshi* [History of Kunju opera] (1989) distinguish three types of domestic troupes:

> From a great deal of relevant information we can see that there were three different kinds of privately kept domestic troupes in the Ming period: 1) domestic troupes composed of singing-girls, commonly called female domestic troupes; 2) domestic troupes composed of singing-boys which we can call domestic boy troupes; c) domestic troupes composed of professional performers which we can call the domestic red-pear-garden [liyuan, i.e., theatre]. After the rise of Kunqu, domestic troupes in the Ming were mostly female, next were the boy troupes. Rarely were they made up of professional performers. Almost all of these domestic troupes performed Kunqu.
>
> (191)

Hu and Liu, and other theatre historians, also provide examples showing that these girl actresses were often between the ages of 11 and 13.[45] Apart from pointing out that female players predominated in the private theatre, Hu and Liu also attribute much greater historical importance to this kind of private theatre than did Lu Eting, who wrote before them.

This private theatre was historically situated in a position "reserved to a small circle and distanced from the masses," a class association that could easily be dismissed, and often was, in various contexts in communist China, especially at times when conservative leftist ideology prevailed. On the whole, people have been less concerned about adhering to a dogmatic Maoist-Marxist historical perspective in the era of the "four modernizations" which began in the late 1970s. Thus although Hu and Liu were scholars writing in mainland China, they faced fewer political constraints since they were writing in the 1980s. In fact, they state straightforwardly that family troupes were "an extremely important performance context of Kunju, and had influenced tremendously the art of singing and acting, as well as the creation of plays of Kunju" (188). Whereas Lu Eting, in his groundbreaking study in stage history, *Kunju yanchu shigao* [Performance history of Kunju opera], had a definite political agenda that affected his interpretation and evaluation of the contribution of female troupes and family troupes (including the boy troupes). This work, although published in 1980, is essentially a manuscript finished in 1963, as Lu tells us in the postscript (359). Lu's political agenda was to re-place the historically ultra-elitist Kunju opera in today's cultural space in the People's Republic of China by rewriting a "people's history" for this high theatre:

> There obviously existed in the performance history of Kunju two types of staging. One was the performance by people's troupes in market places (including theatres). This was much beloved by the masses. Another one was the so-called performance on red carpet by domestic troupes. This was reserved for the enjoyment of a small number of people. Although on the surface they influenced each other, *the former was actually the mainstream.*
>
> (7; emphasis added)

It is clearly an arbitrary judgment to conclude that public performance was the mainstream practice of Kunju opera in the Ming and Qing periods. The literati's leading position in the creation of scripts, criticism of the art of performance, and promotion of this theatre, as well as their penchant for the private girl troupes (as reflected in their theatre writings, which mostly concern the private theatre) had made private performance a major mode of production. Gender and class are entangled in Lu's historical discourse: the "mainstream" is presumably male and rooted in the common people; existing outside this central proper is the female "alternative" which was cherished by the refined higher class.

Lu's evaluation of the significance of female troupes differs from

Hu and Liu's in its different attribution of agency to actresses. Lu acknowledges actresses' specialties and contributions to the development of the "drama of young male and female" [*shengdan xi*], though placing them within the "necessarily and naturally given" all encompassing male influence on the stage:

> Needless to say, female troupes' acting had been influenced by male players. However, they had their characteristics too; for instance, excellence in plays for the young male and female roles. This was determined by their own specific conditions. Therefore, in terms of the creation of the characters of the young male and female, the achievement of female players, including those outstanding gestures and expressions, could possibly in turn have influenced male players.
>
> (248)

This implied gender hierarchy in theatre is reversed in Hu and Liu's narrative:

> Kunqu in the Ming period, which was predominantly composed of young male and female plays, was often performed by domestic troupes, especially those female troupes. The complete acting system of the art of the young male and female plays in Kunqu and its unique artistic style, were formed in the course of the development of domestic troupes, and especially domestic female troupes.
>
> (202)

In Hu and Liu's discourse, the family female troupes are transformed into agents creating and formulating the uniqueness of the art form that excelled in performing plays featuring the young male and young female roles. The question of the interrelation between female and male players and their mutual influence on the theatre in late imperial China, especially during the earlier transition from Yuan to Ming, remains obscure. A huge undertaking of primary historical research, if relevant archival records could still be rediscovered, would be necessary to clarify the related issues since there are too many missing links and discontinuities in the preliminary reconstructed performance history of Chinese theatre. How, if it did really happen, did the art of acting become monopolized by men and imbued with a gendered style in the Ming period? What happened to the Yuan actress tradition? How and when did the first dominating male acting model (if it ever existed) come into being?

The girl players in domestic troupes were trained by either female or male teachers — the very famous thirteen-member female troupe of Qian Dai was coached by two retired female players who were in their 50s and 60s (*Bimeng xu* 3240). It is clear that men did not monopolize the training of girl players. The teaching of girl players and the other ways in which female players, who obviously had a strong presence in theatre history though under male domination, asserted their agency in creating the history of the Chinese stage, requires and deserves another full length study.

For the moment, I want to emphasize that female players in the conventional theatre history of the Yuan, Ming and Qing periods have been represented and treated as an Other, and inserted as a particular category distinctive from the norm in a grand historical narrative which always presumes the subject as male. These narratives on the performance history of Chinese theatre reveal an uneasiness in dealing with this "object" of Otherness.

In two important recent works on the history of Chinese drama and theatre by mainland Chinese scholars — Zhang Faying's *Zhongguo xiban shi* [History of Chinese theatre troupes] and Lu's *Performance History of Kunju Opera* — focusing on stage performance and theatre troupes, female players are given specific chapter(s) with titles marking off this "particular category" of theatrical practice based on gender difference, marking off "female theatre" from some presumed theatrical norm which is not named while the narratives on the *male* transvestite stage are never marked off as "male." Here, the absence of the subject already assumes that it is male. Yet the significant and persistent historical presence of female performers and the female theatre continually disrupts the stability of the male narrative and exposes its incoherences in the representation of the female.

In chapter 3 I shall examine the representation of a defiant, cross-dressing girl actress in an anecdote recorded by a Qing playwright to illustrate how female agency causes disruption in male writing and is simultaneously contained by the male discourse. In chapter 4, the subversion and containment of women dressing in male clothes will be addressed in a critique of the representations of the woman warrior — potentially the ultimate female figure of resistance — in both classical texts and contemporary performances.

TEXT

THREE

A THEATRE OF DESIRE:
THE CONCUBINE AND THE HEGEMON KING

Lasciatemi morir: The Girl Actress Who Played the Hegemon King

"*Lasciatemi morir*" ("Let me die") — Catherine Clément opens the "prelude" to her engaging book, *L'opéra ou la défaite des femmes* (1979)[1] with these delirious words from Vincenzo Bellini's heroine Elvira in the opera *I Puritani*.[2] Koestenbaum says that, European opera not only kills its women, "opera kills the things it loves" (199). This is not the common pattern however in the tradition of Chinese opera, although from time to time there are heroines killed on stage. The Chinese operatic tradition represents happy union as a general structural device. However, the expression chosen by Clément to epitomize her feminist-psychoanalytic critique of European opera could well provide the title for an eighteenth century Chinese anecdote concerning a domestic singing-girl who excelled in playing the macho role of the legendary Hegemon King on stage.[3] Constrained by an exploitative patriarchal system, the eighteenth century girl actress who played the Hegemon King so well took the initiative to *let herself die*, to metaphorically and literally liberate her body from containment as a slave girl owned by a master. Before going into further analysis, let me give a translation of this short anecdote in its entirety. While in its original classical Chinese it can no doubt be read as a charming piece of literary work, the translation here serves the purpose of conveying narrative accuracy but not literary quality:

> Qing'er was a girl actress of the house of Liang Si in the town of Zhu. Liang's wife was originally a sing-song girl from Jiangsu. She was good at playing the musical instrument *pipa*. After she was married to Liang, she bought some young girls as maids and taught them acting and singing. Qing'er was defiant and often escaped from lessons. The surrogate mother whipped her every day. The other girls all tried to persuade Qing'er to comply. She said, "To get my obedience, the precondition is to let me change from the female role to the painted-face role. In this way, I could at least make use of the hero's disguise to vent my indignation." From then onward, Qing'er became unsurpassed in performing *The Thousand Pieces of Gold*.[4] A scholar named Zhan Xiangting was waiting to take up an office in Jinling. He and his friends stayed temporarily at Liang's. One night *The Thousand Pieces of Gold* was staged. When it came to the act of "Farewell to the Concubine," everyone had his heart on the concubine except for Xiangting, who alone regarded the Hegemon King as lovely and charming. All others broke into uproarious laughter. When the girl players removed their makeup, everyone saw that the veteran Hegemon King was much more beautiful than the beauty in the tent. They gasped in admiration of Xiangting's insight. The next day a feast was held under a crabapple tree. Scholars and beauties sat next to one another. Qing'er was born in Anhui and Xiangting in the neighboring Jiangxi. The two thus expressed their affection for each other in their hometown dialect. Others at the banquet could only smile to one another, without knowing what Qing'er and Xiangting were talking about. After some days, Xiangting's scholar friends all left by boat. Although he had already stowed his luggage, Xiangting still stayed behind because he could not forget about Qing'er. He thought of buying a boat to take Qing'er home. However, Liang, Qing'er's master, took her to be a rare commodity that may be kept for a better price. He also wanted to retain her to lead the troupe. Some time before a millionaire had failed to get Liang to sell Qing'er. Now face to face, Xiangting and Qing'er shed tears. Xiangting pondered anxiously but could not come up with any suggestion. Qing'er said, "How incompetent you are in finding solutions! The reason that they take me as a not-for-sale rare commodity is that they use me to make big money for them. After you go away, certainly I will not live. Then it won't take a thousand pieces of gold to buy my corpse for burial."

Xiangting was in great grief, but he could do nothing. He gave her his farewell blessings and left. Less than two months after Xiangting arrived home, the news of Qing'er's falling ill and subsequent death came. Xiangting said, "We'd pledged to keep our promise faithfully in front of the flowers. You didn't go back on your words, how could I go back on mine?" He hurried to Jinling and bought the body and a coffin with three hundred pieces of gold. Qing'er was buried to the north of Bridge Tongjing. Madam Wang and Cao Moting wrote epitaphs for her; several celebrated scholars lamented her death with elegies. I [the writer of this anecdote] wrote the music drama *A Smile of Thousand Pieces of Gold* and had it performed by the troupes. Ah! Not being able to serve one's love alive, thus one reunites with one's love through death. Is it not a thought that a person in love would follow when caught in a desperate situation? And because of this Qing'er is not dead.

(Ren *juan* 3: 28a-b)

This incident is recounted in more than one source in traditional informal writings. It is related briefly in the Qing notation book *Xu banqiao zaji* [Sequel to *Miscellaneous Notes from a Wooden Bridge*] by Zhuquan Jushi, where the author tells us that he heard it from a fellow townsman. This account differs from the version quoted above in that Qing'er's identity as a girl actress is not mentioned and what remains is a sorrowful love story between a scholar and a woman (5056–7).

The passage quoted is taken from a detailed version included in the large anthology of dramatic criticism *Quhai yangbo* [An extensive collection of writings on music drama] (1940), edited by the Chinese drama historian and Dunhuang scholar Ren Zhongmin.[5] This version was originally written by the Qing writer-scholar Shen Qifeng (1741–?), known today mainly as a prolific playwright at the time of Emperor Qianlong. The story comes from his *Xieduo* [Harmonious bell], a collection of stories in the classical literary language much under the influence of the great work of short fiction *Liaozhai zhiyi* [Liaozhai's records of the strange] by Pu Songling (1640–1715). A contemporary noted that Shen's book was well known and ranked it second only to Pu's work itself (Jiang Ruizao 185; Wang Yongjian 647).

The writer of *Sequel to Miscellaneous Notes from a Wooden Bridge* tells us that on one occasion he was too late to catch a stage performance of Shen's *A Smile of Thousand Pieces of Gold* [*Qianjin xiao*] and regretted having missed the play, though his fellow townsman had seen it (5056). Based on this information, it is evident that the play mentioned by Shen himself was actually written and performed. Shen wrote some thirty to forty plays, and they were much sought after by performers. However this play was lost[6] along with many others and only four of his dramatic works have survived, all with plots involving female into male cross-dressing (see Introduction n4).

It is important to trace a brief history of the story's textual circulation for several reasons. First, it should be pointed out that this short piece of narrative by Shen, like many works categorized as *xiaoshuo* [narrative; literally "small-talk"] in traditional Chinese literary criticism, crosses the boundary between historical writing and literary writing. The narrative is both an anecdotal entry presumed to be factual (at least to a certain extent) and a piece of literary work included in Shen's collection of classical short fiction. Second, the narrative's multilevel-intertextual references are highly revealing for the study of theatre and drama from various perspectives: conventional and avant-garde, historical and theoretical. The narrative itself, as a textual representation of the tragic career of a beautiful teen actress who dies for a scholar, is paralleled by a canonical play about a concubine who commits suicide for her king. The rewriting of this narrative into another play by the same author, Shen, adds further interest to the generation of the story's textual representation. Shen's dramatic version, *A Smile of Thousand Pieces of Gold,* could very likely have a happy ending, judging from the title.[7] Third, the story is interwoven with various gender issues: cross-dressing, the construction of masculinity and femininity, and the oppression of women. All these attributes make this story a significant discursive representation of a particular moment in Chinese theatre, with multivalent cultural implications.

A major primary source for academic research, the records in notation books and informal writings have been used repeatedly by literary and cultural historians, yet this anecdotal narrative with its multiple dimensions has thus far escaped the attention of scholars writing histories of Chinese theatrical players, troupes or performance.[8]

This seems unusual, since the anecdote's apparent exposition of the patriarchal oppression of women in imperial times should easily have made it an example *par excellence*, in line with the rather unsophisticated Mainland Marxist criticism of feudal society in pre-communist China regularly used to emphasize the evils of "old feudal China" in contrast to the "new China" under the leadership of the Chinese Communist Party. Mainland critics often arbitrarily gave oversimplified critiques — based on textual information much scantier than the Qing'er anecdote — of the literati's class exploitation, and offered tremendously disproportionate *re*interpretations of any courtesan-entertainer in imperial times as a virtuous figure of resistance against oppression.[9] My point here is not in any way opposed to the Marxist (as broadly defined) critique of culture and society. On the contrary, I am suggesting that more delicate theoretical thinking on the subject and reflections on one's political agenda and position are indispensable in seeking to expose injustice in society past and present, and to achieve an effective critique of any hegemonic ideology in culture. An effective exposing and dismantling of political agendas (hidden and overt) requires sophisticated theoretical investigations into cultural productions and the production of culture.

In the narrative under discussion it is perhaps all too obvious that Qing'er is first and foremost a figure of female transgression. As a domestic girl actress slave of the master of the house, her recalcitrant rejection of theatre training and subsequent demand to play her subjective choice of the masculine role-type (the painted-face) in order to vent her grief are no doubt acts of resistance against patriarchal oppression. The tone of the narrative is implicitly sympathetic toward Qing'er as a representative of the doubly oppressed — a woman under patriarchal containment and a victim of the institution of slavery in imperial China. There is a more subtle interest in Qing'er's story lying behind her overt resistance.

I would like to look at her action as a radical gesture of resistance intended to appropriate strategies of representation and to subvert representation. Qing'er is a strong, talented, and intelligent woman who first resists learning the female role, then excels in performing the masculine role. When the crisis comes, it is she, not her boyfriend

Xiangting, who understands perfectly the operation of patriarchal power and her commodification. Her action of letting herself die disrupts the patriarchal exchange of woman as commodity.

The politics of representation in this short narrative are also intertwined with the dominant intertext — the Ming play *The Thousand Pieces of Gold* by Shen Cai. Perhaps the insertion of this play into Qing'er's story was the artistic choice of the writer Shen Qifeng; or perhaps it formed part of the facts the anecdote was supposedly built upon. In any case *The Thousand Pieces of Gold*, as an intertext, functions as a counterpoint to the narrative.

This dramatic story of the Hegemon King and his concubine was based on a well-known historical incident from the third century B.C.E. The Chinese empire was in an uproar at the fall of the short-lived Qin Dynasty (221–207 B.C.E.), whose First Emperor [Shihuangdi] built the awesome imperial tomb with thousands of terracotta warriors in today's Xi'an. Struggling for mastery of the empire were the Hegemon King of Western Chu, a formidable warrior and initially the region's most powerful warlord, and Liu Bang, the King of Han and the future first emperor of the Han Dynasty (206 B.C.E.–220 C.E.). At the time of the Hegemon King's final disastrous defeat, his loyal mistress Concubine Yu, failing to cheer him up and unwilling to burden him further, committed suicide by cutting her throat with his sword. The Hegemon King later broke out of the encirclement by Liu's forces, but he felt great shame at his failure and he too killed himself.

This household story of the downfall of a historical tragic hero and his virtuous concubine who died for him at first constituted only a short episode in the 50-act play *The Thousand Pieces of Gold* written in the late sixteenth century. Throughout the history of Chinese opera, this play has been a standard work in the repertoire of Kunqu, the theatre that dominated the Ming-Qing stage. In traditional drama criticism, there are frequent references to the dramatic text, its performance on stage, and the actors who excelled in playing the Hegemon King (Lü Tiancheng 226; Jiao 200; Li Dou 14a; Ren *juan* 3: 28), though not the concubine. We can extrapolate that the center of focus had always been the male protagonist. The act of "Farewell to the Concubine" [*Bieji*], number 37 in the Ming playscript, gradually became the most popular episode, performed as a "select-scene play." This act ends with Concubine Yu's suicide and is nowadays almost always performed independently, without the following act in which the Hegemon King commits suicide, signifying his failure in the struggle for (male) power.

This pair of characters, the Hegemon King and Concubine Yu, represents the ultimate in the gender construction of the ideals of the masculine and the feminine in Chinese theatre. But from the beginning this binary opposition in the representation of the male and female genders was neither stable, nor coherent. In Shen Cai's *Thousand Pieces of Gold*, the stage directions stipulate that the character of Liu Bang, the King of Han is not to be assigned to a male role-type, but is to be played by a female role-type player — the *xiaodan* [minor or secondary *dan*] (Act 13 "Huiyan" [The banquet], *Qianjin ji, Liushizhong qu* 35). The role of Liu Bang is in fact a minor one in this Ming play, the hero throughout is Han Xin, Liu Bang's greatest general. This downgrading of Liu Bang's masculinity by casting a female role-type to play him in order to heighten the contrast with the ideal masculinity of the Hegemon King turned out to be a destabilizing element. The Hegemon King has remained a domain of the masculine painted-face player to the present day. The player underneath a role-type could in fact be either male or female, and in this instance the deliberate dislocation in the representation of the "natural" gender relations between the role-type and the character had complex consequences.

The gender condition was further complicated by a circular movement back to the convention that enabled a female player to perform a male role-type and thus play the Hegemon King on stage — this is what we see in Shen Qifeng's narrative of Qing'er. Qing'er's oscillation between these two gendered poles in their extreme manifestations, both on and off stage, is the cause of disruption in representation. Qing'er is portrayed as the prettiest and most feminine young girl in the domestic troupe, as is seen in her first being assigned the young female role and the revelation of her beauty to Xiangting and his friends later in the narrative. She *is* the perfect woman for the conventional female roles typified by the "concubine," a stage figure of the most conventional woman constructed by society. Yet the narrator, in telling us that she rejects this representational imposition, and also implies that in her own effort to pursue the opposite, she becomes more than successful in cross-dressing as the Hegemon King. Her unsurpassed playacting of the Hegemon King — a figure of the *most masculine* kind on the Chinese stage — constitutes an attempt to create a moment of "spacing-off"[10] of representation in a hegemonic discourse, that is also "a movement from the space represented by/in a representation, by/in a discourse, by/in a sex-gender system, to the space not represented yet implied (unseen) in them" (de Lauretis, *Technologies* 26). This space-off is created by the tension and contradiction between the two gendered poles which Qing'er juxtaposes in their extreme form.

But Qing'er's effort to locate herself in a radical position — to create and navigate in a liminal space between the bipolarity of male and female genders — cannot escape the inscription of gendered representation. Her feminine beauty is masked behind an *almost* perfect impersonation of one of the arch "tough guys" in Chinese culture. Only one of the spectators is able to penetrate her masculine mask, and reach her feminine prettiness. She is dragged out of her space-off by a male gaze; she can successfully veil her feminine prettiness self from all men except the one who turns out to be her true love. It could be that the girl actress's cross-dressing was what attracted the scholar in their first encounter — when Qing'er playacts the Hegemon King and Xiangting casts his spectatorial gaze on "him/her." This ambivalence is not a question of the deception of gender identity, everyone in this story knew that all the performers were girls since the Chinese theatrical tradition is that a private troupe was either all girls or all boys and no mixing was allowed by convention. In terms of gender tension this performance context is similar to that of the early modern English stage of Shakespeare and his contemporaries: the spectators knew that the women on stage were played by boys. The ambivalence in the Qing'er narrative lies in her androgynous body, in her subversive attempt to mask her feminine prettiness behind the thick beard of a physically rugged stage character. Unlike the late Ming courtesan whose androgyny reaffirmed the feminine identity, Qing'er's androgyny is a crossing-over of gender division. Her femininity underneath her masculine disguise is recognized only by the eye of the true love — we see the essentialist notion of romantic love as pure, natural, honest and free of any disguise at work here.

After she is unmasked (when she removes her makeup after the performance), her true appearance is exposed and she is fixed in the ideal of femininity for the rest of the narrative, there is no more Hegemon King, no more gender-crossing. The narrator neutralizes her radical meaning and finally turns the story into a male narrative of desire, and male anxiety at this unconventional woman's spacing-off movement is overcome by once again containing the woman within the heterosexual matrix of the male narrative of gender. Qing'er's last words to her beloved — "After you go away, certainly I'll not live. Then it won't take a thousand pieces of gold to buy my corpse for burial" — amount to an aria that declares: "Let me die!" The metaphoric tune of *Lasciatemi morir* is one that Qing'er had refuted and rejected: she was to sing this in the role of Concubine Yu had she not struggled successfully to play the Hegemon King. But in the narrative, Qing'er is ironically made to sing the tune of death in her real life. In another twist of irony, we can also ask: "Is Qing'er's death not a repetition of the Hegemon King's sense of failure?" The female body that at first functioned as a celebration of rebellious strength and artistic creation is in this sense contained in the patriarchal discourse in the end. But this female body is both dead and not dead, as the narrative aptly concludes. Qing'er has been re-presented by a flux of writings not just by men, but also a woman, Madam Wang, as recounted in Shen Qifeng's anecdote. The writings are dedicated to the dead — epitaphs, elegies, and the play *A Smile of Thousand Pieces of Gold*, but they are also a promise of immortality through writing. Qing'er is therefore silenced and not silenced, Shen Qifeng's play ironically reconstitutes her aria, her voice, and her presence. To use a musical metaphor, Qing'er and Concubine Yu constitute an *invertible counterpoint*: whether it is heard at the top (as the host text) or bottom (as the intertext), the aria "Let me die" sounds equally "good." The two figures constitute a double counterpoint in which the two voices interlock; each depends on the other to interweave a web of ideological subversion and containment.

Patriarchal Containment: Mei Lanfang's Concubine

The play about Qing'er has been lost, but the original play about the Hegemon King and the concubine survived and prospered. In 1921 Mei Lanfang created his Beijing opera version — *Bawang bieji* [Hegemon king says farewell to the concubine] — and the dramatic story began another phase of its life in which the focus was shifted to the concubine. The play has enjoyed unsurpassed popularity ever since. Mei, the supreme Beijing opera actor of modern times (specifically, a male *dan*,) successfully reinvented this theatrical representation of woman through his aesthetic transvestism and at the same time, on a certain level seemed to have reduced male dominance or at least to have balanced the male/female power relation within the narrative.

His success in reviving this play has been considered one of the great steps in his acting career, and Mei's Beijing opera version has been so influential that it has affected today's Kunju opera in the staging of the "farewell scene." Many Kunju opera scripts have been inherited directly from Ming and Qing plays but in two recent performance versions of the Beijing Northern Kunqu Opera Company [Beijing beifang Kunqu juyuan], the traditional text formerly adopted from the Ming play *The Thousand Pieces of Gold* has been almost completely altered and the performances followed Mei's version by shifting the focus of attention to the concubine. Mei's addition of the sword dance to the play has become so classic that all other regional operas, including the most prestigious "mother of all Chinese operas," Kunju, have adopted it.[11] Mei's *Hegemon King Says Farewell to the Concubine* has become so paradigmatic that it now virtually "represents" Chinese opera insofar as Beijing opera has come to "represent" Chinese opera. Today the most representative dramatic figure from Chinese opera to a *world* audience (both Chinese and foreign) is undoubtedly the concubine in the "farewell scene" of this Beijing opera. For better or for worse, Chen Kaige's *Farewell My Concubine* has put the concubine figure as well as (a stereotyped) Chinese opera in the international limelight.

Mei Lanfang's representation of the weaker sex via a reinvention of the concubine figure through the male transvestite body is quite an inversion of Qing'er's female appropriation of the space of representation dominated by the male. Before Mei, the play's center of attention in the history of Kunju performance had been the Hegemon King, while in the original Ming text, the Han general Han Xin is the protagonist in the 50-act drama. In both cases, it is the masculine body that dominates. In this regard, it is useful to point out once again that the character of Liu Bang, the arch-rival of the Hegemon King, is assigned to a female role-type of the secondary rank in the Ming play, making the Hegemon King's ultimate rival, in a sense, a "woman." The gender assignment on the level of role-types serves to call our attention to the ultra-masculinity of the Hegemon King figure and the character of the Hegemon King became one of the most important roles for actors specializing in the painted-face role-type.

The concubine character given greater prominence by Mei began humbly, appearing in only two acts in the Ming play (Act 14 "Yeyan" [The night banquet] and the "farewell" act). Furthermore, even in the "farewell" act she is only given a few lines (119–21). The presumed genders of the subject and the object are quite clearly implied in the title of the act: "Farewell to the Concubine." Who is saying farewell to whom? The implied subject is the universal male: an implication that Mei's title, *Hegemon King Says Farewell to the Concubine*, concretizes by filling in the male proper noun as the subject in the text. At this point a paradox emerges concerning the stage performance of Mei's reinvention of the play. Some people have complained that Mei's versions should really be called "The Concubine Says Farewell to the Hegemon King" since the augmented female role now overshadows the male role. The greatest "Hegemon King" in traditional Kunju opera Hou Yushan complains in his memoirs *Youmeng yiguan bashinian* [An acting career of eighty years]:

> Today, the prevailing performance version focuses on Concubine Yu (the lead was changed to the female role-type after Mr Mei Lanfang), . . . therefore some people say that the current version is not "Hegemon King says farewell to the concubine" but "the concubine says farewell to the Hegemon King."

(237)

But how much has Mei really inverted the subject hierarchy of the masculine over the feminine? In modern China, where the women's movement has become a conscious social struggle, Mei's representation of a number of strong women characters (woman generals, among others) seems to have been in line with progressive social awareness. To many people, one effect of Mei's *Farewell* has been a subversion of the sexual hierarchy through the displacement of the male character from the center and the insertion of a much strengthened female character in his place. Read closely however, Mei's version can be seen as paradoxically constituting a more subtle misogyny than the Ming version or an older Beijing opera version collected in *Xikao* [Collection of plays].

In the Ming play *The Thousand Pieces of Gold*, the misogyny is stark naked and shameless. The Hegemon King, encircled by Han troops and lamenting his disillusioned military deeds, asks Concubine Yu:

> [King] My beauty! I care not if I die; I am just loath to part with you. Where will you head for?
>
> [Yu] You should know, my Great King. A loyal minister does not serve two kings, a virtuous woman does not serve two husbands. If anything inauspicious happens to you, I will not think otherwise [but dying with you].
>
> [King] No, no, no. You'd better go and serve the King of Han. I am to part with you, forever.
>
> [Yu] My Great King, *you need not be suspicious of me.* Grant me your sword and I shall kill myself first.
>
> [King] My beauty Yu, *you are really this virtuous.* Aye, *I shall give you my sword.*
>
> [Yu] My Great King, I shall leave you. We would not meet again unless in dreams. You can go and break out of the encirclement without worry.
>
> [Yu kills herself.]
>
> (121; emphasis added)

More or less the same text is kept in the version in the *Collection of Plays*, though the Hegemon King also adds that the King of Han is a voluptuous man (*Bawang* [*Xikao daquan*] 595). In Mei's version, the Hegemon King never reveals any worries about losing Concubine Yu to his enemy as he does in the earlier versions, never giving voice to his fear of having his woman taken by another, which, in a power struggle between men, signifies the greatest blow to the virility of a man. Nor does the Hegemon King in Mei's play ever doubt Concubine Yu's loyalty as he does in previous versions, leading him to test her faithfulness by suggesting that she surrender to the King of Han. In Mei's version the Hegemon King is a righteous hero whose love for his concubine is pure and eternal, and therefore it is Concubine Yu who takes the initiative in suggesting she kill herself so that she will not hinder his attempt to break out of the Han army's encirclement. Mei's Concubine Yu says:

> If I go with you, I will tie you down. No, no. I will take the sword hanging around your waist to kill myself in front of you . . . .
>
> (*Bawang* [Ed. Wei Lianfang] 42)

In one of the most touching moments in Beijing opera, we hear another woman's utterance of "Let me die!" but the deeply loving Hegemon King refuses to give up his sword. Yu, however, steals it from him by trickery and uses it to slash her throat. While being moved by this modern tribute to the good woman, we must note that the veiled misogyny is just as unacceptable as unreserved misogyny. The man is portrayed as a superior, and the woman as even more virtuous than in previous versions. She takes all the responsibility for her action and its consequence — death. Her action is also a violent devotion materialized in suicide. It is a violent devotion impelled not by her own fear and agony, but by the wish to free the man of his worries and burden so that he will have a chance to survive a military defeat. The addition of the now classic sword dance further heightens the concubine's body as an object of physical desire cast by the king's male gaze. Mei's own words show that he created Concubine Yu on such terms:

> Concubine Yu is a person of goodwill, experienced, passionate, faithful and unyielding. She hates war, longing for peace. Her love for Xiang Yu [the Hegemon King] is total. She even sacrifices herself for love.
>
> (*Mei Lanfang wenji* 134)[12]

Such is the behavior required of a woman in love. The ideal virtuous woman must sacrifice herself. This is the romantic ideal of woman constructed on patriarchal terms and it is reiterated over and over in representing conventional woman in the male discourse. Concubine Yu joins many women on the European operatic stage who sacrifice themselves for love and die in the name of the Father, for man.

A 1990 book-length study on Mei Lanfang has this comment on his stage interpretation of the concubine character: "The unsurpassed faithfulness in her self-sacrifice and the tragic sublime in the sword dance embodied the most typical virtue of ancient Chinese woman" (Xu Chengbei 169). The male attribute of the "tragic sublime" is perhaps a fitting description of Mei's artistic achievement (let us assume that we can bracket off "art" from ideology for just a moment) for the concubine is a theatrical representation of a conventional woman by a man and the creation of a "perfect woman" through the transvestite body. This passed-as-woman male body is more a part of the process of the reaffirmation of a male self than a subversion of the patriarchal gender system. Mei's representation of Concubine Yu posits a construct of a feminine ideal based on masculine desire.

This rather self-contained and stable theatrical representation by Mei is inverted by the Qing'er story as read in the present analysis. The representational rupture in the Qing'er narrative lies in the contradiction that in order to achieve the containment of woman, the narrative first has to represent Qing'er's transgression. In fact, the certainty of textual containment "is destabilized by its own necessary representation of female transgression" (Traub 145). It is also a sign of the impossibility of the patriarchy ever completely containing female transgression within the stereotype of the so-called "most typical virtue of ancient Chinese woman." This is despite that "*Lasciatemi morir*" is still sung by the *dan*/diva, and "faithful and virtuous" women are obliged to slit their throats or conduct the ritual suicide of Cio Cio the Butterfly in order to comply with the patriarchal ideology of "*Con onor muore / chi non può serbar vita con onore*" ("He dies with honour / who can no longer live with honour") (Puccini 152) — all supposedly for the love of men. But as Koestenbaum points out, Butterfly can at once be read differently by focusing on her entrance rather than her death:

> When heterosexuality unveils itself as *sumptuous* and *delusional*, the libretto shatters, and shadow-knowledges speak: by loving Butterfly's entrance more than her death . . . I can hear Butterfly as the emissary of sex-and-gender ambiguity. By listening sentimentally and interminably, by never outgrowing this entrance phrase, I can speak a different Butterfly.

> (200; original emphasis)

Just like the schmaltz of Puccini's opera, Shen Qifeng's narrative in its original indulgingly elegant classical Chinese easily overwhelms the readers and makes us forget gender politics. However, by "interminably" contemplating Qing'er's defiant transvestism, we can speak a different Qing'er by rewriting her desire, a desire for a sexuality and love that dream of "wide-open spaces, and cause strange flows to circulate that do not let themselves be stocked within an established order" (Deleuze and Guattari 116), a desire to become man (by playing the Hegemon King), and the desire for freedom and love. On and off the stage, the interminable circulation of transgressive desire is operating like a phantom behind the imposed veil of chastity through the female cross-dressed body.

FOUR

(CROSS-)DRESSING UP TO POWER:
WOMAN WARRIORS

The woman warrior is one of the most threatening unconventional female figures to the patriarchal imagination. There has been no lack of this unsettling "warlike woman," to use Edmund Spenser's phrase, in literature and theatre from different corners of the world: Hua Mulan from a Chinese poem of the Northern Dynasties (386–550) who reappears in fiction and on the stage (in traditional opera and spoken drama) to the present time; Spenser's Britomart who carries on a mission that involves saving British civilization (Shepherd 10) and the sexually threatening "Amazon" Radigund in the *Faerie Queen*; Ludovico Ariosto's Bradamante (*Orlando Furioso*) who is the model of Britomart; Torquato Tasso's Clorinda (*Gerusalemme Liberata*) who is the unknowable woman who must be unmasked to find "a positive image that reveals [her] true nature" (Petroff 40); Richard Wagner's Brünhilde (*Der Ring des Nibelungen*) whose laughter at Siegfried's death presents "a thorn in interpretations of her character" (Abbate 208) which oscillate between "tragic heroine" and "romance victim" (209).

These woman warriors, as different and culturally specific as they are, share one common behavior; they act in defiance of their assigned gender role. Many of them transgress the dress code and disguise themselves as men; and many are put to death in the end. How the body of the woman warrior negotiates gender ideologies is what I intend to investigate here through an analysis of the theatrical representations of Chinese woman warriors.

Rereading and Reinventing Mulan

The term "woman warrior" will remind many Anglo-American readers of Maxine Hong Kingston's now canonical work *The Woman Warrior: Memoirs of a Girlhood Among Ghosts* (1976) in which Fa Mu Lan (Hua Mulan),[1] the legendary Chinese woman warrior, and a household name in the Chinese cultural tradition is reinvented into a hybrid construct by Hong Kingston in the context of American muticultural politics. Hua Mulan was first immortalized by an anonymous Chinese poem which tells the story of how Mulan disguised herself as a man and joined the military in her elderly father's stead for ten years. In the end she returns home with glory and awes her male camp mates when she removes her disguise and reveals herself as a beautiful woman.

Hong Kingston's Fa Mu Lan is a far cry from traditional Chinese representations in that her woman warrior is virtually no longer "Hua Mulan" but a composite figure of a woman warrior reconstituted as a hybrid of different Chinese warriors from folklore, legends and histories.[2] These underlying warrior figures include several females and at least one male. An obvious male warrior figure appropriated is the national hero General Yue Fei (1103–1141) of the Northern Song Dynasty (960–1127), whose mother tattooed the four characters *jingzhong baoguo* ("serve the country with adamant loyalty") on his back. Hong Kingston's woman warrior's back was tattooed by her parents with oaths and names.[3] Mixing Yue and various traditional Chinese woman warrior figures, the woman warrior reconstructed by Hong Kingston had, in her own words, the "power to remind" her that she would not "grow up a wife and a slave," but a "warrior woman" (20) and "female avenger" (43). It can also remind us to pay attention to how the representations of the woman warrior in traditional Chinese opera function in the patriarchal ideology in Chinese society.

Decades before Hong Kingston's Chinese-American reinvention of Mulan in narrative fiction, Mei Lanfang had already re-presented this woman warrior in his Beijing opera play *Mulan congjun* [Mulan joins the army], first performed in 1917, with the intention of arousing the nationalism and patriotism of the Chinese people against foreign imperialism and promoting sexual equality between men and women. The legend of Mulan was also re-adapted by Chinese opera playwright Ma Shaobo several times between 1943 and 1951 for the sake of "encouraging the revolutionary fighting will of the People's Liberation Army and the Chinese people" (Preface 2).[4] It was the "patriotism" of Mulan that was put in the foreground in the early 1950s during the Korean War in which the People's Republic of China fought the U.S. imperialists (Yan Huizhu i). But before any modern playwright or Chinese opera actor usurps this legend, Mulan has to be, before anything else, appropriated as a Han-Chinese by race — since the historical authenticity of Mulan and her ethnicity has long been lost in the traces of textual reproduction. In Ma's adaptation, Mulan is presented as a native of Yan'an — the holy land of the Chinese communist revolution.

Hundreds of years before Mei and Ma, the late Ming writer and painter Xu Wei had already adapted the story of Mulan into a short *zaju* play that had a great influence on the representation of women in Chinese drama by later playwrights, both male and female. Xu's play *Maid Mulan Joins the Army in Her Father's Stead* differs from Mei and Ma's versions of Mulan, in that it places more emphasis on filial piety and chastity than nationalism and patriotism.

The scene in the first act of Xu Wei's play in which Mulan unbinds her bound feet in order to disguise herself as a man before she embarks on her military adventure reveals an oppositional dynamic of containment and subversion at work. This foot-binding motif is not found in the original "Ballad of Mulan" which dates back many hundreds of years to a period when foot-binding was not yet prevalent. It is common knowledge today that the bound foot as a fetish signified the ultimate subjugation of women in late imperial China. Xu's insertion of the most oppressive patriarchal constraint on women is itself revealing enough and needless to say, in modern versions, including Mei's, the figure of the bound foot is totally erased.

Xu's Mulan, in order to put herself in the shoes of a man, has to undo (although only temporarily) the containment of the patriarchy epitomized in foot-binding. The undoing of the fetish unleashes the female from male control and renders her power that surpasses man's. Her later actions justify what she says before changing into male disguise: "standing on earth, supporting the sky" [*lidi chengtian*] (352). Mulan's military prowess is fully demonstrated in this play, as there is no lack of acrobatic fighting indicated in the stage directions. Yet unbinding her feet causes her to worry about how she will get married when she returns from the battlefield with a pair of enlarged feet. Readers and spectators in the past would feel relieved when Mulan immediately tells of a magical soaking treatment that can re-shrink the feet to the size of the "golden lotus" (352). In this way, the unconscious feminine subversion is immediately contained by naturalized masculine values and this is further illustrated by the theme of chastity running through the whole play. Mulan gets her parent's consent to playact as her father's double only on the condition that she keeps her virginity — the most valuable price of women as commodities of exchange in the imperial past. In response, Mulan sings, "Be at ease, mother. I'll return to you a virgin daughter" (354), and she does keep her promise. Upon her return after more than ten years of absence, she employs a metaphor for her virgin body in her joyous tune: "returning to you the same non flower-bearing bud" (361). The androgynous body is immediately kept in check by the non-deflowered female body within and her subordination to the patriarch — the father — is taken for granted. Mulan's crossing of gender lines is only provisional. At the end of the day, as all Chinese familiar with the story will know, Mulan is decorated by the emperor, returns home, removes her male garment, is reunited with her family and, in Xu's version, gets married as arranged by her father. She comfortably fits herself into the space prescribed by the Confucian gender system.

With frequent references to other women paragons throughout the text, Xu's Mulan was constructed in the Confucian tradition of the "virtuous woman." In the early decades of the twentieth century, Mulan was constructed by Mei as a patriot and a voice for women's equal rights. Early in the play she says, "I wish to share my country's sorrow. This is the same to men and women" (*Mulan congjun, Xikao daquan* 575). As an ideology, patriotism supercedes gender boundaries and tames Mulan's potentially subversive androgyny. Very near the end of the play, Mei speaks through Mulan with a modern consciousness of sexual equality, but within the limit of the national:

> You warriors should realize that if women are determined to establish themselves, they become the same as men. Since women's education does not prevail in our country, ordinary women all become trash. Were all our country's men as strong as Mulan, we would have nothing to fear of the barbarian countries, even if there were ten folds of them.

> (593)

However, all progressiveness and transformative potentiality, overt or hidden, is ultimately translated into the traditional values of filiality (for the family) and loyalty (for the country) that run through the text and are given one last fanfare at the end of the play (594).

After a survey of historical records of military women and imaginary representations of the Chinese woman warrior in Chinese opera, Barbara M. Kaulbach argued that "[n]one of the woman warriors on the Chinese stage are allowed activities that could potentially bring about social change" (77), and concluded that structurally they "behave in principally the same way: brave fighters in times of war, they resume their woman role at the end of the war" (80). Joseph R. Allen also argues that the traditional version of Mulan is not "primarily the story of military action but rather of returning home" (346). Focusing on visual depictions of Mulan across centuries, he further argues that "the most recent and culturally most divergent versions are ultimately also tales of domestication" (346). Xu's Mulan is in the beginning fighting for the cause of man, as the play's title suggests that she "joins the army in her father's stead." She is entirely a substitute for man. Nothing can be more symbolically powerful than the scene in Mei's version in which Mulan's father orders his old military uniform to be altered to fit Mulan's body (*Mulan congjun, Xikao daquan* 576). Mulan's male garment in this specific condition is as empowering as it is domesticating.

Also obviously blended into Hong Kingston's construction of the Chinese woman warrior are the legendary stories of the Yang family generals and their women, also from the Northern Song period.

According to the legends told in traditional drama and fiction,[5] three generations of the family's men were killed in battle against invading "barbarians"; their widows, who were audacious warrior women, took up their husbands' roles to protect their country and fight against the alien enemies.

Stories of the Yang family woman warriors enjoy great popularity in today's regional operas. The ever popular full-length Beijing opera play *Yangmen nüjiang* [Women generals of the Yang family], was first adapted by Fan Junhong and Lu Ruiming in 1960 and subsequently made into a classic Beijing opera film. This full-length play was also staged by the China Beijing Opera Company [Zhongguo Jingju yuan] at the Bicentennial Anniversary of Beijing Opera held in Beijing in January 1991.

Like Mulan, the Yang family woman warriors are substitutes for men, but this time the men are dead men. On one level, the women are represented as a projection of the male, as man's complementary opposite. However, more space of resistance has been negotiated out of this text. This Beijing opera on the one hand reinforces a sexual hierarchy which hides and sanctions the way gender is imposed by force; yet on the other hand this patriarchal discourse, in re-inscribing, re-presenting and re-producing itself is caught in a paradoxical condition of chronic self-dismantling, which culminates in the total absence of the "Father." In order to contain the powerful and transgressive woman generals, the Father has to make himself *absent* and *invisible* – it is news of the death of the last male general of the Yang family that touches off the plot of this play.

Also of special interest concerning the figuration of the Chinese woman warrior is the episode in which Hong Kingston's woman warrior gives birth to a baby in the midst of a war while hiding in the battlefield (40). This is not part of the literary tradition of the Mulan legend but is reminiscent of a stock scene in several *daomadan xi* ("sword-and-steed woman warrior plays")[6] in which a woman warrior, either a Han-Chinese or a "barbarian," gives birth while fighting in a ferocious battle and then either wins or loses the battle on account of this biological-sexual function, the battle's result depending on the play of cultural politics in specific contexts. This thematic episode recurs often in plays relating to the military adventures of the Yang family against alien enemies.

In contrast with European opera and drama, the woman warrior role-type in Chinese opera is unique in its widespread presence in the general repertoire and in its imposing representation of the power of women — in terms of sociopolitical status, physicality and supernatural power, depending on the individual character depicted. (The closest Western operatic counterpart that one can think of being perhaps Wagner's Valkyries, especially Brünnhilde, in the *Ring* cycle.[7])

The physicality of the Chinese woman warrior in the use of the body in dancing movements and acrobatic acting has made this role-type a distinguished lure. As displayed in the physical prowess of the body of the *daomadan* and *wudan* performers and the characters' dangerous potential to displace men, the Chinese woman warriors appear as a fabulously strong female sex that is a potentially disruptive force in the patriarchal order. Yet the theatrical representation of this figure is repeatedly imbued with layers of gender politics and frequently entangled with racial domination in which woman as the Other is often subordinated in one form or another. In addition to returning home, the woman warrior can be undone through captivity, like Hu Sanniang in *Hujia zhuang* [the manor of Hu], one of the most popular *wudan* plays in both Beijing and Kunju operas. This disorderly woman is first relegated to an object of desire by the deformed Wang Ying, nicknamed "short-legged tiger," and is defeated and captured in the end. The woman warrior can even be condemned to death like the "barbarian" warrior princess Bright Pearl [Mingzhu] in *Tiangang zhen* [The Big Dipper battle formation], though it is also in this extreme form of silencing that more subtle textual politics of resistance can possibly be played out.

The Virtual Cross-Dresser and the Alien Other: Princess Bright Pearl

I shall move on to a close reading of a current performance text of *The Big Dipper Battle Formation*, a "sword-and-steed woman warrior play" from the most prestigious and historically influential Kunju opera, that enacts an episode from the saga of the Yang family generals: the sixth son of the family sets forth to fight against an inimical Other — Princess Bright Pearl, a pregnant "barbarian" woman warrior of the kingdom of Liao, which is challenging Song China's hegemony over the great landmass of East Asia. Through a critique of the ideological assumptions of this play, I shall demonstrate how the patriarchy is obliged to simultaneously empower the subversive feminine — the woman warrior figure — while appropriating and containing it within an oppressive representation posed and masked as natural. As feminist theatre critic Gayle Austin states, "[plays] combine verbal and nonverbal elements simultaneously, so that questions of language and visual representation can be addressed at the same time, through the medium of an actual body. They contribute a unique field of examples of women's representation" (3). The present discussion will take into account the acting and costume — the body — as well as the dramatic text.

The Big Dipper Battle Formation is a "select-scene play" which originated from an episode of a chuanqi play, Xianglin xian [Birth of the lucky star] written by the late Ming playwright Yao Ziyi.[8] The performance of The Big Dipper had been preserved for generations in the traditional repertoire of the Northern Kunqu school. The play was one of the showpieces in the repertoire of the noted Northern Kunqu performer Ma Fengcai (1888-1939), a transvestite actor specializing in the daomadan.[9] In the following generation another transvestite actor, Wu Xiangzhen (d. 1990), who was recruited into the Beijing Northern Kunqu Opera Company in the 1950s was renowned for his performance of this play. Yang Fengyi, the current leading player of Big Dipper learned it from Wu.[10] The play was revived by the company in 1983. A rendition that made major changes to the traditional version was completed in October 1988, taking into consideration the new cultural context for the production and reception of Chinese opera in late 1980s China. The immediate success of this version has made it the standard text ever since. It is classified as a play in the category of "preserved repertoire" [baoliu jumu], indicating the play's status in the company's repertoire, and the fact that it is considered valuable and officially endorsed. The following analysis focuses on this new version and is based on a performance script dated July 16, 1989, a live performance that I saw in Hong Kong on November 17, 1989, and a video recording of a performance at Jixiang Theatre [Jixiang xiyuan] in Beijing on November 26, 1988. At critical points in the analysis, I shall also examine the differences between the new and the traditional version. The following is a synopsis of the play. The story takes place in China during the Northern Song Dynasty. Yang Yanzhao, the sixth son of the loyal Yang family and one of the legendary "Yang Family Generals," is defending Song against the kingdom of Liao (916–1125) on the order of the Emperor. The Liao army has set up the "Big Dipper Battle Formation"[11] as its fighting unit. The commander of the "Big Dipper Battle Formation" has been killed in a confrontation with the Song army and the plot of the play commences at the point of his death, thus he plays no part in the dramatic action. Princess Bright Pearl, wife of the deceased commander, therefore takes up his position to fight against Yang and his army. Yang is at first hesitant about launching an offensive attack because Bright Pearl is expecting a child. Although he is unwilling to take advantage of her precarious position he is soon persuaded to attack by his deputy generals Meng Liang and Jiao Zan and gives the order to strike. Bright Pearl, a strong woman with an indomitable will, has studied warrior techniques and strategy since she was a child. Determined to avenge her dead husband, she is resolute and unflinching in leading her army against Yang, regardless of the fact that she is about to give birth. Her subordinates Xiao Tianyou (a man warrior) and Huang Qiongnü (a woman warrior whose name means "jade girl") fail to dissuade her from her decision.

On the battlefield, Bright Pearl defeats the four Song generals Meng Liang, Jiao Zan, Yue Sheng and Chen Lin with ease, but she soon feels worn out because she is about to give birth. She confronts Yang, who tells her to surrender on the grounds that she is no longer able to fight because of her pregnancy. Bright Pearl rejects Yang's proposal and is then defeated by him. Soon afterwards she is chased to the edge of a cliff by the four Song generals whom she had defeated earlier. The four Song generals repeatedly demand her surrender, but in desperation Bright Pearl rides her horse off the cliff and manages to escape. Upon the annihilation of the "Big Dipper Battle Formation" and hearing the newborn baby's cry, Yang orders his soldiers not to hurt Bright Pearl, and recalls his forces. Bright Pearl returns to fight Yang and his troops after giving birth to her child, and she dies as a result of overexerting herself.

Structurally, the dramatic situation and action of the play are derived from and move forward in rigid pairs of binary oppositions of contradiction, resistance and oppression. Two levels of hierarchical oppositions can be discerned: one is the gender opposition of male and female, the other the racial and cultural opposition of the "civilized" and the "barbarian": Song-China versus Liao. Not only is the dramatic world of the play patriarchal, the ideological underpinning and discursive perspective are also ethnocentric. At the beginning of the play Yang swears to wipe out the *hu'er* ("barbarians"), and the four Song generals in the course of combat shout repeatedly to Bright Pearl, "Barbaric girl, surrender!" The Liao people were viewed by Song-China as less civilized people lurking along the Empire's border. Adopting a self-elevated ethnocentric point of view, which regarded itself as civilized and occupying the center, China gave itself the designation *Zhongguo*, literally "the Central Kingdom."

The play's main protagonist is the Liao princess, but the dramatic perspective is Chinese and male. Bright Pearl also speaks from a Sinocentric viewpoint, when she commands her troops, she addresses them twice as *xiaofan*, meaning "little alien barbarians." This is not an exceptional case, as it is a convention in traditional Chinese theatre that non-Han characters refer to themselves as "barbarians."

This kind of unnaturalness underpinned by a culturally biased perspective has been overwhelmingly naturalized in Chinese opera. This play of the cultural politics of gender is further implicated in the power politics of contemporary China where racial minorities are subordinated to the Chinese Communist Party under the guise of "ethnic autonomy," the best known example being the question of Tibet. Because of ethnic politics, at least the outer appearance of the "barbarians" on stage has been turned as respectable as Han people. Cultural hegemony, racism and sexism are always intermingled. In this case, woman/Bright Pearl is represented as the Other/Liao and man/Yang is represented as the Self/Song (China). In *The Big Dipper*, the opposition between man and woman at the same time implicates racial and cultural contradictions.

The leading role in this play is a woman, Bright Pearl, and it is a drama of the tragic death of an admirable, gallant and unyielding woman. But Yang and his men, representing man and the civilized, are the first to come on stage and the characters who remain alive and triumphant on stage in the end: in the last moment of the play the dead body of Bright Pearl — a woman — lies in front of a group of warrior men, Song generals and soldiers, who freeze in triumph in a theatrical pose of stylized convention of *liangxiang*, literally meaning "showing (the) face," a consummation of emotions and manifestation of power relations in a momentary freezing of facial expression and body gesture in Chinese operatic acting.[12] A man also has the first as well as the last lines in the play. Hence, in the beginning are (civilized) man and his words and in the end it is again the same (civilized) man and his words, the predominant female presence is "wrapped up" in a male narrative, a system of patriarchal jurisdiction, a universe of the Law-of-the-Father, in the Name-of-the-Father. The play's overall structure is interweaved in a series of bi-directional movements between female empowerment and its containment.

The play begins with Yang's entrance. He sings:

> Heroic generals and soldiers,
> Men like tigers and leopards.
> The might of the army is great,
> Earth moving and mountains shaking,
> I shall sweep away the Tartars [*hu'er*].[13]

Finishing the tune,[14] Yang recites:

> Entrusted with the imperial edict, commanding the army to withstand the Great Liao.
>
> Tartars advancing here will have their souls annihilated.
>
> Over the three barriers, my mighty name makes people tremble, With a loyal heart, I protect the Song Dynasty.
>
> I, Yang Yanzhao, am guarding the three barriers on imperial edicts. The repugnant Liao army has repeatedly violated the border. Not long ago the scout reported that the principal general of the Big Dipper Battle Formation had been killed in battle. Taking advantage

of this fine chance, I shall destroy the Big Dipper Battle Formation. Meng Liang and Jiao Zan have been sent to find out about the strength of the enemy but haven't reported.

Elements of the two hierarchical oppositions of man/woman and civilized/barbarian are inscribed in Yang's short opening tune. Men, described as heroes, are represented in the metaphoric allusions to fierce animals, or more accurately, predators: tigers and leopards, and Sinocentrism is registered in the term *hu'er* that Yang, a Song-Chinese general, uses to refer to the Liao army. In traditional Chinese historical discourse, various insulting terms meaning "barbarians" have been set against *Han*, a word often used to also mean "Chinese" and implying a highly developed, advanced civilization (the adoption of the term from the mighty Han Dynasty). From a Sinocentric point of view, the Song Dynasty was weak and vulnerable from the beginning, in contrast to the Han or Tang dynasties, for instance. Throughout its history, the Song Dynasty was threatened by the other inimical "barbaric" races — in opposition to the "civilized" Chinese self, since these alien peoples fringed the borders of the Chinese empire. The arch-challengers to the Song Empire were the Liao and the Jin (1115–1234), who "conquered" land formerly under Song rule and established their own kingdoms, challenging Song's claim to sole hegemony. The Song Dynasty was so weak that it had to share half of its land with the foreign Jin Dynasty, which ruled a large part of northern China, hence the historical division between the Northern and Southern Song dynasties. In the end Song-China and Jin were both overcome by another alien race, the Mongols, who set up the largest empire in human history — the powerful yet short-lived Yuan Dynasty.

The *hu'er* in the play *The Big Dipper* are represented as "invaders." The "repugnant Liao army," fighting against the Chinese, "has repeatedly violated the border." They are the alien Other threatening the power of Song-China. The regime that Yang, a man, represents is the legitimate center; the alien race represented by Bright Pearl, a woman, the Other, is illegitimate. In this representational construction, the two levels of contradictory oppositions of man/woman and civilized Chinese/primitive barbarians are contaminated to the extent that they are presented as natural and given.

After Yang's opening lines, his subordinates Meng Liang and Jiao Zan return from the battle front and report:

> *Meng* The commander of the Big Dipper Battle Formation was killed. Princess Bright Pearl has taken up the important task in his stead.
>
> *Jiao* That Princess Bright Pearl is pregnant. How can she lead the army to fight a battle? We should take advantage of this great chance to launch an assault.

In response Yang says, "I have not the heart to take advantage of someone's precarious position." It is Jiao Zan who convinces Yang by saying: "Supreme commander! It has been, ever since the ancient times, a necessity of war to take advantage of the enemy's weakness. Supreme commander, you shouldn't miss this great chance." Earlier on, Yang's words ("With a loyal heart, I protect the Song Dynasty.") have shown his virtue of being "loyal to the emperor and loving one's country," a virtue required of a righteous men in imperial China. Now he is depicted as a self-righteous Confucian military hero, a great man who does not take advantage of someone's precarious position, but he soon puts aside his moral conscience temporarily to strive for a practical objective. This pragmatism may not be un-Confucian after all.

On the part of Bright Pearl, pregnancy is a metaphor for a body in danger, a moment of the weakening of the empowered female body. It is largely because women in the past had no control over pregnancy — yes or no, where and when — that they were at the mercy of the patriarchal order. Even though a woman was as physically powerful as a man and to an extent challenged the coherence and stability of the patriarchal order it was difficult for her to escape from its containment and victimization. Meng Liang's words "Princess Bright Pearl has taken up the important task in his [her husband's] stead" reveal how the role of woman is understood from a male perspective: woman is only a substitute, a substitute for man. Later on this notion of woman as substitution is also spoken through the words of Bright Pearl herself.

Bright Pearl makes her first appearance in the second scene of the play. As a general, she performs the *qiba* [literally "the overlord rises up"] — a sequence of patterned, stylized, valiant dance movements representing a warrior's preparation for war.[15] There are two points to be made here. First, in the traditional version, Bright Pearl's initial entrance was played out in the conventional set piece of *dianjiang* ["reviewing the army and assigning tasks to the officers"] which requires no acrobatic dancing. Second, now that the more static scene has been replaced by an action sequence, further female empowering is in place. Woman warrior characters in other plays, while dazzlingly demonstrating military skills in the *qiba*, also unmistakably and at once reveal their feminine fragility. The acclaimed performance as Hu Sanniang in *Hu Jia Zhuang* by Wang Zhiquan, the distinguished *wudan* from the Shanghai Kunju Opera Company, being an example *par excellence*.

The characterization of Bright Pearl in this post-1988 theatrical representation has been changed from that of a traditional woman warrior type who is no less feminine than any ordinary woman, to a forthright and fiery man-like woman. But the stage appearance of Bright Pearl is "man-like" only in terms of temperament since a physically pretty female face has been cast as this warrior princess. On stage this figure embodies an ambivalent crossing of intense femininity and excessive masculinity — seen in the frequent and strenuous acrobatic fighting sequences throughout the play. The actress is required to perform this *qiba* in a masculine and powerful manner. More importantly for the present analysis, conventions and movements originally belonging to the *qiba* of the male military role-type [*wusheng*] are borrowed to strengthen Bright Pearl's masculine characterization, constituting another "infringement" of a specific male domain (Figure 1). In this version of the play Bright Pearl is an unusual woman warrior in Chinese opera, she differs from the traditional examples because she is a super-powerful woman who resolutely rivals men in physical power.

She sings while performing the *qiba*:

> I am here in military uniform and full of vigor,
> In charge of the Big Dipper Battle Formation, wielding the spear and wearing the armor.
>
> Born an enchanting and fragile beauty,
> I didn't care to take up a needle,[16]
> Love only to play with swords and spears,

> Leading brave troops and maneuvering battle formations,
> I dare say that even grown men are frightened.

And then she recites:

> I am Princess Bright Pearl. My husband was the commander of the
> Big Dipper Battle Formation. Because he was unfortunately killed
> in fighting the Song army, I am taking up this important task in his
> stead. Previously the scout reported that the Song army was about
> to assault our Big Dipper Battle Formation. Therefore, I am in full
> battle array, ready to meet the enemy.

Figure 1   Yang Fengyi as Princess Bright Pearl, the woman warrior and 'virtual
cross-dresser' usurping the power of the man-general. Notice the flag in the
background embroidered with the male-gendered term *shuai* [general]. 1994. Photo:
Siu Leung Li.

There is a recurrent theme in Chinese narratives, drama, historical
narratives and legends that on occasions when the man dies fighting
for his emperor and country, and is thus absent from "his-story," the
woman will act as a substitute for him in order to accomplish the
unfinished cause. To sacrifice oneself for the emperor and for the regime
was the highest ideal and honor for a great man in the feudal tradition
of China. If in an emergency situation it was necessary and unavoidable
to let a woman take up a man's job, she was only considered a mere
substitiute, acting only as a deputy of the absent man, as in Mulan's
case in which her father is "out" and virtually absent due to old age.

Women finish the incomplete job for men and are represented as men's complement. Bright Pearl — the woman — is not represented as fighting for her own cause, but for the man: a he-self in opposition to the she-other, a supposedly real and universal self that is absent from the play yet still tightly holds the power to dominate. Let us not forget that allowing the Hegemon King the chance to breakout from encirclement by the enemy without hindrance is what Concubine Yu willingly dies for.

Bright Pearl's masculine stylized movements in the *qiba* and the contrast between a weak and a strong image of woman in her lyrics show that she is powerful to the point of physically surpassing man. She is threatening because of her potential to displace man and disrupt the hierarchical social binary of male/female — a violent hierarchy in which the former governs the latter. However, just like the socially constructed representation of woman as "enchanting, fragile beauty working with needles," Bright Pearl the woman warrior is also always a male-construct. She is fabricated by the patriarchal consciousness out of its constant fear of the destabilizing female Other — in Bright Pearl's case, an ever-empowering woman whose determination equals that of a "tragic hero." The male narrative thus attempts to deprive her of independence and autonomy. Socially, Bright Pearl has no identity of her own. Her position of commander is inherited from her husband. It *origin*-ally belonged to a man: in a patriarchal system, men of course ally the *origin* with themselves and mask it as natural. When Bright Pearl announces, "I am Princess Bright Pearl. My husband was the commander of the Big Dipper Battle Formation . . . " she is defining herself as predicated on her husband's entity, attributing herself to her husband. Her statements after the utterance of her name and title undo her as a female *subject*. In this theatrical representation, the constitution of a woman's identity is constructed as dependent on the center of the male-*I* that displaces any space for a female-*I*. This specific representation of the woman warrior is a paradoxical effect of the patriarchy's *failure* to suppress woman's recurring subversion and its simultaneous need to reiterate containment.

In her effortless victory over Yang's four deputy generals and her undisputed leadership of the Liao army, Bright Pearl displays a prowess surpassing that of most men. But in the narrative she is unable to sustain her victory due to the biological actuality that she is shortly to give birth to her baby. This biological-sexual difference determines her failure. Just before confronting Yang she sings:

> Ah! Knowing that a woman hero can overcome a grown man,
> Enduring the pain in the stomach, pushing the horse.
> My hips feel as if they were stabbed by swords,
> Bursts of war drums rolling altogether.

Bright Pearl is thrown into a predicament — giving birth during a battle — by factors out of women's control, the inability of controlling pregnancy. In this case, she is doomed by her biological sex as a woman. Yet the general representation of the pregnant woman warrior giving birth at the battlefront is not a coherent one since childbirth can also be a factor leading to victory. The "battle formation," which carries sorcerous power, is a unique concept in the traditional Chinese military novel and is a recurring device in the Yang family saga. At times it is because a woman warrior gives birth while trapped in a formidable battle formation that the formation is dismantled, due to the desecrating presence of the unclean blood from the delivery that is an exclusively female function. Whether represented as beneficial or ruinous on the battlefield: the blood from delivery is always a formidable feminine force of destruction. Male power is incompatible with unique female physical capabilities since man has not been given the female multiple physical capacities of gestation, birth and lactation. By "referring to his [literary] creation as to his child," man has been "appropriating the life-giving act of childbearing" in literature (Trinh 37) and is also able to abuse the woman who performs these physical capacities through a textual victimization of her. Bright Pearl is unable to maintain her usurped male power, for in this specific theatrical representation she has to give birth in the midst of a battle and this exclusively female physical capability dismantles her resistance.

After she is defeated by Yang, Bright Pearl expresses her grief and sorrow in a type of tune borrowed from Beijing opera because existing Kunqu music was not considered effective enough in portraying the emotional intensity of dejection. Again, this is a major change made to the traditional Kunqu version. A *daoban* (the "Interjective Aria")[17] characterized by its intense, stirring and tragic quality is added:

> Trembling with fear, pain in the stomach, body without strength,
> Dry and cold, empty valley, hanging cliff, where to shelter?
> Pity me, cherishing lofty but empty aspirations,
> Hard to escape the dangerous situation.
> Pity me, swathed in iron clothes,
> Hard to fight the stubborn enemy.
> Looking at the Big Dipper, looking at the Big Dipper,
> Bursts of grief, tearful eyes, blurred and misted.
> Dreadful, dreadful, flag falls and the person annihilated,
> Verging on a hopeless situation.
> Oh, my husband!
> Fighting desperately to avenge my husband, will unbending.
> Defying death, will unbending.

Commenting on the tragic grief of the great ancient poet Qu Yuan (ca. 340–278 B.C.), the renowned historian Sima Qian (145?–90? B.C.) wrote, "Heaven is the origin of humankind. . . . People in destitution cannot help but cry to heaven" (*Shiji* [Records of the historian]: *Qu Yuan liezhuan* [Biography of Qu Yuan]). In the play *The Big Dipper*, we have the representation of a woman in destitution crying to her (dead) husband. Why is it that man in distress cries to heaven — "the origin of humankind" — while woman cries to her husband? Does man come from heaven and woman from man? Is this a culturally dislocated echo of the description of the creation of woman in the Judeo-Christian *Genesis*? When Bright Pearl is "verging on a hopeless situation," what she cries out is "my husband" and what she has on her mind at that moment is avenging her husband's death. Even on the threshold of death what she regrets is her failure to avenge her husband. That which has driven her to fight and defy death is the naturalized role for a woman as a substitute and complement of man. Earlier in the play, an overemotional inclination is seen in Bright Pearl's rejection of her subordinates' advice not to personally lead the army against the Song troops. After giving birth Bright Pearl returns to fight to her final death, further implying that she is irrational in throwing her weak body back on the battlefield in order to rekindle an already finished battle. Ironically, the forthright and fiery elevation of the masculine characterization of Bright Pearl in this new version of the play also leads her to her own destruction.

In the last moments of the play, Bright Pearl appears in a representation of woman as victim, wearing soft white "fighting skirts" [*zhanqun*] — her shoes have been white throughout the play. Having taken off her hard *kao* (the technical term for military armor in the system of Chinese stage costume) and *kaoqi* (military pennants), symbols of male power that she has temporarily usurped from men, she is now displayed as a fragile female body. Here we see a subtle play of sign systems and the body in the Chinese theatre that produces delicate meanings. The Prague School semiotician Karel Brůsák has commented aptly on the sign systems in the Chinese theatre: "[it] has devised a complicated and precise system of signs carrying a large and categorically diverse range of meaning" (60), and further elaborates on the structure of signs of theatrical costume in Chinese theatre:

> Chinese theatrical costume observes strict conventions . . . [and] is a complicated structure of signs. It differs from Western theatrical costume not only by its plurisignification but also by the nature of the referents. It reveals not merely the wearer's social status, age, and so forth, but his worth, character, and so on. It reveals an interesting interdependence between aesthetic outlook and questions of technique. For the costumes used are always made from high quality, expensive materials painstakingly put together to fulfill to perfection the demands of stern convention, while at the same time upholding the immutability of that same convention by their own durability.
>
> (64)

A new set of *kao* in light blue and white was made to suit the new version of the play for its premiere on November 17, 1988 in Beijing, and Bright Pearl's intention of seeking revenge and the final disposition of her body were further inscribed in her costume. The dominant color of her military armor is blue, the color of mourning to the Chinese, while her fighting skirt and shoes are white, the color of mourning and death itself. Since the beginning of the play Bright Pearl has been a mourner, mourning the death of her husband; and she dies in white —

as the saying goes, "the dead wear white." Fighting against the "perfect man," she, an "imperfect man," is destined to be defeated. The traditional representation of the woman warrior on the Chinese stage is from the beginning a male construct, the woman warrior is an imperfect (castrated) man, she is irrational, the weaker partner, always the weaker sex — the way Plato and Freud have defined woman in the West, as already demonstrated by Luce Irigaray in *Speculum of the Other Woman.*

As shown above, the choice of color for costumes and for the painted-faces is no casual undertaking in Chinese opera (Zheng Chuanyin, *Chuantong wenhua* 30–66). For instance red is often taken to symbolize happiness and another woman warrior, Liu Jinding, often appears in red armor in stage representations — in *Nü shasimen* [Slaughtering four generals: the female version] for instance — since she is about to get married. In the traditional version of *Big Dipper* which we can still see on video, Bright Pearl is not a widow, and is thus not an avenger. She is not in mourning and she too wears red. She does give birth at the battle in this version and therefore loses. The curtain falls as she retreats under the protection of her deputy generals.[18] She is still a defeated woman warrior, but without the tragic flaw of the insistence on a cause which leads to the tragic hero's downfall as embodied in the new characterization of Bright Pearl. In this respect, a certain modern cultural sensibility was imbued into this late 1980s reinvention which responds to and reflects upon the traditions of Chinese opera.[19]

Of the different types of costumes in Kunqu, Beijing opera and other regional operas, *kao,* the military armor of the characters of both the man-general and woman-general, is fundamentally a male garment. "When it comes to physical labor, women's attire has almost always, of necessary, been the same as men's" (Solomon, *Re-dressing the Canon* 178). The *nükao,* or female military armor worn for military physical labor, is the most male-oriented and *masculine* of the female costumes worn by female role-types. Symbolically, the woman warrior in Chinese opera is already dressed like a man, and let us not forget that in the cross-dressing tradition of Kunju and Beijing opera, woman warriors were played by men. In fact a female performer playing the woman warrior role-type is virtually (cross-)dressing up to power. The actress playing the woman warrior is in this sense always inherently cross-dressing.

Carol Gilligan has noted that: "The sex differences depicted in the world of fairy tales, like the fantasy of the woman warrior in Maxine Hong Kingston's . . . recent autobiographical novel . . . indicate repeatedly that active adventure is a male activity, and that if a woman is to embark on such endeavors, she must at least dress like a man" (13). Hong Kingston's Fa Mu Lan is given "men's clothes and armor" (33): "I put on my men's clothes and armor and tied my hair in a man's fashion" (36). Figuratively, the Chinese woman warrior on the stage is clad in a male garment, with cosmetic modifications to represent woman's femininity, rather than femaleness.[20] One must not overlook the fact that in traditional Chinese theatre, it is a convention that "feminine beauty" in the stage representation of a female character played by a *dan* performer, no matter whether a female *dan* or a male *dan*, is an indispensable constituent factor of a successful and great *dan*. The woman warrior, who is physically strong yet displays a male-defined feminine beauty, is defined in the terms of man. The woman warrior's body on the stage is like a tailor's peg-doll, in that its function is to carry sartorial attributes.[21] Her identity and power and all other attributes are granted by the garments she wears — the garments she has "stolen" from men. Even though she is clad in *kao* — the symbol of male power and of the perpetuation of that power as symbolized by the enduring quality of its material and the painstaking artistry of its tailoring — and has usurped (provisionally) a man-general's position of power, Bright Pearl the woman warrior always remains an "imperfect man." The costume has paradoxically become a trope of female appropriation of male power as well as the imprisonment and oppression of the female body. The woman warrior's female subject is ironically put under erasure in her act of usurping male power by taking up a man's clothes (the military armor) and position (commander). The usurpation of male power coincides with the erasure of the female subject. Always an object and a complement of man, she is never allowed to be a successful rival to man. At best, she is acting as a deputy for the man who once owned her and continues to imprison her: obsessed with the dead man, Bright Pearl fights to avenge his death.

In her last spoken line Bright Pearl cries out to the Song troops who have won the battle and are ready to withdraw, orders them to stop their reckless provocation and states that she is there to fight them again. At this moment, she identifies herself to the Song army as *guniang*, which can be translated as "girl" in English. Earlier on when Bright Pearl was first asked by Yang to identify herself ("You who are approaching on a horse, are you Princess Bright Pearl?"), she answered, "Indeed, I am the supreme commander." From the status of a "chief commander" [*shuai*] to that of a "girl," Bright Pearl's different linguistic utterances are self-reflexive of her respective situations, first as a woman who is in a position with the power of a general/man, and then as a vulnerable woman, a male stereotype of a defenseless "girl."

Behind Bright Pearl's demonstrative strength as a warrior woman is the hidden condition that she is participating in a war game — a men's war game. She is to follow man's rules of the game, and the rules are to play with bodily violence, metaphorized in her love of playing with swords and spears. Struggling inescapably in a man-centered world, Bright Pearl is inexorably entangled in this male war game. Her husband's early death leaves her to complete man's highest manifestation of the noble spirit of loyalty — that of no retreat, no surrender. The last line of the play is uttered by the Song general after Bright Pearl dies in front of him and his men on the stage . The final line turns out to be the ultimate homage that one warrior pays to another: "This is a true hero among women! Bury her corpse with good care. Withdraw!" [*zhennai nüzhong haojie, jiang qi shishou haohao yanmai, shoubing*]. The white, fragile, dead female at his feet is thus transformed into a most respectable enemy, comparable to any man. It is important to note that part of the code of the man warrior and the hero is that he respects his strong and decent enemy in the Chinese military tradition, as best exemplified by many instances in the great classic long narrative *Sanguo yanyi* [Romance of the three kingdoms]. This heroic code of behavior is equally applicable to women, and the female body of Bright Pearl is given deferential treatment as an honorary man.

In the modern times, women warrior figures in traditional Chinese opera have gained great popularity with the rise of the *dan* role-type. The emerging prominence of the *dan* in the early decades of the twentieth century was attributed to the growing awareness of women's rights in China. At the very beginning of her 1938 book on Chinese drama, which is dedicated to Mei Lanfang, Cecilia Zung says that "the Movement for the Emancipation of Women . . . accomplished the leadership of the "tan" [*dan*]" (xxiii) in Beijing opera. It is true that from the 1920s to the mid-40s, it was the *dan* that dominated the traditional Chinese stage and it is also true that Mei's genius contributed enormously to the rise of the *dan*. The 1920s and 30s saw the rise and prosperity of the so-called "four great *dan*" artists, with Mei the leader among them.[22] But it is important to keep in mind that they were all male *dan*, male "female" act*ors*, men. Just how the Chinese women's movement in the early part of the century affected the rise of the *dan* in Chinese opera (if the causal relationship did, in fact, exist), Zung did not explain. It would take another full-length study to examine this issue in detail, but it should be pointed out that the long tradition of the domination of the public theatre by men, especially in Kunju and Beijing opera, saw a phenomenon of men playing the role of women on stage in order to appeal to the almost exclusively male audience (oftentimes women's access to public theatres was severely limited or even denied). In a man-centered culture, man constructed the female stereotype for himself, on stage and off stage. Man has attempted to appropriate the stage representation of woman, trying to immerse destabilizing female figures in the patriarchy. Female *dan* players were generally considered inferior in their artistic achievement, and interestingly enough, the stage image of the four great male *dan* performers were arguably "prettier" than that of their contemporary female *dan* performers, judging by the high quality plates of male and female *dan* performers in Zung's book, for instance.

Nowadays in Kunju and Beijing opera as a general rule (there are very rare exceptions), *dan* role-types are taken by women while some female performers still play the *sheng* roles, a situation that has a lot to do with the Chinese communists' attitude toward gender and sexuality. The communists consider male cross-dressing unnatural and have unofficially stopped the training of the male *dan* (see chapter 8). In any case, the naturalized feudal patriarchal discourse still underlines Chinese opera, regardless of the disappearance of the male *dan* and the rigorous reform of Chinese opera. Feudalism has reinscribed itself in a traditional art form censured by the Chinese communist regime as an oppressive feudal ideological residue, especially during the Cultural Revolution. The communists' regulation of Chinese opera in the past fifty years, while destroying much of the cultural heritage, has not only failed to unmask and stop the functioning of the feudal patriarchy with its ideology of the domination of the Other, but has perpetuated this discursive practice. The formation of the Chinese Communist Party functions fundamentally as a patriarchal political organization (Gilmartin, "Gender in the Formation of a Communist Body Politic"). Chinese women, while ironically metaphorized as "half of the sky" [*banbian tian*], still largely play a subordinate role in a patriarchal system that has blended Western communism and feudal Chinese ideology — Chinese women have not been given, but have been supporting, "half of the sky."[23]

Toril Moi has said that contemporary feminism is "about transforming the existing power structures — and, in the process, transforming the concept of power itself" and rejecting the notion that "women's relationship to power is . . . exclusively one of victimization" (148). The traditional Chinese woman warrior, a powerful Other who poses a potential challenge to man's power and destabilizes man's *I* and its centrality, is mostly reduced and represented in a male discourse as a "potential same-to-be, a yet-not-same" (Godzich xiii). Her subversiveness is continuously oppressed and rendered as another stereotype in the universe of male writing. In today's revival and reinvention of the traditional play *The Big Dipper Battle Formation*, the representation of the woman warrior shows several tension points where a complex negotiation between the empowered and empowering woman and an oppressive but posed-and-masked-as-natural male narrative is subtly played out. The search for a power-transforming female representation in Chinese opera may not have circumvented victimization. However, as Judith Butler argues in *Bodies That Matter* (1993), that the normative "regulatory ideal" can never complete its materialization of "sex" through reiteration of regulatory norms, the repetitive subjugation of the feminine in Chinese opera through a reiteration of victimization is a sign that the regulatory patriarchal containment is necessarily never complete, and that the possibilities for revictimization open a fracture in the discursive space that can be used to turn the patriarchy against itself and call into question the hegemonic force. The extraordinary escalation of both the intensity of empowerment and victimization in the reproduction of the figure of Bright Pearl both textually and in performance is instructive. The possible implosion of this contending site of representation, embodied in the woman warrior, can be reclaimed as a space of hope for which to begin. This liminal space is also where the significance of rereading the representations of the woman warrior on the Chinese stage lies.

FIVE

UN/QUEERING THE LATENTLY QUEER AND TRANSGENDER PERFORMANCE:
THE BUTTERFLY LOVER(S)

Of the two best known stories of cross-dressing in traditional Chinese culture — the heroic adventure of Hua Mulan and the tragic love story of Liang Shanbo and Zhu Yingtai — the latter, best known as "the Butterfly Lovers" in English, has recently been in the spotlight of contemporary cultural politics in connection with the ambivalent queer tensions derived from the multi-level cross-dressing performance in the cultural representations of this tragic romance. Arguably the most celebrated folk tale in Chinese culture, surpassing Mulan and the White Snake, the earliest textual record of the "Liang-Zhu" story has been traced back to the Tang Dynasty (Lu Gong 10).

This legendary romance has been repeatedly retold in popular cultural forms from Yuan-Ming plays to various traditional and modern cultural forms, including prose narrative, folk ballad, regional theatre, classical poetry, modern novel, film, musical, concerto, ballet, modern dance, comics, and TV drama, and the list could go on. The plethora of Liang-Zhu texts in various art forms have been compiled into anthologies over the past few decades (Lu Gong; Qian Nanyang, *Liang-Zhu xiju jicun*), including a three-volume monumental collection published by the esteemed Zhonghua Press in Beijing in 1999. Entitled *Grand Collection of Liang-Zhu Culture* [Liang Zhu wenhua daguan] (1999), this collection pulls together works ranging from traditional operas to score excerpts from the violin concerto *Butterfly Lovers*.[1] The fact that this compilation of some 2,500 pages includes the term "culture" in its title signifies the cultural status given to this legend in mainland China. The predominant position of the role of Chinese opera in the history of this "Butterfly Lovers" saga is because it is essentially from this traditional art form that the modern generations of playwrights, filmmakers, composers and the like have drawn inspiration to re-appropriate this theme and produce their own modern variations constituted in, and at once constituting, specific historical moments and cultural contexts.

The plot line of Liang-Zhu varies in details from text to text, so it will be useful to summarize the essential plot elements of the story before further examining the gender trouble generated.

- Teenage girl Zhu Yingtai disguises herself as a boy to attend school in the provincial capital — Hangzhou — despite her parents' objection.
- Zhu meets the boy Liang Shanbo at a pavilion on her way to Hangzhou.
- Zhu and Liang spend three years studying together and become close friends. Liang does not know the true sex of Zhu.
- One day Zhu has to return home at her family's request.
- Liang sees Zhu off and walks her to the same pavilion where they first met — the Eighteenth-Mile Pavilion.
- On the way, Zhu gives many hints about her true sex to Liang, implying that she has fallen for him. Liang fails to read through Zhu's tropic expressions.
- Before they part, Zhu tells Liang that she has a twin sister. She wishes to make a match between her twin sister and Liang and asks Liang to visit her family to make a proposal.
- Later, Liang visits the Zhu mansion. At the rendezvous, Zhu reveals her true sex to Liang. The "twin sister" is in fact Zhu herself.
- By that time, her father has already arranged Zhu's marriage into another family.
- Liang is heart-broken, and returns home where he becomes seriously ill and dies.
- Zhu fights against the arranged marriage. Finally she assents, on

the condition that she will be allowed to visit Liang's tomb on her way to her future husband's family on the wedding day.

- On her wedding day Zhu mourns at Liang's tomb. The tomb cracks open and Zhu jumps into it.
- Zhu and Liang are transformed into two butterflies.

In Chinese theatre, it is recorded that this story was already being staged in Yuan times, but none of the Yuan plays exist in their entirety today. The earliest extant dramatic texts are three tunes with lyrics from a Yuan play[2] and some fragments from plays dating back to the Ming Dynasty.[3] The present discussion will include these Ming dramatic fragments and the following significant modern versions:

(1) *Liuyin ji* [In the shade of willows], Chuanju opera (premiered 1952);

(2) *Liang Shanbo yu Zhu Yingtai* [Liang Shanbo and Zhu Yingtai], Zhejiang Yueju opera[4] (premiered 1952); film version 1953 (also China's first color film);

(3) *Liang Zhu henshi* [The regretful story of Liang and Zhu], Hong Kong Cantonese opera film, directed by Li Tik, 1958;

(4) *Liang Shanbo yu Zhu Yingtai* [Liang Shanbo and Zhu Yingtai], Huangmeidiao opera film directed by Li Han-hsiang, produced by the Hong Kong Shaw Brothers Studio, 1963;[5]

(5) *Liang Zhu/The Lovers*, Hong Kong film, directed by Tsui Hark, 1994;

(6) *Liang Zhu/The Lover*, a musical written by Hong Kong playwright Raymond To Kwok-wai, 1998.

The Liang-Zhu story concerns a woman who refuses to be grounded, who transgresses the boundary of the private family compound and travels freely in the public realm. In modern times, the Liang-Zhu saga was first catapulted into a new height of popularity in mainland China in 1952, when two operatic versions — the Chuanju opera and the Yueju opera — were hits with critics and audience alike at the first national Chinese opera festival held after the establishment of the People's Republic of China in 1949. In subsequent developments, it was the Yueju opera version that disseminated the Liang-Zhu text beyond the boundaries of mainland China to Taiwan, Hong Kong and other overseas Chinese communities. This turning point signified the power of a modern medium — film. The Yueju opera Liang-Zhu was made into a film in 1953 and was shown to international audiences. The climactic moment in the film's global career came at the 1954 Geneva Conference, when it was shown to a cross-cultural audience, which included Charles Chaplin and China's Premier, Zhou Enlai (1898–1976). This Chinese opera film soon became a precursor text for later remakes in other regional operas.

The important aspect of Yueju opera most relevant to the present analysis is that it is today an (almost) all-female theatre. This regional opera first matured in 1906 (Shengxian wenhuaju 1) as an exclusively male theatre and the first female Yueju troupe appeared in the mid-1920s, only to fail miserably in Shanghai. Female Yueju troupes gradually gained success and displaced male ones in the 1930s (Gao Yilong 48–9, 71–4). Today Yueju opera in mainland China is basically female and is dominated by female players, although there are often a couple of male actors in each troupe. The most accurate description of the theatre thus being "an (almost) all-female theatre." The Liang-Zhu play is the definitive work in the repertoire of this regional opera which is necessarily a cross-dressed theatre.[6] The archetypal imagination of the male character of Liang Shanbo is constructed through the body of the female cross-dresser. Film director Li Han-hsiang's 1963 Huangmeidiao opera film also features an actress (Ling Po) playing the part of Liang. This film was a legendary success in Chinese communities outside China, especially in Taiwan. The Hong Kong Cantonese opera film *The Regretful Story of Liang and Zhu* (1958) also has Liang played by a female cross-dresser, Yam Kim-fai, a legendary figure in Hong Kong's popular imagination. Constituted by this decades–long cultural practice, it is now expected that Liang will be played by a woman.

Hong Kong playwright Raymond To Kwok-wai's 1998 musical *The Lover/Liang Zhu* is a "queer" version which starred a young stage actor in the role of Liang while a famous Cantonese opera male impersonator played her own sex in the role of Zhu in this production. This straightening out of gender roles, contrary to the traditional practice in operatic representations of this folk tale, appears even more ironic when we remember that this version was intended to queer the story. Tsui Hark's 1994 box-office hit entitled *The Lovers/Liang Zhu* also has a "natural" assignment of gender roles but with an intent diametrically opposite to that of Raymond To. Tsui Hark's straight cast is a result of his intention of remaking Liang-Zhu into a down-to-earth straight love story.

With reference to this variety of art forms retelling the Liang-Zhu story, I shall address the following issues: What is the latent subversion in sexuality in this story? How do we account for the cultural obsessions in relation to the dislocation of gender in this story and its associated theatrical form(s)? Why has the story been so popular in a female theater? Does Liang Shanbo have to be a "woman" (i.e., be played by a woman) to be embraced by Chinese operagoers? If so, why? Is it a manifestation of the patriarchy's anxiety: suppressing differences, maintaining bipolarity, resisting gender b(l)ending, and restoring order? Can the example of the Japanese all-female Takarazuka Revue throw new light on the present case study? Can the subalterns maneuver possible disruptions in the text and turn it into a reenactment of an unsettling undercurrent in culture? In this respect, how does Raymond To's "queer" musical version subvert and/or uphold compulsory heterosexuality?

Transgender activist Leslie Feinberg in her/his *Transgender Warriors: Making History from Joan of Arc to Dennis Rodman* (1996) uses "transgender" as "an umbrella term to include everyone who challenges the boundaries of sex and gender" (x). By this definition Zhu Yingtai is well-qualified as a transgender warrior, through her challenge of established gender ideology. Simultaneously, from the perspective of contemporary queer theory, it is conspicuous that in this legend the dominant structural device of female cross-dressing — and double female cross-dressing in the frequent case of an actress playing the role of Liang Shanbo — necessarily renders the seemingly heterosexual romantic love story unstable and multivalent in terms of desire and sexuality. However, the dominant heterosexual matrix has long constructed as natural a *straight* collective cultural memory of this legend, seen for generations as a boy-girl romance, in which, like Romeo and Juliet, the boy and the girl die for (heterosexual) romantic love.

We had to wait a thousand years after the first appearance of this tale in Chinese folklore for the inherent incoherencies in its narrative to be publicly attended to, by a film director and a playwright in 1990s Hong Kong. These two contemporary representations tried to resolve or make visible the queer tensions by way of requeering and/or unqueering the narrative. In addition, the undoubtedly female focus in the fundamental narrative structure of the story had incited earlier feminist-oriented reinterpretations, as seen in some film versions, especially the 1958 Hong Kong Cantonese opera film.

Although the character Zhu Yingtai is the active cross-dresser in the story, thereby challenging the existing patriarchal gender institution and its values, in today's female theatre of Yueju opera, through which the Butterfly Lovers was canonized, the actress who plays Liang Shanbo is also always cross-dressed. Zhu is the wilful woman whose sexual transgression is contained in the play. Wilful women "have acted autonomously by choosing their own sexual partners. The public stage provides a didactic platform in which the punishments for this crime can be enacted" (Ferris, *Acting Women* xiii). Whereas Zhu's containment is represented "over her dead body" (Bronfen), another well-known female character from Chinese opera — Du Liniang in *Mudan ting* [The peony pavilion], also a wilful woman in the sense that she imagines sex in dreams and insists on choosing her own sexual partner — is resurrected in the play to be co-opted into the patriarchal institution. Zhu however is a more subversive figure who pushes the plot to a defiant climax. The patriarchy, like the feudal ruler, cannot control that moment which escapes its power, that is, suicide, "a way of usurp[ing] the power of death which the sovereign alone, whether the one here below or the Lord above, had the right to exercise" (Foucault 138). Stephen Greenblatt's vein of the new historicist view of all-encompassing power and inescapable containment after Foucault may carry its argument through in view of the singing-girl's "*Lasciatemi morir*" and the final undoing of Princess Bright Pearl, the woman warrior discussed earlier. However, subversion is already represented by the act of containment: the singing-girl Qing'er lets herself die to prevent her master from making a fortune out of her body, Bright Pearl fights on in her own no-retreat-no-surrender determination, and

Zhu Yingtai's suicide prevents the arranged marriage. As Foucault has already hinted at the possibility of usurpation of power from the one above, the disruptive effect of the human agency of taking one's own life in one's own hands (both literally and metaphorically) in an attempt at transforming the world must be prioritized to envisage the alternative of thinking, reading, writing, and living differently.

Three Major Readings of Liang-Zhu

The "Butterfly Lovers" story has been a site of ideological contest ever since its first appearance in the writings of the literati. Throughout the ages, we can see a continuous rewriting and rereading of this story as each institution in power appropriated the story for the reinforcement of a specific ideological discourse. During imperial times, the dominant reading of the story served to uphold feudal patriarchal hierarchy, while in contemporary China, anti-feudalism has been the controlling political rhetoric in the reinvention of the story. Popular cultural re-imaginings of this story centering around sexuality — the queer/straight negotiation which generated effects of destabilizing the long time assumption of the stable heterosexual construct emerged at the margin of China in 1990s Hong Kong.

The first written records of Liang-Zhu from the Tang and Song dynasties without exception foreground the image of the "the virtuous woman" [*yifu*]. Zhu's death was brought to the attention of the Emperor of the Jin Dynasty by Prime Minister Xie An and her tomb was enshrined by the court as "the virtuous woman's tomb" [*yifuzhong*].[7] The central figure in the prose accounts from the Tang and Song dynasties through the county annals of the Ming and Qing dynasties are more often than not Zhu Yingtai, the woman, rather than Liang Shanbo, the man.[8] The earliest record from the Tang period seems to have locked into most subsequent prose recounting the key imagery of the virtuous woman/tomb, at least throughout the imperial period. The ideology of *lienü* and *jiefu* (both terms also mean "virtuous woman") in the thousands of years of Chinese traditional culture dominates the Confucian moralistic interpretation, co-opting this potentially subversive story to a mythology (in Roland Barthes' sense) to reinforce patriarchal values.

Since the founding of the People's Republic of China, an opposite dominant reading in the vein of socialist ideology has emerged to "de-doxify" the patriarchal appropriation, and the "Butterfly Lovers" has become a convenient vehicle for anti-feudalism. The preface to *Grand Collection of Liang-Zhu Culture* (1999), contributed by the renowned folk-culture scholar Zhong Jingwen, says, "The story of Liang-Zhu has profound ideas. Zhu Yingtai disguises herself as a man for the purpose of searching for the equality of men and women and questing for knowledge; courageously disobeying her parents' arranged marriage to quest for true love" (Zhou Jingshu 1). Four decades before, Lu Gong wrote that it was a "typical story" embodying "people's intense will to fight vigorously against feudal society, reflecting the courageous struggle of a young couple," and "representing the experience of thousands and millions of young men and women" (7). The pair of young, tragic lovers has been elevated to the dimension of a model for the masses to follow in the unceasing quest for freedom of marriage and equality for women. The Chuanju and Yueju opera versions of the early 1950s are no doubt first and foremost embodiments of this PRC rereading.[9]

In the late 1950s, some ten years after the establishment of the communist regime in mainland China, Hong Kong echoed the broad line of interpretation as seen in the Chuanju and Yueju operas in the Hong Kong Cantonese opera film *The Regretful Story of Liang and Zhu*. This film version has been hailed as pioneering feminism — female journalist Fung Tze regards it as "an avant garde Chinese opera film from head to tail" and calls this character construction of Zhu Yingtai "a feminist from head to tail" (84). Whether this version is "feminist" or affirmatively "from head to tail" led the times is subject to discussion, but the film does lean extraordinarily toward the female protagonist Zhu Yingtai, played by one of the greatest Cantonese opera "divas," Fong Yim-fan.[10] Liang Shanbo is only a supporting character in the film. However, the role was not casually cast. As mentioned above, Liang is played by Yam Kim-fai the great male impersonator in Hong Kong Cantonese opera. In many ways, this Cantonese opera film version was a heavyweight production. This rendition also adheres to the paradigmatic Liang-Zhu operatic structure in which Liang is played by a woman.

In this version Zhu plays a much more predominant part than in previous versions. The climactic moment of Zhu's feminine self-positioning is the classroom scene in which she confronts the authoritative old teacher concerning Confucius' teachings about women. In her opinion, the saint's teachings are "feudal topics" [*fengjian lunti*] and "biases" [*pianjian*] against women. The significance of this text is that in other versions, for instance, the 1952 Chuanju opera *In the Shade of Willows* Zhu takes Confucius to task in a private conversation with Liang. In Li Han-hsiang's 1963 film version, Zhu complains about this sexual inequality issue to Liang after the class, not by confronting the symbol of patriarchal power — the teacher — in front of the whole class. The classic Yueju version does not stage this episode at all. In the Cantonese opera film Zhu is immediately labeled "betrayer of the saint" [*shengren zhi pantu*] by the teacher. Represented here is a disobedient woman who not only desires education and knowledge, but also finds her own voice. The preponderance of the female lead in the singing and performing in this version has ironically led to a complaint, by the novelist and Cantonese opera connoisseur Xinqishi, that the imbalance is totally out of proportion (21–3).

The rewritings and rereadings examined above — the imperial-patriarchal and the modern socialist-feminist — are opposed to each other on one level, yet the feminist reading can in a way be tied in with the anti-feudal discourse, since the oppression of women was an integral part of the feudal patriarchy. These two approaches to Liang-Zhu share one conservative gender move: the attempt at rendering invisible the queer tension, erotic indeterminacy, and ambivalence of desire which are in circulation in and between the texts of Liang-Zhu — at least to the queer eye. If, to gay people in the United States, the Broadway musical has been "a place for us" (Miller), Liang-Zhu has been "a collective memory and gay myth" for (Hong Kong) Chinese *tongzhi* ("homosexuals"),[11] as indirectly pointed out by film director Stanley Kwan ("Stanley Kwan, Artist-in-Residence" 12, 16). But in these various Chinese opera films the queer dimension constituted by transgender performance in Liang-Zhu has been relegated to a liminal margin, consigned to the unspeakable in a heterosexual matrix.

Yet the stage as a site of ideological contest is never foreclosed. There is no single sweeping victory won by one party. To many, theatre is already subversive, and cross-dressing — whether on stage or in real life — is by itself potentially transgressive. The necessity of double cross-dressing in the gender performance of Liang-Zhu constantly interrupts the stability of the textual surface. The slippages and incoherences in the presumed heterosexual world of the feudal and socialist readings of Liang-Zhu are betrayed by an old question asked by generations of readers and spectators: How could Liang not have seen through Zhu's disguise and guessed her real gender after three years' of studying together, much less after he is given so many further hints by Zhu during the farewell trip and parting at the Eighteenth-Mile Pavilion? I recall that in my childhood my mother (who was very fond of Cantonese opera then, but less so now) often resorted to the simple and straightforward explanation that Liang was just too stupid. This is no joke at all. This is how the legitimate question of why the veil of gender disguise is not lifted has been swept under the carpet and thus suppressed in the common imagination of the public for generations. A simple explanation can often be an effective dissimulation for not seeing what is there. Today, we must ask further questions: How could Liang, after knowing Zhu for so long as a boy, at the blink of an eye so comfortably accept Zhu's gender bending and have a change of heart, falling in love with the female Zhu once she reveals her true sex? Could the person that Liang loves deep down, without self-awareness, be the "male" Zhu at school? For, after all, Liang loves all the "qualities" that both the female and "male" Zhu possess. Can one switch one's gender (signifiers) and remain the *same* person?

Two of the possible ways of resolving the gender tension, sexual anxiety and contradictory logic are that we imagine otherwise:

(1) Liang has known from day one, or from very early on, that Zhu is a woman and soon they naturally start a romance. This is Tsui Hark's straight solution.

(2) Liang is simply gay and falls in love with the "male" Zhu without realizing her true sex — Raymond To Kwok-wai's requeering of the story follows this queering logic.

This un/re-queering third reading of the Liang-Zhu story — after the imperial-feudal and socialist-feminist readings — focuses on one of the most highly debated social and cultural topics of daily life in the late twentieth century, that is, gender and sexuality. Raymond To's queer reading is an attempt at reinventing "a gay collective memory and myth," as opposed to the heterosexual appropriation of the story hitherto most thoroughly done by Tsui Hark.

The queer reading is by no means a far-fetched, over-interpretation of the Liang-Zhu story. Coincidentally echoing the Liang-Zhu story in the parallel operation of the enigma of sexuality, is the forever mysterious case of the "Butterfly Scandal" of Shi Pei-pu and Bernard Boursicot that was put to trial for espionage in France in 1986, on which David Henry Hwang's *M. Butterfly* and the "true events" this play was based upon. With so much exposition and discussion of this "M. Butterfly" saga in real life, including the high-profile *20/20* Barbara Walters' interview (1992) with the Frenchman Bernard Boursicot and the ex-Beijing opera transvestite actor Shi Pei-pu (interviewed separately), as well as the biographical non-fiction work *Liaison* (1993) by Joyce Wadler, we still have not gotten to the "truth" of this matter. The knot of the enigma is similar to that posed by Liang-Zhu: How could Bernard Boursicot not discover Shi Pei-pu's true sex after so many years of intimacy and, in this case, allegedly begetting a child? From *20/20* we know that Boursicot had had relationships with women and that at the time of interview he was living with a male partner. But Boursicot insisted that he had truly believed that Shi Pei-pu was a woman during their long relationship. We also learned in the interview that Shi Pei-pu was beyond doubt biologically male from the very beginning. He worked for the Chinese secret service and disguised himself as a woman in an attempt to gather intelligence information from the French military attaché stationed in Beijing. To meet the modern quest for rationality, one possible "logical" explanation is that Shi was such a true master of transgender performance on and off stage that his female impersonation fooled even his sexual partner, but common sense must ultimately reject the possibility of such a perfect impersonation. Another possible explanation is that Boursicot saw the true sex of Shi from day one and maintained the relationship and pretended to take Shi as a woman because he was gay. This would mean that their relationship was in fact a closet homosexual relationship conducted by Boursicot for himself under the veil of a stealthy heterosexual affair that began during Mao's Cultural Revolution. With a metaphorical turn of critical perspective, Hwang's M. *Butterfly* proposes a postcolonial critique of the real life event. In this play, Rene Gallimard fails to recognize Song Liling's true sex because of his Orientalism: Asian men are women, they can never be real men. As Song Liling says, ". . . I am an Oriental. And being an Oriental, I could never be completely a man" (83), while Gallimard is a man "who loved a woman created by a man" (90). In Hwang's own words, M. *Butterfly* is a "deconstructivist *Madame Butterfly*" (95).

The "Butterfly Lovers" (Liang-Zhu) story played a vital role in the intriguing transgender performance in the "M. Butterfly" incident, for that story of the "butterflies" was also the story of this "butterfly." Shi Pei-pu told Boursicot the Liang-Zhu story (Wadler 36) in order to strengthen his alleged cross-identity as a female brought up as a man, drawing a parallel between "herself" and Zhu. But in reality, Shi Pei-pu was a man who claimed to be a female disguised as a man. Shi's story does not so much share the gender crossing structure of Liang-Zhu as that of the double gender disguise shaping the narrative of Blake Edwards' film *Victor/Victoria* (1982). *Victor/Victoria* features Julie Andrews in the role of a heterosexual female singer who disguises herself as a gay male drag cabaret entertainer. However, *Victor/Victoria* ends in comedy with the restoration of the order of gender and a heterosexual marriage (between Andrews and James Garner) while the "M. Butterfly" saga ended in a conviction for espionage and sexual suspense — "suspense" in both its literal sense and the sense of the suspension of the boundaries of gender and desire. Is the truth out there? Does anyone deserve the truth? Can we handle the truth? What was the truth of the sexual relationship between Shi and Boursicot? What is the truth of the sexuality circulating in the Liang-Zhu legend? The "truth" might not be accessible after all, and in the end, the "truth" might not reveal much about how we live our (sexual) lives. It is perhaps how we (re)imagine, how we represent or fail to represent the "truth" of sex in our cultural production that matters.

The latent homoeroticism in Liang-Zhu might not have been easily visible to the heterosexual imagination in the past, but it was not that heavily veiled from the queer perspective. The apparent coherence of the textual surface of the tale had already been fissured here and there in the earliest extant Ming dramatic fragments and up to the regional operas of recent decades.

In the six texts of the eighteen collected in Qian Nanyang's *A Collection of Extant Liang-Zhu Dramas* (1956) that include the rendezvous scene in which Zhu's true sex is revealed we find in five of them that Liang continues to use the *male* pronoun to address the *female* Zhu in front of him, using mostly "my dear brother" [*xiandi*] and other common variations of this form of address. These texts range from the Ming fragments through nineteenth century regional plays to recent regional operas. Namely they are:

(1) "Fangyou" [Visiting a friend] from a Ming Dynasty chuangqi play;
(2) "Fangyou" [Visiting a friend] from Cuiqiang opera;
(3) "Liang Shanbei tanpeng" [Liang Shanbei visiting a friend] from a Hongdong opera of the nineteenth century;
(4) "Liang Shanbo fangyou" [Liang Shanbo visiting a friend] from a Chuju opera;
(5) "Zhuzhuang fangyou" [Visiting a friend at the Zhu mansion] from a Chuanju opera (Qian Nanyang, *Liang-Zhu xiju jicun*).

In each of these five plays, the text persists in restating the male signifier after Zhu resumes her female identity, stealthily creating a fracture between the sign and referent. Interestingly enough, in the Hongdong opera "Liang Shanbei visiting a friend" (36–8), Zhu Yingtai even uses the male pronoun to refer to herself. If we stretch our reasoning far enough to insist on the compulsory heterosexual reading, this dislocation of gender might be glossed over by arguing that Liang had just become used to calling Zhu a boy after all their years of studying together and thus momentarily failed to switch to the female pronoun. But this is not credible in real life, where after one or two slips of the tongue under "normal" circumstances, the dislocation should be refitted. In the dramatic examples cited here Liang sticks to the male pronouns all the way through the scene. There is no switch from the male to the female form of address — the male pronoun has become structural.

The "exception" in Qian Nanyang's collection — the play that sees Liang switch the gendered pronoun — is a Shaoxing *wenxi* opera dating back to the 1920s (94), entitled "Liang Shanbo at the Lotus Pond" [Liang Shanbo ouchi] (92–4). My suggestion is that this and other later versions that switch to the "proper" gendered pronoun are attempts to tame this disruptive textual indeterminacy by changing the disruptive term to the "appropriate" one of "my dear sister" [*xianmei*]. I would also like to suggest that this fracture in meaning and the resultant anxiety have been felt, and that measures have been taken to fix the disorderly moments in the text. The interesting connection here is that the Shaoxing *wenxi* is the forerunner of today's Yueju opera which, not surprisingly, also follows the practice of "remedying" the gender indeterminacy. An enlightening contrast is the Chuanju opera *In the Shade of Willows*, which came out at the same time as this Yueju opera, but follows the traditional use of the male pronoun, as it is in an earlier version of a Chuanju opera "Visiting a friend at the Zhu mansion" collected in Qian Nanyang's anthology.

In comparing the Yueju and Chuanju operas Huang Shang noticed this discrepancy and called it a "very little difference" [*xiaoxiao de chayi*] ("Liang Zhu zaji" 82). He regarded the treatment by the Chuanju opera as effective in moving the spectators:

> But the special point of this very little difference in the Chuanju opera has deeply moved many spectators. . . . Every time when Shanbo utters "Zhu the Second Master [*Zhu erye*]," it not only reminds the audience of the love between the two of them, but also their three-year studying together and profound friendship that is like *brotherhood* [*xiongdi*]. There is no question that the audience immediately realizes the *foundation* [*jichu*] of their intense and truthful love.
>
> ("Liang Zhu zaji" 82; emphasis added)

The "foundation" of the romantic love between Liang and Zhu is the three years of shared school life. The logic seems to be coherent and convincing up to this point, yet the textual instability is that the "friendship" is founded on "brotherhood" — the homosocial that can easily be implicated with the homoerotic, depending on the eye of the beholder. *Tongzhi's* translating of Liang-Zhu into a gay myth and Euro-American film critics' reading of homoeroticism in John Woo's films are two cases in point. The homosocial is entangled with the homoerotic and the heteroerotic concurrently in Liang-Zhu. On the surface level of the story, the "brotherhood" develops and is translated to the heteroerotic of boy-girl romance. The ambiguous transition and transformation between the homosocial "brotherhood" and heterosexual romantic relationship begs a rational explanation to satisfy heterosexual logic. To "correct" or not to "correct" the gendered pronoun has become an unavoidable either/or decision for the modern author in the remaking of this tale. Two novels, both entitled *Liang Shanbo yu Zhu Yingtai* were written in 1954 by two famous writers, Zhang Henshui and Zhao Qingke, and each follows a different direction in the gendered pronoun matter. Zhao continues the textual indeterminacy whereas Zhang follows the modern attempt at neutralizing the tension resulting from the confusion of gender signification.[12] It cannot be an innocent question anymore for modern authors and perhaps it was never an unsophisticated textual strategy from the beginning.

There have been further attempts to re-channel indeterminate sexual desire toward the heterosexual, in addition to the "correcting" of the gendered form of address at the critical moment of gender revelation in the story. In the farewell scene as enacted in the operatic tradition, Zhu (still in the male disguise) gives Liang numerous hints about her gender via many vivid tropes of male/female romance (e.g., the mandarin ducks, the Cowherd and the Girl Weaver legend, etc.). The scene, in which Liang innocently fails to read through all the tropes for Zhu's true sex is vivified by Liang's comic mismatching of gender in Zhu's romantic suggestions. Liang either complains that Zhu is comparing him to a woman, or that Zhu is not a woman. Liang's inability to set in order the gender style and the corresponding biological sex in the binary male-female system is in sharp contrast to his immediate recognition of a latent romantic desire in Zhu's rhetoric. In Li Han-hsiang's Huangmeidiao opera film, at this heightened romanticized moment Liang says to Zhu, " 'Tis a pity that you're not female, or I'd fall in love with you."

On the one hand, this direct assertion using the expression "falling in love" between "male and female" makes explicit the possible existence of romantic desire, with the intent of reinforcing the order of heterosexuality. A male-male relationship is not allowed. However, on the other hand, is it not possible that Liang already in a way has feelings for the "male" Zhu? For what he sees, regardless of the numerous hints given to him by Zhu, is persistently a "man." Isn't it true that the attempt to reinforce the heterosexual norm and channel desire to that of the heterosexual at once betrays that there is an underlying latent homosexual desire? Or at least that the potential desire is ambiguously gay and/or straight? An interesting reverted specular image would be the "Ambiguously Gay Duo" animated sketch seen on US television show *Saturday Night Live* in the late 1990s. The "ambiguous" in this playful burlesque of comic-strip American superheroes is a sign in an inverted referential relation with its referent — as the two characters Ace and Gary are unambiguously gay in their sexuality and relationship. The specularity of this example of the ambiguously gay textual strategy and the unambiguously gay postmodern parody is instructive. The unambiguously gay may not have emerged in contemporary China and Hong Kong, but the *ambiguously* gay tactic of intervention is not necessarily less effective in de-territorializing desire. It is no mere coincidence that *tongzhi* have taken the Liang-Zhu legend as a gay myth and their collective memory. Liang does not deny his desire for the "male" Zhu, only because (Liang thinks that) they are of the same sex and they cannot be a couple as forbidden by social conventions. The textual disruption is constituted by the simultaneous presence of the desire and the prohibition.

In a cross-dressing theatre staging of Liang-Zhu, the underlying eroticism is further complicated by the true sex of the two performers on stage. In the legend's most successful renditions, in Yueju opera (theatre and film) and the Hong Kong made Huangmeidiao opera film, Liang is played by a woman. Today, after the flux of queer, feminist and new historicist rereadings of the early modern English stage, it has become all too common for us to point to the gender politics of two female (or male) players playacting a heterosexual couple on stage. In the staging of Liang-Zhu, on the physical level of the players, there are two women; while on the level of dramatic representation of the characters, it is a man and a woman. Coincidentally, in Yueju opera as with the Japanese Takarazuka Revue, it is the young actresses who play men who attract the largest share and the most enthusiastic of fans, and more often than not, these male impersonators are the real stars. Supporters of the Takarazuka and the Yueju opera are also mostly women, as is commonly known. Clearly the dislocation of gender and the cross-channeling of eroticized energy weave a complex web of desire. The hidden performance of lesbianism beneath the masked bodies of the characters on stage is intertwined with the male gay subtext on the textual level in the Liang-Zhu folktale, resulting in a multivalent and polyvocal matrix of desire and anxiety radiating from this theme. In fact, the significance of the theatricality of the Liang-Zhu phenomenon extends beyond this level of crossing the stage and the text. In addition to inciting ambivalent desires that circulate on the stage and between the stage enactment and the audience, the fact that the most memorable modern stage renditions of Liang-Zhu are distinguished by their casting of female cross-dressers who do not in the least look convincingly male in the role of Liang raises further issues of the construction of masculinity and femininity in traditional Chinese culture.

The failure of the young scholar Liang Shanbo to gain a prominent office is the key to the understanding of the politics of gender construction in regard to this story. Audiences and critics naturally tend to focus their attention on the clever and capable Zhu Yingtai, but the dimwitted Liang Shanbo is equally significant for our gender interrogation here. I would like to suggest that the reason Liang is best played by a woman, is that he is a "woman." The traditional Chinese construction of masculinity manifests itself in a variety of representations and was derived from cultural structures that are in many ways different from today's Euro-American notions of masculinity.[13] While it is true that the classic figure of the gentry-scholar on the Chinese operatic stage has always been "effeminate" compared to the military-roles of generals and soldiers (e.g., the Hegemon King), it is also true that the "fragile scholar" was one ideal type of masculinity in imperial China. It has been argued that the concept of "masculinity" in pre-modern China was conceived in the network of hierarchical social and political power in a homosocial context rather than in opposition to "woman" in a hetero-sexual/sexist matrix (Song). The characterization of Liang in the story is that of a "man" who neither aspires to, nor achieves the ideal of the gentry-scholar in imperial China — scholarly honor and official rank [*gongming*]. Following this vein of argument, Liang falls short of the ideal scholar for he has shown no concern or ambition to strive for maximum masculine power through distinguishing himself at the imperial civil examinations, not to mention gaining top graduate status [*zhuangyuan*]. The classic structure of the "scholar and beauty" [*caizi jiaren*] romance in traditional narratives and drama is that the scholar overcomes all obstacles public and private to attain the top graduate honor, is decorated by the emperor and wins the beauty legitimately, resulting in a happy reunion at the closure of the story. The paradigmatic "scholar and beauty" text is the Yuan play *Xixiang ji* [West wing]. By these standards Liang Shanbo is too self-indulgent in lamenting his unfulfilled love for Zhu Yingtai since romantic love, even if it is the personal priority of a scholar, must succumb to the pursuit of scholarly honor and official rank. Liang and Zhu's ill-fated love is the result of the intervention of the patriarchy, represented by Zhu's father, who has agreed to marry his daughter into the powerful Ma family. There is clearly a dimension of class and social power underlying the love story. The construction of masculinity in imperial China depended substantially on social power and in this regard, Liang does not qualify, as Zhang Sheng does in *West Wing*, as "masculine." The fact that Liang does become a magistrate of the county of Yin (in Zhejiang Province) in some versions of this tragic romance does not change the argument. In the first place, a magistrate is an insignificant position in the hierarchy of power and in the second, the episode of Liang's gaining an office is simply omitted in the leading Liang-Zhu texts, including the Yueju opera, the Chuanju opera, and the Huangmeidiao opera film.

Liang is not masculine but feminine, and this story is most successful when a woman plays the part of Liang since he is an effeminate man, almost a "woman." The comparison between Liang-

Zhu and the canonic *West Wing,* in which the two lovers secure a happy ending in marriage through Zhang's success in securing the top graduate title is a revealing one. There is no cross-dressing in the dramatic story of *West Wing,* but there is the same intervention in love and marriage by the parent — but only the top graduate will get the bride.

Unqueering Liang-Zhu

The representations of Liang-Zhu in traditional forms — both as texts and theatre events — have betrayed incoherences and instabilities in desire and sexuality. In the 1990s, before *tongzhi* had the chance to reappropriate publicly the legend of Liang-Zhu as a queer myth, it was first sabotaged by film director Tsui Hark's heterosexual recuperative reinterpretation. Tsui's quick neutralization of the potential queerness of Liang-Zhu is not unique. In Euro-American popular culture, the potential queerness of the cult tough woman figure Xena, from the 1990s TV series *Xena: Warrior Princess,* has also been, as pointed out by Sherrie Inness, understood by some critics "as nothing more than a pseudo-superhero who — with her short costumes and long legs — appeals primarily to men, not women" (160).

The queerness of Liang Shanbo is neutralized in Tsui's film *The Lovers* (1994), in which he directly confronts the gender and sexual ambivalence of the legend and is to a great extent successful in erasing the problematizing potential in the conventional plot. The patriarchal anxiety over non-heterosexuality is given a good cure in Tsui's unqueering rewriting. In the film Liang sees through Zhu's gender disguise almost right away, and the two teens have their sexual union in the farewell scene. In effect, Liang-Zhu has become a teenage romance, an interpretation reinforced by Tsui's casting of two teen idols in the leading roles. Tsui also introduces a "real" gay character called Ting Wangchun: an effeminate stereotype of gays as seen through the eyes of homophobes. The possible redemption for the stereotyped representation perhaps being the heart-of-gold characterization of this gay character.

In *Yin ± Yan: Gender in Chinese Cinema* (1996), the documentary film that he made for the British Film Institute, Hong Kong director Stanley Kwan (lately celebrated for his award-winning gay film *Lanyu* [2001] set in contemporary Beijing) interviews Tsui Hark about his treatment of Liang-Zhu. From a *tongzhi* perspective, the narrative voice of the documentary explains that:

> The original version of the story is part of every Chinese gay man's memory and growing up experience. I wonder if Tsui Hark had any hesitation about rewriting it in such a blatantly heterosexual way.[14]

Kwan regards the story of Liang-Zhu as "a quintessential statement of adolescent sexual ambivalence"; however, "Tsui's version eliminates all the ambiguity and turns the story into a conventional heterosexual romance" ("Stanley Kwan, Artist-in-Residence" 16). From the perspective of *tongzhi*, Kwan further asks "Was he [Tsui] conscious of appropriating and destroying a gay myth?" (16). Kwan directly asks Tsui, "If people criticized you of robbing [*lüeduo*] a collective memory/ myth from the homosexual people to reinforce heterosexuality, how would you respond? ("Zhuxiao yishujia Guan Jinpeng" 12). Kwan's own reading of the Liang-Zhu story is wholly a queer, alternative reading of the folklore that brings out all the inherent sexual tension and gender anxiety from the fissures on the textual surface. Tsui is well aware of these incoherences, although not in a theoretically informed way as presented by Kwan. The incoherences constitute the reason that Tsui's film attempts to resolve the problem as he sees it. First, in the documentary film, Tsui tells us that he went to see Liang-Zhu with his first love (he does not specify whether it was a Chinese opera or some film version). This accounts for his highly personal relationship with the story. Second, Tsui analyzes the story extremely rationally, saying that since Liang is thinking of revisiting a "friend" he should not have such a fatal emotional trauma when he discovers the true sex of this friend. In his film Tsui also rationalizes Liang's death, it is the result of a violent assault by the servants of the Zhu family, not of a broken heart. In addition, Tsui points out that had Liang really been in love with Zhu all the time, it should be the Zhu *at school* that he loved, not the Zhu he saw at the family mansion. Tsui is nevertheless an artist of great sensibility and sees through all the ambivalences in the traditional narrative of Liang-Zhu. He explains that he didn't know how to deal with the situation of "a man becoming a woman" in the traditional story — he could not figure out what to do with Liang's "attitude" at that point. Tsui's solution, for his own vision of this story, was an unqueering process. The ideological structure of Tsui's film is built upon a reinforced binary opposition of the homosexual and the heterosexual. He ingeniously adopts in the film a pair of common terms from Chinese culture originally having no reference to sexuality to represent a "traditional equivalent" of the contemporary notion of gay and straight, namely, *xu* and *shi*, literally the unreal/empty and the real/substantial.[15] The evaluative effect of this pair of terms is straightforward, as Kwan aptly points out in *Yin ± Yan*. Putting aside queer politics, Tsui's approach is a most rational and effective rewriting strategy to make all things straight. However, this does more than destroy a gay myth, it also diffuses all the tantalizing romantic ambiguities, be they lesbian, gay, bisexual, heterosexual, or transgender that have captivated audiences from all walks of life for many generations.

Tsui's film is a critique of the oppression of women and at the same time a reproduction of the containment of women. The film is given a concrete historical setting, the Eastern Jin (317–420) period, with some significant details of the class hierarchy and aristocratic lifestyle portrayed accurately. This aspect of Tsui's film is very different from the relatively a-contextual, a-historical representation in Chinese opera in which it is often just loosely understood to be a story of the feudal past. Tsui's remake represents the brutal oppression of able and strong-willed women under a patriarchal system in the Chinese tradition. The reinvention and full development of the character of Madam Zhu, Zhu Yingtai's mother, as a strong woman in her younger days who finally succumbed to patriarchal containment and became an efficient and capable woman who manages the Zhu household implies a condemnation of the oppression of women and the patriarchal system. Along with the monk (invented by Tsui Hark) who was once her youthful lover, Madam Zhu knows what is happening in reality and foresees the tragic fate of her daughter and Liang. Madam Zhu experiences the greatest tragedy as she sees her daughter re-enact her own story of futile resistance, step by step. The difference between herself and her daughter is that Madam Zhu chose to be contained and took the role assigned by the patriarchy; whereas her daughter chooses her uncompromising resistance as a disobedient woman "over her dead body."

Yet at the same time as Tsui Hark expresses sympathy toward women and criticizes the brutality of patriarchy, he also caricatures women. In sharp contrast to tradition and for comic effect, he reinvents Zhu's character as a dumb and useless, though innocent, teenager who indulges in romantic love, in contrast to the very consistent portrayal of Zhu in traditional operas as intelligent, talented, self-conscious, and rebellious. Tsui also erases the potential feminist subversion seen in the Cantonese opera film and Li Han-hsiang's Huangmeidiao opera film (though Tsui's treatment of some scenes shows traces of Li's film). Tsui's version of Liang-Zhu is an "incorrect" text in several ways in terms of gender politics. But it is visually charming and in effect refashioned an old wine almost forgotten by today's young generation into the new bottle of the late twentieth century's global idol culture and scored a great commercial success. In the end, it is successful in unqueering Liang-Zhu, disentangling all the gender ambiguities in the traditional story.

The Queer Turn: Tongzhi Rewriting

Four years after Tsui Hark's unqueering of Liang-Zhu, Raymond To's requeering attempt, *The Lover*, came out in the form of a stage musical which ran from late 1998 to early 1999. This production, presented by the commercial theatre Spring-Time Stage Productions Ltd, received waves of publicity preceding its premiere and during its run. Apart from heavy press publicity, two 30-minute promotional featurettes (one in English[16] and one in Cantonese) featuring praise from celebrities were aired on Hong Kong's leading television network at strategic moments during the show's run. The bulk of the publicity focused on selling this musical remake as anti-traditional in terms of its homosexualizing of the Liang-Zhu story. This commercial production generated a great deal of noise, received a lot of attention, and incited many reviews. To put things in context, it is important to keep in mind that this queer version did not come out of a cultural void. It can be seen as the culmination of almost a decade of queer fashion in Hong Kong popular culture dating from Tsui Hark's milestone swordplay film *Swordsman II* in 1991. *The Lover*'s reinterpretation of Liang-Zhu demonstrates a complex negotiation between individual cultural intent and institutional commercial considerations, the expression of marginal desires and the regulation of normalizing social morality.

The official English title of To's musical used the singular noun "lover" (see the house program and VCD cover), not "lovers" and without a "butterfly" either, thus signifying a one-way love. There are two crossed-lovers: each of whom falls in love with a self-imagined other, a gendered other whose sexuality and gender identity is misread and misconceived by the self. Liang mistakes a heterosexual female for a gay man while Zhu mistakes a gay male for a heterosexual man. In both cases there is *a lover* with an absent and imagined "lovee."

Unlike Tsui Hark's *The Lovers* which very successfully ironed out the irregularities in the traditional narrative from a straight perspective, Raymond To's *The Lover* is an incomplete "queering" project. *The Lover* is a "queer" text constituted in contradictions and ironies and at the beginning it looks novel, bold, and subversive. To's Liang is simply gay. He is also a rebel against established values in general. In this musical, the scene in which Zhu confronts the teacher in the Cantonese opera film, or, the scene in which Zhu confronts Liang on the issue of Confucius' comments on women as seen in the Chuanju opera and Li Han-hsiang's film, is interestingly transformed into one in which Liang, the gay man — instead of Zhu, the heterosexual woman — confronts the old teacher by asking whether the great ancient poet Qu Yuan was gay. The problematizing of the sexuality of Qu Yuan has a long history. The last heated debate on the subject, between the conservative sectors and the pro-queer voices, took place in June 1999 when the *tongzhi* circle in Hong Kong proposed making the Dragon Boat Festival, the fifth day of the fifth month of the Chinese lunar calendar, also "Tongzhi's Day" [*Tongzhi ri*]. There was a bitter exchange of incisive articles in leading Hong Kong newspapers.[17] Raymond To did not make a random choice when he replaced the debate on Confucius' teachings on women with one on the sexuality of Qu Yuan. A voice of feminist critique has been displaced by a calling for gay rights. To further underline his point, To added a confrontational scene between Liang and Ma Wencai (Zhu's fiancé) in which they argue over which is "natural" — gay or straight. Yet in the end the musical seems to be arguing for a universal notion of love that transcends differences in sex and desire, where "love" is neutral, and independent of gender and sexuality. This is a compromised argument probably to tame the musical's gay turn and make it less uncomfortable to the majority of the middle-class audience who were likely to be heterosexist at heart but would pretend to be open, liberal, and modern (thus buying tickets to watch a "queer" musical).

While Tsui Hark successfully sidestepped the traditional enigma/ ambiguity of how Liang failed to realize Zhu's true sex by adding a scene where Liang sees her female body beneath the dress, To's queer version ironically fell back on the traditional story. This time, the gay Liang, like the traditional straight Liang, failed to realize that Zhu is a woman. To is self-contradictory when he tells us in the *Making of the Lover* that in his opinion it is incredible that Liang does not discover Zhu's sex after three years of friendship in the traditional story.

But To's queer turn was in several ways self-cancelling. The production's most significant change to the most successful traditional performance practice was assigning a male actor to play Liang. At the same time, it cast a young woman — a well-known Hong Kong Cantonese opera *male impersonator,* Koi Ming-fai — in the role of Zhu, again contrary to the practice in previous Chinese opera versions. At first glance, the musical seems to play upon the popularity of male impersonation in Hong Kong Cantonese opera by obviously cashing in the theatrical connection. It also seems to be effective aesthetic logic to have a male impersonator play Zhu, since the character disguises herself as a boy in the story. In the end, the musical reverses the previous cross-gender assignment. In other words in this "queer" version there is paradoxically a straightening of the gender dislocations practiced in the traditional operas. Of course, we must also note that today's Beijing opera performance of Liang-Zhu, for instance, have a "straight" cast. But the play Liang-Zhu is not a major work in the repertoire of Beijing opera (the play *The Hegemon King Says Farewell to the Concubine* belongs to and represents Beijing opera, in the same way that *The Peony Pavilion* is the first and foremost magnum opus in Kunju opera repertoire). Liang-Zhu is an identity marker of Yueju opera. Ironically the stage appearance of Zhu Yingtai in To's musical is by far the most identifiably feminine even in male dress. In fact, to attain sustaining subversion of gender and sexuality Zhu should be played by a masculine man, just as Hwang insisted in the casting of *M. Butterfly*.

To's queer Liang-Zhu also shows a continual marking out of the "otherness" of the female. The stage image of Zhu as played by the young Cantonese opera *male impersonator* does not appear more "masculine" than her counterpart in previous operatic versions. In an episode invented by To, the woman is once again a substitute — following in the footsteps of Princess Bright Pearl, Hua Mulan, and the woman generals of the Yang family — Zhu is a substitute for a man, her brother who died young before the play begins, without finishing his quest for knowledge. At the beginning of the musical Zhu says to her father, "Father, my brother and I were twins. Our hearts beat as one live and dead. . . . I want to attend the White Deer School for my brother . . . " (To 34). Thus it is to fulfill the male will for knowledge that To's Zhu disguises herself as her brother and leaves for the city to attend school.

This queer musical relies on the romantic notion of "true love" to overcome the anxiety of sexuality differences. The effect is, as discussed above, a degenderizing of desire — "true love" transcends gender, just as the lesbian heroine in the film *Chasing Amy* (1997; directed by Kevin Smith) finds her "true half" in a heterosexual man. At the end of the day, To's gay Liang seems to turn "straight" by accepting Zhu in the afterlife, as shown in the closing sword dance, again an invention of To's. Or could it be that the gender-transcending true love, with a real woman and a real man dressed in unisex white costumes performing the sword dance signifies a genderless moment? Perhaps the sword functions as phallic symbol once again and the blissful final sword dance signifies a gay relationship?

Despite Raymond To's failure to thoroughly queer Liang-Zhu, he has at least refashioned the traditional story into a "mainstream" queer text. The story cannot be read the same again. Today we see *tongzhi* clubs — however small and marginal they may be — being run by college students on many campuses in Hong Kong, and we can claim To's *The Lover* as part of the "public assertion of 'queerness'" that has to a certain extent resignified "the abjection of homosexuality into defiance and legitimacy" (Butler, *Bodies That Matter* 21).

ARTIFACT

SIX

THE CRISIS OF GENDER REPRESENTATION:
THE YUAN THEATRE MURAL

Gender is often an unsettling cultural category that resists stable interpretations. Just as the continuous reinventions of the Liang-Zhu story have effected further problematization of the inherent ambiguity of sexuality in the texts, the "gender trouble" of the players in Yuan theatre has caused ruptures in the conventional discourse on Chinese theatre, a discourse that strives to construct a unitary plane and to sidestep its own representational incoherences. The debate on the gender of the leading singer-player in Yuan theatre (chapter 2) points to the uncertainty of reconstructed textual history, which can only be a representation of a representation. No scholar can put forward definite proof for their argument; or, conventional wisdom tells us that more historical evidence will emerge in the course of time (if one believes that it is possible to grasp the whole picture of history) but in the end, new evidence still may or may not be definitive. At present, we have at best an approximation of historical truth, based on certain speculations that sound more convincing than others. In any case, we can conclude that it is probable that the general performance practice in Yuan theatre slanted toward women: actresses cross-dressed to play men.

Apart from textual evidence (ignoring the question of how puzzling historical textual fragments can be), further evidence is available in an extremely important historical artifact — a colored mural in a temple in Shanxi province that depicts a Yuan theatre troupe, with 11 men and women including performers and musicians, on stage in both dramatic costumes and ordinary clothes. Yet this piece of additional evidence, the players represented in the painting, that supposedly informs us of the "facts" of gender representation in Yuan theatre, simultaneously generates more queries about gender trouble concerning the representation's corresponding historical reality. The incoherent representations of this most iconic cultural artifact of classical Chinese theatre — the "Zhongdu Xiu" mural of the Yuan Dynasty — compel us to rethink issues of gender ambiguity and the crisis of representation itself.

Representing the Representation of Gender

The "Zhongdu Xiu" mural first attracted attention of scholars in the 1930s, and is preserved in the Mingyingwang Temple of Guangsheng Monastery in Hongdong County, Shanxi. In the mural the figures are lined up in two rows, with five in the front and six in the back. Two of the players have painted faces. Four are bearded, though one is obviously wearing a false beard hung over the upper lip from a metal wire very similar to the *rankou* still used in today's Chinese regional operas. A line of Chinese characters written from right to left on top of the painting reads "Dahang player Zhongdu Xiu is acting here." Two vertical lines of small characters adorning the right and left of the horizontal line say respectively: "Beloved in Yaodu" and "Fourth month, the first year of Taiding," that is, May 1324. From these characters we know that the painting shows a Yuan theatre performance in the heyday of that period.[1]

This mural provides many clues to critics and scholars attempting to reconstruct various performance practices of the time. Like Xia Tingzhi's *Green Bower Collection*, no serious contemporary study of Yuan theatre can afford to ignore this cultural artifact, which began to attract scholars' attention in the late 1930s (Shih 200). From the perspective of the present critique, this wall painting betrays significant uncertainties in the representation of gender — perhaps not so much in the troubled gender identity of the cross-dressed female players depicted, but rather in the instabilities and uncertainties in the very mechanism and process of representing gender.

With specific reference to their statements about, and analyses of, the gender identity of the figures in the mural, I shall address these ten pieces of writing, listed in order of their publication:

(1) Qi Gong. "Lun Yuan dai zaju de banyan wenti" [A discussion of the question of impersonation in Yuan theatre]. 1955.

(2) Liu Nianzi. "Yuan zaju yanchu xingshi de jidian chubu kanfa" [Some preliminary reflections on the performance practice in Yuan *zaju* theatre]. 1957.

(3) Zhou Yibai. "Yuan dai bihua zhong de Yuan ju yanchu xingshi" [The performance of Yuan drama as represented in Yuan wall paintings]. 1959.

(4) Chung-wen Shih. *The Golden Age of Chinese Drama: Yuan Tsa-chü.* 1976.

(5) William Dolby. *A History of Chinese Drama.* 1976.

(6) "Hongdong Mingyingwangdian Yuan zaju bihua" [The Yuan drama mural of the Hall of Mingyingwang in Hongdong county]. *Zhongguo da baike quanshu: xiqu, quyi* [The great Chinese encyclopedia: traditional music drama, folk musical art forms]. 1983 (contributed by Liu Nianzi).

(7) Zhou Guoxiong. "Shanxi Hongdong Mingyingwangdian xiqu bihua xintan" [A new investigation of the Yuan theatre mural in Shanxi Hongdong]. 1985.

(8) Liao Ben. *Song Yuan xiqu wenwu yu minsu* [Cultural relics and folk custom of the music drama of Song and Yuan dynasties]. 1989.

(9) "Hongdong Mingyingwangdian Yuan zaju bihua" [The Yuan drama mural of the Hall of Mingyingwang in Hongdong county]. *Zhongguo xiquzhi: Shanxi juan* [Annals of Chinese music drama: Shanxi volume]. 1990.

(10) Chou Hui-ling. "Striking Their Own Poses: The History of Cross-Dressing on the Chinese Stage." 1997.

A brief account of the mural's depiction of cross-dressing and the players' gender is given by Qi Gong in his 1954 article. He points out the fact that both female and male players are represented and identifies their gender identities. Zhou Yibai also attempts to identify the gender of the cross-dressed female players in his 1959 article devoted to the study of the wall painting ("Yuan dai bihua"). Chung-wen Shih's description in her English work on Yuan drama (199–202) pays no attention to the gender of the performers, nor does she interpret the significance of gender representation in the painting. William Dolby limits his discussion to pointing out that "the troupe is headed by a woman and there are several other actresses, some playing male parts" (63). He also arbitrarily and inaccurately states that the personage wearing the false beard is an actress (see below), giving no evidence to support his assertion (63). The related entries in *The Great Chinese Encyclopedia: Traditional Music Drama, Folk Musical Art Forms* (117) and *Annals of Chinese Music Drama: Shanxi Volume* (583–4) give succinct descriptions of the figures, and do not forget to point out the female cross-dressers.[2] Liao Ben gives a meticulously detailed account of various aspects of the mural (215–26) and draws on it, together with other evidence, textual and physical, to illustrate the prevalence of female cross-dressing on the Chinese stage in Song-Yuan times. Through analyses of other historical relics dating from the two periods, he also concludes that the evidence "proves the fact that at the time men and women performed together on the stage" (289) — a practice prohibited in the Ming-Qing period.

Unlike the historical studies quoted above, Chou Hui-ling's more recent article (1997) is a feminist rereading of the history of cross-dressing in Chinese opera. In her brief description of the Yuan mural, she writes, without further explanation of her assertion, that "Zhong Du Xiu [sic], the leading *actress* of the troupe, appears in the painting as a Yuan *male* official. *Male actors*, flanking Zhong, are costumed in minor *male* roles" (134; emphasis added). Looking at the discussions of the mainland China scholars, the general consensus seems to be that of the 11 figures depicted, eight (five men and three women) are believed to be in theatrical costumes corresponding to their real genders. It is in identifying the genders of three of the figures in the front row, whose "real" genders Chou has so matter-of-factly identified, that these theatre historians have given contradictory narratives. Surprisingly, these scholars never refer to each other's conclusions about the gender identification of the figures. One reason may be that, unlike the central debate on the gender of the lead singer in Yuan drama, gender was never a major concern in their study of the wall painting. However, these scholars did make efforts to identify the gender of the figures, sometimes with analyses of proof in some detail, and with the assistance of historical and cultural knowledge of daily practices in Yuan times. Once again, the three figures in gender trouble are: the figure in the center (Zhongdu Xiu, dressed as a man in an official's robe) and the two on the outer left and right respectively (whose theatrical costume has led to the conjecture that they are male attendants of the official).

The Proper Name

The "quest for gender identity" began with the *proper name*. In examining the mural scholars first attempted to identify which of the 11 figures the person was the referent of the sign "Zhongdu Xiu" which appeared on top of the mural. Conventions of naming and its relations to gender are historically specific and vary in different historical times and cultural contexts and even within the same cultural-historical context there has not been one single fixed principle in structuring the naming process. In Chinese culture, which operates on the binary logic of gender, names are, as expected, gendered in common practice. Therefore, in most cases a name is also an indicator of the holder's gender identity, although there are some names that are non-gender specific.

In their oscillation between gender borders, and conflation of both genders, theatrical cross-dressers have always put into question the stability of gender categories and upset the desire to ground gender within the heterosexual matrix. In late imperial times, transvestite actors often adopted feminine stage names rather than masculine ones, drawing more attention to their gender during theatrical representations than that during their "real" life. This naming practice by female impersonators was preserved up to the first half of the twentieth century and constantly created a fracture in the plane of signification between the sign and the referent, and thus rendered the signification of gender identity more problematic. Nowadays, instead of creating stage names, Chinese opera performers from the Mainland tend to use names, often their "real" names, which usually reflect their "real" gender identity. But immediate destabilizing effects remain in the case of female cross-dressers who are still endorsed in China (whereas the tradition of male cross-dressing has been discontinued), since their feminine "real" names are at odds with their male stage representations. The question of the proper name of the cross-dresser itself constitutes an aspect of cross-dressing that creates a source of gender trouble.

From historical information, it is well known that in Yuan theatrical convention the majority of actresses adopted the character *xiu* in their names (numerous examples can be found in *The Green Bower Collection*). This character literally means "elegant" and/or "beautiful/excellent." On the whole it sounds feminine, but it is also used by men, depending on the combination with other characters in a specific name. According to Shen Congwen, for Yuan actresses *xiu* also carried the meaning of "being successful" (435). Liao Ben elaborates that "it was a Yuan custom to add the character *xiu* to the name of a place to call those actresses who were outstanding in a certain district" (220). Therefore, Zhongdu Xiu was presumably a famous female player from Zhongdu.

The exact play that is supposed to be in performance as represented in the mural has not been identified yet, despite the efforts of leading scholars in the field. This has in turn posed difficulties in identifying the dramatic characters, not to mention the leading character. In any case, the leading player named in the horizontal sign is generally agreed to be the figure dressed as a *male* official in the *center* of the stage:

> The player who is in the male leading role, in the *center* of the stage, *is* a woman. How do we know? Let us first refer to the title written on the horizontal sign — this leading player is called "Zhongdu Xiu."
>
> (Qi Gong 288; emphasis added)

The person in the *center* . . . is *perhaps* the leading player "Zhongdu Xiu" inscribed in the horizontal sign.

(Zhou Yibai, "Yuan dai bihua" 593; emphasis added)

In the wall painting, the person occupying the center in the front row is obviously a leading role. The person *should be* Zhongdu Xiu as written in the horizontal sign.

(Liao 219; emphasis added)

. . . occupying the center of the stage . . . *should* be the leading role of *zhengmo* played by Zhongdu Xiu.

(*Zhongguo da baike quanshu* 117; emphasis added)

That the central position is the privileged space is taken for granted in conventional cultural operations. With the exception of Qi Gong, the scholars adopt a more cautious, speculative tone by saying that it is *probably true* that Zhongdu Xiu is the figure in the center. To start with, it is clear that the central figure cannot be identified beyond doubt.

Given the historical knowledge that the owner of the proper name "Zhongdu Xiu" *must be* a woman, and that the likeliest candidate is the figure in men's costume in the center of the mural, the next step taken by scholars was to attempt to prove that "he" is a woman. Although the proper name itself is a powerful proof of the gender of its bearer, it is only through *reasonable* speculation that we have established that the figure in the center is probably Zhongdu Xiu, which can only be a name adopted by a female performer according to Yuan theatre convention. Therefore, other evidence proving the *female* identity of this central figure is necessary to prove that "she" can be convincingly identified as Zhongdu Xiu. The usual criteria used to identify gender difference in this, and many other cases, are designs of clothes, depiction of body parts (e.g., face, hands), and jewelry.

The Dress

Qi Gong's major argument that the gender of the leading cross-dresser in the Yuan mural is female is the gendered design of clothes for women and men. According to him, on the stage depicted in the painting all the women are dressed in clothes with a *left opening* (i.e., the right lapel goes over the left) and all the men in clothes with a *right opening*. He adds that although there were men in Yuan times who wore clothes with a left opening, on the stage at least, all women are wearing clothes with a left opening. In Qi Gong's argument Zhongdu Xiu's identity as a female cross-dresser disguised as the male leading role is proved by (among other evidence), her wearing of an *undershirt* with a left opening under the official's crimson robe (288).

It is important to note that this criterion — the left/right lapel distinction — is far from stable to begin with. While Qi Gong says that in principle men's clothes in the Yuan period followed the right opening style, it should be added that both left and right openings were commonly adopted in various styles of women's clothes during the same period by both Mongolian and Han women, as suggested in a recent historical study of Chinese costumes (Dai 179–83). Furthermore, other recent studies hold that the various northern tribes generally adopted the left opening, while the Mongols did the opposite (Hang 14–5; Shi Waimin 88, 107). Interestingly enough, Qi Gong himself realizes that there were exceptions to the so-called male design of the right opening. Realizing the instability of his ground, he argues for consistency *within* the representational world of the mural: all "women" dress in left opening garments and all "men" in right opening garments. But the issue here is, paradoxically, the very *defining* of gender difference. The questions to be answered are exactly "Who are the 'real' men and women in the mural?" and "Which 'male' figures are actually women dressed up as men?" The style of dress can either be a sign of the player's own gender or the gender of the dramatic character the player is portraying. Or, as Qi Gong's *tactful* argument relies on a recognition of a delicate crossing of gender attributes: both female and male dress styles can be embodied in one figure, as exemplified by Zhongdu Xiu. Given such circumstances, what are the ultimate signs for the "real" gender?

As I mentioned earlier on, only three figures in the mural have been implicated in the issue of crossing gender identity. The rest are taken, with good reason, as unambiguous in their gender representation.

I shall leave these seven figures as practically unproblematic since it is not my intention to problematize everything to the extreme on an abstract theoretical level. What I intend to address is the incoherence and instability of the definitions used to ground gender. In the case of Zhongdu Xiu, there is one style of dress (the female, with a left opening) hidden, yet not completely, behind the other (the male, with a right opening), so that the "real" gender of the person is subtly revealed, but only to the highly observant eye. Qi Gong's great attention to detail is shown by the fact that only a minimal part of the collar of Zhongdu Xiu's undershirt is visible — just enough to reveal the crossing point of the left and right lapels. However, the period for closure of the issue cannot be inserted yet, for the depiction of the attire of the "male" attendant on the far right again puts into question this means of defining gender in the mural (in addition to the historical information I quoted above indicating that women in the Yuan Dynasty adopted both ways of crossing their lapels).

This attendant is a problematic figure with the most indeterminate gender representation. First, we can also see enough of this attendant's undershirt to tell that this garment has a *right opening*. Following the logic of gendered attire (as exemplified by Qi Gong's analysis), this should be a man — provided that the logic is coherent and stable. Neither Qi Gong or Liu Nianzi (*Zhongguo da baike quanshu*) refer at all to the gender of this attendant in their accounts of the mural; thus automatically assuming that "he" is male in a discourse that presumes the male as the universal and does not mark out the masculine gender. Liu states that among the 11 figures, seven are male and four are female and his description indicates only the gender of the women figures, who are Zhongdu Xiu and the three "obviously" female-looking figures in the back row.

The Face, the Hand, and the Foot

In identifying the gender of the figures in the mural, Liao Ben states directly, but without providing any reasons, that the two attendants (in male costumes) on the far right and the far left of the front row are women (289). Zhou Yibai, using facial features as signs pointing to the real gender of the figures, comes to the same conclusion, though in a less definitive tone: "These two persons, whose countenances are all so lovely and charming, seem to be both women in disguise" ("Yuan dai bihua" 594). The attendant on the right is really a *counter*part of the one on the left, for his/her gender identity is an enigma whereas the latter's identity as a female cross-dresser has strong supporting evidence. If one assumes that the attendant on the far right and Zhongdu Xiu are both female cross-dressers, a question immediately comes to mind: is it simply *chance* if some actresses in dramatic costumes wear undershirts with a left opening while others wear undershirts with a right opening? If one believes that the attendant is a man, then the so-called feminine facial features ("lovely and charming") are not persuasive at all in differentiating gender identity. In Chinese figurative painting, the descriptions of persons with "neat and elegant eyebrows and eyes, and beautiful-looking" (Liao 220), or a "neat and elegant countenance" (*Zhongguo da baike quanshu* 117) are not restricted to women. These descriptions are also sometimes appropriate for refined young men. But I find the feminine countenance, though unreliable in determining gender, in no way as ineffectual in differentiating gender as the "delicate fingers" or "long and slender fingers" which Liu Nianzi (*Zhongguo da baike quanshu* 117) and Liao Ben (220) cite as one feature proving Zhongdu Xiu's female identity, and in describing other female players. In truth, anyone is able to see that all fingers in this Yuan mural (and in many other traditional Chinese paintings and sculptures), are always depicted as delicate, long and slender, regardless of the gender of the person they belong. Since Liao Ben uses similar descriptions of this body part frequently in his accounts of female figures in theatrical relics (*Song Yuan xiqu wenwu*), this textual representation of *feminine* fingers has become merely a convention and has lost its signifying function in marking gender difference. Intended as a differential category to make a gender boundary, it is self-dismantling and has lost its original function.

While Qi Gong interestingly points out the differences between the lapels on the male and female costumes, Liao Ben in his analyses of the figuration of women in various sculptures and paintings, has noted that women are most prominently represented and identified by their *small feet* (288–9) — a practice probably most prominently illustrated in erotic paintings.

Chinese erotic paintings almost invariably depict women's bound feet, except in a few cases where either fisherwomen are portrayed (see plates on pages 40 and 129 in *Mixitu daguan*) or the *other* ethnic peoples are the subjects of the representation of sexuality (*Mixitu daguan* 59, 105). In these two contexts, women are depicted with *naked* "natural feet" [*tianzu*] and the site of sexual intercourse breaks away from the confines of the house (specific locations vary from the bedroom to the garden) to the natural world of the river and the wilderness. The ideological confinement of sex in Han-Chinese culture has its symbolic location, just as the Victorians confined and moved sexuality into the home (Foucault 3). Furthermore, the bound foot is never shown naked in erotic paintings, metaphorically reinforcing the bondage of women imposed by men. Van Gulik rightly observes, "The erotic picture albums show that women kept on their shoes and leggings during sexual congress when engaged in upon mats and other places where the attending maid servants could see the pair" (*Sexual Life in Ancient China* 222). The revelation of female identity by the bound foot, which represented female genitals, is a recurring motif in Chinese drama and fiction as well. This *man*-made fetish and its relation to the structuring of gender and cross-dressing in culture and society are most prominently represented in a voluminous *tanci* (a genre of storytelling with stringed accompaniment) work by the Qing woman writer Chen Duansheng (1751–1796). In her *Zaisheng yuan* [Love of a life reborn], the strong, talented, and handsome female protagonist Meng Lizun disguises herself as a man and becomes the prime minister. Her real gender identity is revealed in chapter 64 of this 80-chapter narrative through the unveiling of her tiny "golden lotus" — her feet — and not her breasts or long hair (920–27).

While Liao points out that small feet are an indicator of the female gender of figures in various paintings, he surprisingly does not specifically mention the "feet" in his analysis of the Yuan theatre mural. However, when he says that the two male-costumed attendants on the ends of the front row are women, the most convincing proof that he could have drawn on is undoubtedly the evidence of the small feet of at least one of these two figures. The exceptionally small and pointed boots of the attendant on the left side is entirely visible — she is positively a woman in male dramatic costume. The attendant on the right is again a bit ambiguous: only about one half of each of his/her feet can be seen under the long robe. By proportion they seem to be smaller than the feet of other male players' but obviously larger and less pointed than those of the female attendant on the left. The only certain thing about the gender identity of the player portraying the attendant figure on the far right is that it is never certain.

As for the leading player, Zhongdu Xiu, who is in male theatrical costume but wearing a female undershirt (according to Qi Gong), we can only see the rather rounded (not the typical feminine pointed) tips of her feet, which are almost hidden by the long official's robe that she is wearing. The small/bound feet, most powerful signification of the female gender specific to Chinese culture, cannot be applied to further confirm the gender identity of the central figure, who is almost certainly Zhongdu Xiu.[3]

When I said earlier on that Dolby was inaccurate in saying that the performer wearing the false beard was a woman, I was not arguing in terms of facial appearance, since I have already pointed out that it is not reliable to determine the gender of the players on the basis of facial features. Given that female cross-dressing was common in the Yuan period, the face under the beard on stage could be a woman's. However, Dolby was probably not aware of that very important convention of gender representation in painting, the feet: the player wearing the false beard has a pair of normal size feet — he is male. In addition, there are no other feminine attributes to be found in this figure.

The last gender enigma of the Yuan mural that I want to address again revolves around the leading player Zhongdu Xiu. Zhou Yibai, one of the first scholars to publish studies on this mural, observes that Zhongdu Xu "wears a pair of golden earrings" ("Yuan dai bihua" 593), thus providing another piece of evidence that Zhongdu Xiu is a female player dressed in male clothes. Zhou's assumption is that the earrings signify the real gender while the male costume indicates the disguised gender. Tseng Yung-i, probably following Zhou, also notes that Zhongdu Xiu is wearing gold earrings on both ears. As a result, he also concludes that the dramatic personage is "*evidently* disguised by a woman" (43; emphasis added). This *apparently* useful observation of the "earrings" in fact generates more perplexities about gender representation. First, although it does not seem to have been a Han Chinese practice for men to wear earrings, visual evidence reveals that Mongolian and Khitan men did wear earrings as body adornments, the portrait of the Yuan Emperor Chengzong being an excellent example.[4]

In the mural, the dramatic costumes are in Han style, while several of the figures in the back row are clad in everyday clothes of the Yuan period. In fact the bearded male musician clad in daily Yuan style clothes on the far left of the back row does wear earrings (Shen 434, illustration 206). Was he a Mongol? Shall we assume that Zhongdu Xiu is Han Chinese, or Mongol? In any case, the character of the male official that Zhongdu Xiu is playing should not wear earrings, and Zhongdu Xiu *as* a woman would probably have worn earrings in real life. However, if according to the social norm only Chinese women wore earrings, why did the leading actress in the painting not remove her ear-rings while she was cross-dressing as a man? Or are the earrings an addition of the painter, a representational device like the small feet, to signify to the viewer that the person dressed as a male is really a woman? Could it be an "alienating" device, a theatrical convention to remind the audience that a performer of one gender is portraying the other gender, to lay bare the *performing* of gender and to display the illusion of gender, a convention that is prominently used in some other theatres such as the Javanese *ludruk* plays, the traditional Iranian theatre called *ta'ziyeh*, and the Balinese *Parwa* dance drama?[5] In fact, this theatrical practice has its precedents in Chinese theatre. In the southern drama [*nanxi*] *Zhang Xie zhuangyuan* [Zhang Xie the principal graduate], there are examples of the female impersonator drawing attention to his male gender identity under the disguise. The actor of the comic role-type [*fujing*][6] plays several female characters throughout this play. In Act 16 the comedic actor, cross-dressed in the role of an old woman, enters with his big feet naked, exposing them to the mockery of another comic actor (86), and in Act 19, the expression "a real man" [*dazhangfu*] is played upon to refer to the comic actor's old woman disguise (99). As Liao Ben points out, in Song theatrical performance the comic actor [*jing*] always leaves some clues to reveal his gender identity (280). The examples cited above demonstrate that in Chinese theatrical representations of cross-dressing the bound foot again constitutes a primary representational apparatus invented by men to maintain gender difference.

All we are left with after these systematic analyses are the contradictions and incoherences in this whole discourse on gender difference which culminate in the enigma of Zhongdu Xiu's "earrings." Regardless of whether there are satisfactory reasons for a person believed to be a woman to wear earrings when disguised as a man on stage, I have discovered yet another puzzling and slightly droll query: Do the earrings really exist in the authentic mural? Liu Nianzi's entry in the authoritative *The Great Chinese Encyclopedia* tells us that, instead of a pair of "golden earrings," there is an *earhole* found on each of Zhongdu Xiu's ears (*Zhongguo da baike quanshu* 117). Why is there such a metonymic displacement of this cultural sign of femininity? Why has there been in this academic *discursive* practice such a process of metamorphosis of an imagistic element, not without a trace of the "poetic" (a textual process that strongly reminds one of a particular semiotic feature of classical Chinese poetry effectively demonstrated by Francois Cheng in his *Chinese Poetic Writing*)? How has the relation between this academic writing and its object operated? Has the visual evidence — with a supposedly concrete physical existence — remained incorrupt? Has anything happened to the integrity, and thus the stability and reliability of it? It seemed at first that it would not be difficult to examine printed reproductions of the authentic object for verification, since these pictures are so accessible even to ordinary readers. The printed reproductions presumably closest to the authentic wall painting are the ones in *Annals of Chinese Music Drama: Shanxi Volume* and *The Great Chinese Encyclopedia*. These two works include photographic reproductions showing evidence of the corrosion of the original. The best reconstructed picture is that included in Shen Congwen's monumental *Study of Ancient Chinese Costumes* (1981, 1992) which is a color illustration with clearly identifiable details (434, illustration 206).[7] In this reconstructed picture Zhongdu Xiu is clearly portrayed wearing golden earrings. However the photographic reproductions, in relatively low resolution and weak contrast, do not seem to support the existence of earrings, not to mention pierced ears. The truth seems to lie in the authentic wall painting in Shanxi, provided that it has not been destroyed. However, there is still the possibility — in view of the great difficulty, for various reasons, of preserving cultural artifacts in mainland China — that it could have been so damaged that it could prove nothing; or that throughout the some 600 years after its creation, improper maintenance and preservation efforts such as inaccurate repainting could have corrupted the "original."

Of the studies on this Zhongdu Xiu mural that I have consulted thus far, only one author directly states that his study was based on a field investigation (Zhou Guoxiong 100). The focus of this recent article has nothing to do with gender, although the author states in passing that there are three women and seven men performing on stage in the mural (101). Of the other writers, not one mentions the medium — authentic or reproduction — on which they built their description and analysis. It is hard to deny that the authentic work of art still preserves a mysterious power to define and give stability to meaning in an age of mechanical reproduction, yet the "truth" contained in this original mural seems to be continuously deferred.

In the end, this is perhaps not important in verifying the point at hand since both the earrings and earholes refer to the feminine gender of the person portrayed. Is it not the common objective and consensus of these scholars to show that the figure in question *is* a woman and also the bearer of the name in the horizontal sign, i.e., Zhongdu Xiu? However, some basic questions remain to be asked. Why are there such multiple contradictions in these writings on gender differentiation and identification relating to the Chinese stage, which is a theatre with a strong presence of male and female cross-dressing? Is it merely a historical coincidence that the basic information, the wall painting itself, is too corrupt? Was there a problem in the reproduction of the authentic object? If so, why and how? What was the exact object — the authentic mural or a reproduction, and if a reproduction, which one — that each of these scholars examined? Why has the "authentic" wall painting been consistently deferred from any presence in the academic texts woven around it? Or is it more relevant for us to reflect on the question of the (in)coherence of representation — textual, visual, cultural, historical — in relation to the category of gender? Perhaps the socio-cultural construction of the two genders was in the beginning questionable and unstable, so that the stability and consistency of the representational apparatus in sustaining gender differences and the process of representing gender are constantly put into question by their own inherent ruptures. One significant suggestion of this interrogation seems to point to "gender" as a self-implosive cultural category; or, perhaps, that a stable representation of "gender" is more often than not a practice of radical impossibility.

ACTING

SEVEN

GENDER AND PERFORMANCE:
CROSSING REALITY/FICTION AND ACTING THE OTHER SEX

Performing the Real and the Fictional

If cross-dressing and theatre are already subversive in their own making as cultural practices in the realm of *performance*, the inevitable interlocking relation between gender and performance is almost expected. The beginnings of theatre in various cultures seem to be inseparable from cross-dressing and especially male into female cross-dressing. Male transvestite theatres often appear more as the "norm," instead of theatres following the order of mimesis which put women in female roles and men in male roles. What does Chinese opera, a theatre so rooted in cross-dressing, signify in epistemological terms? How does it operate as a site of contestation and negotiation among different ideological forces and resistant voices, specifically in terms of gender?

To investigate issues concerning cross-dressing, sex, and gender in Chinese opera, it will be revealing to first examine the operation of the categories of *zhen* [real] and *jia* [fictional/false/fake] centering around this theatre, as these are broad existential concepts controlling the categorization of sex and gender in Chinese literary, historical, legal and medical discourses.[1] One of the important points about Lu Xun's brief remarks on transvestism discussed in chapter 1 is how immediately and aptly one can correlate the theatre with the real world. This is also the point where the literary concept of *xing* is instructive in reading Lu Xun's passage. In this *xing* type of metaphoric relationship, the two juxtaposed terms have certain invisible connections underlying them which render their relationship an inevitable one, one which is ordained by an overall cultural code.[2] In Lu Xun's essay, the two terms are transvestism and old imperial systems disguised as democratic institutions. The missing connection or the linking communal structure is the trope of "staging," which is insinuated in transvestism. To Lu Xun, corrupt politicians are performing in a democratic disguise, just like transvestite actors who are performing another gender. This idea of the world as stage, manifested in varied nuances in difference cultures, was as prevalent in early modern England as it was in the late imperial Chinese discourse of theatre.

Immediate English examples are the speeches of Jaques in *As You Like It* (II.vii): "All the world's a stage, / And all the men and women merely players. / They have their exits and their entrances, / And one man in his time plays many parts, / His acts being seven ages" (Shakespeare 1622); Antonio in *The Merchant of Venice* (I.i): "I hold the world but as the world, Graziano — / A stage where every man must play a part, / And mine a sad one" (1092); and the Duchess in *The Duchess of Malfi* (IV.i): "I account this world a tedious theatre, / For I do play a part in't 'gainst my will" (Webster 66). These well-known reflections on the world as stage share one implication — that each person performs a role or several roles in life, which is a theatre. In the Chinese context, the Ming writer Xu Wei once wrote an antithetical couplet for the stage in which the second line reads: "Playacting on spontaneous occasions originally belongs to the nature of human life" (Quoted in Cheng Fuwang et al. 3: 166). The Qing critic Li Diaoyuan begins and ends the preface to his *Juhua* [Discourse on drama] with the same statement: "The past and the present are one theatre." In a way, therefore, history is theatre and theatre is history, or in other words, real life or history is performance; people perform their lives. In the same preface Li also writes:

> Not one single day of our lives is not in a play. Wealth, poverty, dying young, longevity, a hundred years of chaos pass like flashes of lightning and sparkles of a flint; reunion and separation, sadness

and happiness, all disappear in a moment of the blink of an eye. All these are just like a transient play that comes to a closure in an instant.

(35)

This view on the relationship between theatre and life in the Chinese context is immersed in the philosophical thought of Taoism-Buddhism. The Ming playwright Tu Long (1542–1605) brings Buddhism into his assertion that the "floating world is a big theatre" which is "fictional" [*jia*] (quoted in Wei and Wu 116). In any case, it is easy to see how often the stage is an apt metaphor for the world. In the West, from early modern times on, the widespread reliance on representations of theatricality as a means of ideological dissemination and social control in the operation of sociopolitics further illustrates that the "illusionistic theatre" and the "real world" are inevitably interlocked and mutually contaminated. Image-making was crucial to the ruler, the "prince" was well aware of the importance of the royal spectacle in the manipulation of power. Queen Elizabeth I said, "We princes . . . are set on stages, in the sight and view of all the world duly observed."[3] The "illusion of power" in theatre at court in early modern England was a "real" display of royal power in the sense that "the truth of the royal productions was the truth of appearances. Power was asserted only through analogies, faith affirmed through symbols" (Orgel, *Illusion* 88).

Modern Chinese rulers, like their Western counterparts, have consciously and skillfully played on representations of theatricality to empower themselves. The ultimate demonstration of connection between theatricality and power being Mao Zedong's eight public presentations of himself, dressed in military costume, to millions of Red Guards in Tiananmen Square between August and October 1966. In imperial times on the contrary, the "son of heaven" ruled by the "inaccessibility" of his body. His figure was too supreme to be seen or even named with the proper noun by the people under his authority. Invested with absolute authority by the mandate of heaven, the emperor was represented by and ruled through his bureaucrats.[4] The interplay of power between the monarch and theatrical production notable in early modern England finds no obvious counterpart in the theatre history of Ming-Qing China. Emperors and nobles in the last imperial dynasties of Yuan, Ming and Qing enjoyed theatrical performances at court,[5] but they did not engage in theatrical action like the early modern English noble spectator who ultimately watched and acted what s/he became in the theatre action. The court masque, which turned the theatrical event itself into an entity, the stage itself into the action, and realized and embodied the truth of the monarchy with the monarch in the center and playing the central role (Orgel, *Illusion*), is not something to which one can easily find a parallel in late imperial China's theatre history.[6] In fact, Ming and Qing laws prohibited the stage representation of emperors, queens, concubines, royal and heroic officials, and sages (Wang Xiaochuan 10, 16, 31–2), although these prohibitions were rarely enforced and obviously often ignored.

From an anthropological perspective, in the still relatively ritualistic performance contexts of the staging of Chinese opera today (let us not forget that the ritualistic origin of Chinese theatre is an influential theory), there are often moments in which the realms of the ritualistic, the theatrical, and the real interpenetrate. Yung Sai-shing has insightfully demonstrated this in a meticulous analysis of the *Beidou xi* ["Big Dipper" opera] in Singapore in the early 1990s (99–131). In such a context the participants, including the sponsors, the performers, and the spectators, are generally not aware of the existence of these coextensive spaces and there is a collapse of spatial boundaries and much interfacing among the different realms.

The precarious relationship between theatrical illusion and social reality is more often revealed in a secular context in descriptions of the equivocal perception by ordinary spectators of the real and fictional roles in the performer/character identity, and in the discourse of the theory of acting. It seems that many Chinese spectators in the imperial past were reluctant to acknowledge a rigid differentiation between the stage and the world, the sign and the referent. Meanwhile, classical writings on acting imply that the perfect performer-in-role is one who transcends the boundary of the real and the fictional; or, in other words, blends real life and playacting. Cross-dressers on stage transgress these boundaries and embody all these uncertainties, constituting a subversive element that calls into question a rigid binary system.

During the Ming Dynasty Zhou Hui recorded a comic incident of a wealthy yet illiterate man's failure to make a distinction between the play-world and the real world:

> There was a supremely wealthy man who was illiterate and knew nothing about the theatre. One day he gave a banquet in his mansion. He entertained his guests with a play staging the story of Cheng Yuanhe.[7] There was the comic actor Liu Huai who was excellent in arousing laughter and moving people's emotions. When the play came to the scene of killing the horse and selling Lai Xingbao [the servant played by Liu Huai], Lai cried and asked to stay with his master. The wealthy man called the actor to come over and filled up a golden cup with wine. Granting him the wine, the wealthy man consoled him, "As your master has determined to sell you, it is not worthy of you to beg to stay with him." Lai said yes and retreated. This is what we call a play within a play, a dream in a dream. Isn't it also what a wealthy man does, being a wealthy man?

(4)

Similar anecdotes of individuals conflating the stage and life are found elsewhere. The influential Qing dramatic critic Jiao Xun (1763–1820), cites four incidents[8] in *juan* 6 of his *Jushuo* [Discourse on drama], in which a spectator, enraged by the abominable villain played (obviously successfully) by an actor on stage, beat up or even killed the actor during the performance (203). The notorious character portrayed by the unfortunate actors in all four cases was Qin Hui, undoubtedly the most treacherous, wicked and crafty character ever constructed in classical drama and fiction out of historical figures.[9]

There are several possible perspectives on how to interpret the significance of these and similar reports which show how spectators could often "mistake" the fictional dramatic world for the real world. One possibility is the superb skill of the actors. Lu Eting cites the record of the actor Liu Huai to illustrate the great artistic achievement of Kunju actors around the end of the sixteenth century (78). The third "Qin Hui" record can also be read in part as a hyperbolic commendation of the player's great mimetic performance, as Zhang Faying does in his *History of Chinese Theatre Troupes* (113). Of the four "Qin Hui" records, this one alone includes a direct commendation of the acting: "the performance was optimal in every aspect of artistic expressions" (Jiao 203).

Given the unique cultural meaning of the Qin Hui/Yue Fei pair, a moral intent seems to be apparent in the recording of these hilarious events. A didactic reading can especially be made out of the second "Qin Hui" incident, which reports the mitigation of the spectator's legal punishment on the grounds that he had struck the actor-in-role dead out of righteous indignation,[10] rendering this story an example illustrating the historical punishment of evil people: "infamy stinks for ten thousand years," as the Chinese idiom goes. From a semiotic perspective, one may refer to a general lack of "theatrical competence," defined as "the ability to recognize the performance *as such*" (Elam 87), among the spectators, as well as a gross error in theatrical framing (88).[11] "Theatrical competence" is a dynamic concept to explain the behavior of conflating the theatre and reality. In Zhou Hui's facetious account, the description of the wealthy man as illiterate and ignorant about life accounts for his failure to distinguish between the play and reality.

However in these records something more is implied concerning the perception of the real and the fictional, and the potential implosion of the real into the fictional and the fictional into the real. When the wealthy man steps into the play-world and offers the poor servant character a golden cup of wine, the comic actor in turn steps out of the fictional world to accept the offer. Zhou Hui's comments at the end of his account of this incident have very strong Taoist underpinnings: "This is what we call a play within a play, a dream in a dream." Is this not a reference to the well-known paradox of Zhuang Zi's (or Chuang Tzu) in which he asks if he is dreaming of the butterfly or the butterfly is dreaming of him?[12] James J. Y. Liu has interpreted this parable in connection to phenomenological literary criticism: "Is Chuang Tzu not 'bracketing' the world in Husserl's sense? For he is neither affirming nor denying the reality of either himself or the butterfly, but suspending judgment on both" (*Chinese Theories of Literature* 61). Elsewhere, Liu further comments that

By rejecting the "either/or" way of thinking and even the "both/and" way of thinking, Zhuang Zi arrives at "neither/nor," which repudiates all binary opposition and admits all paradoxes.

(*Language – Paradox – Poetics* 13)

The mutual contamination of the real and the fictional unsettles the hierarchical order of things and questions the mimetic relation between the real and the fictional in which one is ordered before another and posed as the essence constituting the phenomenal existence of the other.

In the third and the fourth reports of attacks on actors playing Qin Hui, which are the most detailed of the four, there are some sharp contradictions and incoherences that require yet another reading perspective for a better understanding of them. The spectators in both records are shown to be able to recognize the theatrical frame and to differentiate the fictional from the real to different degrees. One spectator, who stabbed the actor playing Qin Hui with a knife, explained when he was brought before the judge:

> I never met that actor before. At that moment I just wanted to die together with Qin Hui; I really had no time to make a distinction whether it was the real person or a fake.

(Jiao 203)

In the fourth report, when the other members of the audience tell the spectator, an illiterate woodcutter, that it was only a play and the performer was not the real Qin Hui, he said:

> I also knew that it was a play, that was why I beat up the actor. If it were the real Qin Hui, his fat would have smeared my axe.

(203)

These two spectators may not be well educated, but they are not theatrically incompetent and are not unaware (especially the woodcutter) of a certain dialectical relation between the two different poles of the real and the fictional, yet at the moment in question they unconsciously refuse to accept this differentiation and its sanctity. To these spectators, there are moments when the distinction between the real and the fictional is suspended and there are points in the continuum of the real-fictional that are both real and fictional simultaneously, when the boundary between the two is eclipsed. The spectator with the knife falls in a bracketed moment where there is an awareness of the categories of the real and the fictional, but their distinction is not important in the ordering of action. The woodcutter beats up the actor because there *is* Qin Hui; but he does not chop up the actor because there is *not* the real Qin Hui. The two spectators see and identify two equally *credible* and valid identities in the body of the actor-in-role. The Qin Hui there before them is neither real nor fictional but can perhaps best be designated as "virtual" — I would posit it as an existential category corresponding to what Majorie Garber calls the "third" in her study of gender and cross-dressing, and describes as "a mode of articulation, a way of describing a space of possibility" (11). There is already a conflation of the real and the fictional which enables the spectators' violation of the rigid binary division, exposing its radical instability. The violation in turn further conflates the two binary poles. The seeming contradictions in the spectators' violating actions and recuperative words reveal that aspects of such oppositional conceptions as world/stage, reality/fiction, and corollary male/masculinity and female/femininity are constantly in crisis, and were being continually inscribed yet also continually undermined in the formation of the theatrical experience in imperial China.[13]

The conceptual categories of *zhen* and *jia* that are always negotiating each other in the discourse on acting constitute an integral and essential theoretical argument pointing to a certain epistemological understanding. It is perhaps best exemplified in literary expression by the famous couplet from the first chapter of the great eighteenth century novel *Honglou meng* [A dream of red mansions] written by Cao Xueqin [Tsao Hsüeh-chin] (1715?–1763?):

> When the unreal is taken for the real, then the real becomes unreal;
> Where non-existence is taken for existence, then existence becomes non-existence.[14]

Dore Levy interprets it in this way: "The couplet therefore signifies not a hard and fast division between truth and falsity, reality and illusion, but the impossibility of making such distinctions in any world, fictional or 'actual'" (15).

The collapse of the distinction between the real and the fictional, reflecting implications of Taoist and Buddhist thinking, has made possible and reinforced the underlying idea of *becoming* the real through *performing* the real in theatre. It is perhaps more than a mere accident that the very first record of playacting in the Spring and Autumn Period (770–476 B.C.E.), the biography of the comic entertainer You Meng by the great historian Sima Qian, is a story of mistaken identity in which the real and the fake, the living and the dead, the low entertainer and the high minister, are all mixed up. The King of Chu was holding a birthday banquet and You Meng showed up in the guise of the deceased prime minister Sunshu Ao. The King was amazed, and thinking that Sunshu Ao had risen from the dead, he wanted to appoint "him" prime minister again (*Juan* 126, 10: 3201).[15]

Performing Gender, Acting Woman

After a thorough delineation of the cultural operations of the real and the fictional, the aesthetic ideal in classical discussions of the performer and the role of *becoming* the real through *performance* can be seen in a new light in relation to gender. I shall reinterpret two frequently quoted classical passages on the art of acting to illustrate my point. The greatest of Ming playwrights, Tang Xianzu (1550–1617),[16] gave the following instructions to young performers in his hometown of Yihuang xian:

> The performer specializing in the female role-type should *often think* [*changxiang*] of herself/himself as a woman. The performer specializing in the male role should *often desire* [*changyu*] to become the person s/he playacts.
>
> ("Yihuang xian" 1128, emphasis added)

The Qing scholar Ji Yun (1724–1805) quotes an unsurpassed transvestite actor on the secret of his success in "acting woman":

> We who take our body as female must at the same time transform [hua] our heart-mind [xin] into female. Then our loveliness and charm will infatuate all those who see us. If there is one degree of the male heart-mind left, there is necessarily one degree of non-verisimilitude with woman. In this situation, how can one fight for the favor given to women? As for performing on stage, I render the heart-mind pure when playing a virtuous woman . . . ; profligate when playing a promiscuous woman . . . ; solemn when playing a noble lady . . . . To express delight, anger, lamentation, happiness, indebtedness and grief, or love and hate, I put oneself in the other's position. I never take it as playacting but as real. People then all see it as real. The other people impersonate woman but fail to retain a woman's heart-mind; imitate women but fail to acquire various hearts/minds of women. That is why I am supreme.

(12:10, emphasis added)

These comments are not in reference to playacting any specific character, but playacting the other sex: what a female (male) impersonator has to do in order to *perfectly* play woman (man) on stage. These passages have been used by scholars in conventional theatre criticism to demonstrate how meticulously actors pursued the art of acting in the past, and how classical Chinese acting theory is distinguished by the emphasis on capturing the *shen* [essence/psyche] of the person to be impersonated — a concept referred to as *chuanshen lun* [theory of retaining the essence/psyche] in modern discussions of traditional theatre aesthetics.[17]

In my view, these passages on acting also point to what we today address as issues of gender, performativity and performance (Parker and Sedgwick; Butler). It is instructive that these classical remarks on stage performance amount almost to saying that gender is performance. Yet it is of course imperative to pay attention to the ontological differences between these remarks from imperial China and today's poststructuralist, Euro-American discourse on queer trouble asking one to consider "how it is that queering persists as a defining moment of performativity" (Butler, *Bodies That Matter* 224).

These classical Chinese theories on impersonating the other sex are vested in the binary oppositions of form/appearance [*xing*] on the one hand, and essence/psyche [*shen*] on the other. This cultural operation is still based on a system of binary gender, the structure of the female "heart-mind" versus the male "heart-mind" is still operating as the basic epistemological principle. It would be going too far to assume that there is a dismantling of the two-gender system in these commentaries. Instead, these Chinese opera practitioners believed that it was not enough to merely take up the clothes (form/appearance) to make a male cross-dresser a woman. Interestingly, on this point, it seems that leading queer theorist Judith Butler may share something with these ancient Chinese, since she has said, "I never did think that gender was like clothes, or that clothes make the woman" (231). But the parallel stops there. Butler's concern is the philosophical-deconstructive interrogation of performativity and citationality, subjectivity and agency. To her, any appeal to an interior, a priori identity is futile because it does not exist. But let me emphasize here that Tang Xianzu and the transvestite actor were essentialists in that they believed in the essence of a biological sex as given. In capturing the essence/psyche of the female sex, a male transvestite can be transformed into a "woman" that everyone takes as "real." External appearance has to be integrated seamlessly with internal essence to perform the "real woman." The secret skill required for a man to *become* a woman is to transform one's "heart-mind" [*xin*] into that of a woman. It is not just for the short duration of acting on stage that the Chinese stage cross-dresser "identifies" with the opposite sex,[18] in contrast to Konstantin Stanislavski's theory of the actor/actress as an artist who identifies with the character, and for the duration of a performance "becomes" the character s/he plays. The Chinese stage cross-dresser has to *always* [*chang*] retain the "heart-mind" of the opposite sex and transform his/her own "heart-mind" into that of the opposite sex. The Chinese transvestite actor writing in the eighteenth century may sound similar to the contemporary performance artist from the 1970s "who tries not to make a distinction between herself and her role" (Solomon, *Re-dressing the Canon* 167). But whereas the contemporary performance artist's role is her own self, the Chinese female impersonator's role is his *transformed* gendered self which is not his own, nor is it any longer the same sex. The key word in the Chinese context is *hua* [to transform, transformation]: "We who take our body as female must at the same time transform our heart-mind into female," thus spoke the incomparable transvestite actor from the eighteenth century. This discourse in acting can be related to the Taoist epistemological conception of "the transformation of things" (Burton Watson's translation of *wuhua*]), as presented in the chapter "Discussions on Making Things Equal" ["Qiwulun"] in the Taoist classic *Zhuangzi* (*Chuang Tzu*). In fact, the whole discourse in theatre concerning the epistemological view of reality and fiction is immersed in Taoist-Buddhist thinking.[19]

A discourse of gender as mutable in its very performance derived from the Taoist/Buddhist notion that things are fluid and transformable.[20] The possibility of transforming into another gender — in order to make a fictional playacting become real — is acknowledged in the classical writings discussed above. Regardless of the requirement of the capturing of the essence/psyche, genders (femininity, masculinity) in this context are implied to be culturally constructed and are independent of the corresponding sex (woman, man) — a man can become a "real" woman. Femininity or masculinity (construct) has no necessary relation with being female or male (essence). Femininity and masculinity are not to be defined as real or fake, because the constitution of either of these two categories is performance, not any given essentiality. A compulsory mimetic relation between the two genders and the corresponding two sexes was not enforced in these classical writings concerning theatrical cross-dressing. The belief being that a man could perform the feminine; a woman could perform the masculine — as *real*. Furthermore, with the benefit of hindsight, we can see a hidden contradiction in this emphasis on the essence/psyche in the act of impersonation. As we see in the transvestite actor's words the essence/psyche, which is assumed to be an essential constant, can somehow be reiterated. If "essence" is transferable and reiterative, it has to be redefined and understood in a different way, and this iterality reinforces gender as a performance act — even the "essence" can be performed.

The possibility, at least in discursive practice, that a man can *become* a woman (and vice versa) in the theatre is validated by the unsettling and conflation of the categories of the real and the fictional, by the blurring of the boundary between real life (the world) and performance (the stage), by the transgressing of, or making equal of, the rigid mimetic order of the world (the real) and its representation (the fictional). The anecdotes in which audience members fail to see stage personalities as actors may or may not be true, but this legacy has continued into modern times. The *Jingju erbai nian zhi lishi* [Two hundred years' of history of Beijing opera] (1926) records that a Japanese envoy once watched a performance by Mei Lanfang and was overwhelmed by Mei's feminine beauty. Since he did not know that Mei was a man he referred to him as a woman, inciting a chortle from his companions (Hatano 216). According to the author, who was also Japanese: "it is impossible to differentiate whether Mei is female or male when he appears on stage with the makeup" (216).

The Order of Gender

This mixing up of gender, and hence of the hierarchical order in society, is exactly what the dominant discourse tries to repress, and is also where the subversion of a cross-dressed theatre lies. The transgressive aspects of the stage have presented a resistance against a dominant discourse that has from the beginning categorized gender into a hierarchical order.

Evidence from the section on music in the ancient text of the *Liji* [Book of rites], dating from the Han Dynasty, aptly demonstrates how oppositional the Chinese music theatre has been in a hierarchical cultural structure (all emphasis added in the quotations):

> By the sackcloth worn for parents, the wailings, and the weepings, they defined the terms of the mourning rites. By the bells, drums, shields, and axes, they introduced harmony into their seasons of rest and enjoyment. By marriage, capping, and the assumption of the hairpin, they *maintained the separation that should exist between male and female*. By the archery gatherings in the districts, and the feastings at the meetings of princes, they provided for the correct maintenance of friendly intercourse.
>
> (*Li Chi: Book of Rites* 2: 97; *Liji: yueji* 11: 9; 128)

If these processes [of nature's change and growth] took place out of season, there would be no [vigorous] life; and *if no distinction were observed between males and females, disorder would arise and grow:* — such is the nature of the [different qualities of] heaven and earth.

(*Li Chi: Book of Rites* 2: 104; *Liji: yueji* 11: 12; 129)

Therefore the ancient kings [in framing their music], laid its foundations in the feelings and nature of men; they examined [the notes] by the measures [for the length and quality of each]; and adapted it to express the meaning of the ceremonies [in which it was to be used]. They [thus] brought it into harmony with the energy that produces life, and to give expression to the performance of the five regular constituents of moral worth. *They made it indicate that energy in its Yang or phase of vigour, without any dissipation of its power, and also in its Yin or phase of remission, without the vanishing of its power.* The strong phase showed no excess like that of anger, and the weak no shrinking like that of pusillanimity. These four characteristics blended harmoniously in the minds of men, and were similarly manifested in their conduct. *Each occupied quietly in its proper place, and one did not interfere injuriously with another.*

(*Li Chi: Book of Rites* 2: 108–9; *Liji: yueji* 11: 14; 130)

The purpose of setting up all kinds of institutions, including music and gender, is to fix all people and things in a hierarchy so as to maintain order. The differentiation and separation between the male and the female is central to maintaining social stability. The stability of *yin* and *yang*, each in its own "proper" place, is the controlling trope of order. This order is also authorized by ancient rites (as presented in the *Book of Rites*). However, there are always "new" and deviant things arising to challenge the past and the ancient:

But now, in the new music, [the performers] advance and retire without any regular order; the music is corrupt to excess; there is no end to its vileness. *Among the players there are dwarfs like monkeys, while boys and girls are mixed together,* and there is no distinction between father and son. Such music can never be talked about, and cannot be said to be after the manner of antiquity. This is the fashion of the new music.

(*Li Chi: Book of Rites* 2: 117; *Liji: yueji* 11: 18; 132)

Theatre that mixes men and women is dangerous. Performers from the beginning were relegated to an inferior rank, compared with animals and consigned to the category of deviants: among them were the "abnormal" dwarfs.

This anxiety deriving from the mixing of men and women, as I point out in the second chapter, is the major cause of theatre censorship. It is noteworthy that in the history of Chinese theatre, attacks on male transvestism have been infrequent. So far I have encountered only two instances of direct attacks on cross-dressing as disturbing social custom and domestic morality, both dating from the early Ming period (fifteenth century), before the theatre reached its height later in the period. Lu Rong (1436–1494) writes in *Shuyuan zaji* [The Shu garden miscellany] that among those actors of *xiwen* plays, "the ones who disguise as women are called counterfeit female [*zhuangdan*]. They speak softly, walk slowly and greet charmingly — always appearing to be like real women. The literati who wish to rectify the morality in their households should detest and dismiss them severely" (112–3). Another gentry-scholar Du Mu (1458–1525) remarked that in the capital city there were actors from the Wu county performing Southern dramas whom the imperial guard Men Da reported to the emperor as "using men to disguise as women and disrupting customs and morals" (49–50). Plays like *West Wing* and *Yuzan ji* [The jade hairpin] were regarded as a bad influence on young men and women. In the words of the Ming scholar Tang Laihe, these plays are "despicable for their incitement to promiscuity" (8531). By contrast, in early modern England, male transvestism was thought to incite male homosexuality, and constituted a major source of male anxiety.[21] Part of this anxiety arose from the fear that a man might become a woman in practicing transvestism. The relatively open attitude toward homosexuality and sexuality in general in early imperial China (Van Gulik 1961; Hinsch; Liu Dalin, *Zhongquo gudai xingwenhua*; Shi Fang; Xiaomingxiong) has probably shaped the anti-theatre prejudice toward attacking the stage as disrupting the morality of young males and females.

BODY

EIGHT

AESTHETICS AND POLITICS OF
THE PERFORMING BODY:
FEMALE SCHOLAR AND MALE QUEEN

Gendering Genre: The Dialectic of Prettiness-Eroticism and Artistry

Chinese theatre has been accused by moralists of corrupting women, among other things; however, it is notable that Chinese theatre itself has been gendered as feminine and narrated by way of feminine tropes. As for the player, Sophie Volpp has argued that the actor in seventeenth century Chinese theatre was "symbolically coded feminine," and that the "feminization of actors" was "one of the primary themes in late-imperial Chinese representations of the actor" (139). In traditional critical writing, it was not just the theatre but also dramatic lyrics that were feminine-gendered. Indeed, it may well be proposed that the entire theatre event[1] of Chinese opera has often been coded as feminine.

This already gendered theatrical discourse, combined with a performance aesthetics which privileges a binary pair of notions: *se* ["prettiness-eroticism"] and *yi* ["artistry"] — which are mutually enhancing yet restraining — plus the obfuscation of gender and sex categories brought about by cross-dressing, have caused a (self)dismantling effect in gender representation in both the dramatic text and stage performance in Chinese theatre. It is necessary here to reflect on the translation problems posed by the highly cultural specific term *se* before moving on to further discussion of the dialectic of *se* and *yi* in connection with the feminization of Chinese theatre.

The Chinese term *se* carries at least four, sometimes partially overlapping, levels of meanings depending on the individual usage in context: (1) "color," e.g., *yanse*; (2) "prettiness" as in describing a woman as having *zise*; (3) "eroticism/erotic desire," e.g., *seqing*, or recently gaining more currency in academic discourse, *qingse*; (4) "reality/appearance" in Buddhist philosophy, mostly paired with *kong* [emptiness/void]. Most relevant to our discussion here are the implications of numbers two and three, and these two senses of the word are more often than not intertwined. Generally speaking, *se* as "prettiness" already implies a certain degree of underlying erotic desire. For the sake of readability, in the subsequent discussion I shall use "prettiness-eroticism" or simply "prettiness," whichever is more appropriate in a specific context, in referring to *se*.

The "(self)dismantling effect" constituted in the complex interpenetrating operation of the gendered theatrical discourse and the aesthetics of "prettiness-eroticism" and "artistry" exposes and unsettles the incoherences, instabilities and uncertainties of the heterosexual matrix itself through its suppression of gender and sexual transgressions in society. While in the dramatic world, the patriarchal order is often (apparently) restored in the end, and its ideologies of female virtues and heterosexual demeanor reinstated. A critique of this radical ambiguity in representing gender, which galvanizes on the one hand the problematic relations between the fictional/constructed/social and the real/unconstructed/natural, and on the other hand the question of power hierarchies and gender, makes the study of Chinese opera highly relevant to contemporary cultural studies. This critical inquiry is as much about the construction of gender as the undoing of it in traditional Chinese theatre.

Chinese drama, as a literary genre as well as a performing art, has been feminized in some major criticisms in the classical dramatic discourse. In the critical writings of the Ming period, both the literary-dramatic and performance aspects of the art form are textualized in feminine terms. In his theoretical-critical work *Qulü* [Rules of dramatic songs] (prefaced 1610), which is one of the seminal writings in traditional dramatic criticism, Wang Jide draws an analogy between composing *qu* [dramatic lyrics] and a pretty woman's meticulous embellishment of her beauty and elegance, from the face to clothes to gestures; he also states that *ci* [lyrics] and *qu* "should not be heroic and marvelous, but only lovely, charming, and colorful" (4: 179). Wang is in fact following a long critical tradition of assigning the general characteristic of *ci* to the realm of the "graceful and restrained" [*wanyue*]. Relatively speaking, being "vigorous and firm" [*xionghun*] is usually regarded the as the orthodox characteristic of the genre of *shi* [poetry]. But it must be emphasized here that this opposition, which suggests a masculine/feminine binary, is a general description asserted by individual schools of classical poetry criticism and is not meant to generalize the style of all the authors and works in a poetic genre as one monolithic mode. For instance, in Chinese literary history there was a "bold and unconstrained" [*haofang*] school of *ci* in contrast to the "graceful" school, at the same time however, there was the dominant assertion that the orthodox style [*zhengzong*] school of *ci* should be "graceful and restrained." This critical practice of gendering genre in Chinese literary criticism through the use of gendered terms to generalize the vital characteristic of a genre is my focus of attention here. The feminist analysis of this "sexed character of discourse" follows this logic: "Man seems to have wanted, directly or indirectly, to give the universe his own gender . . . anything believed to have value belongs to men and is marked by their gender" (Irigaray, *Je, tu, nous,* 31). It is common knowledge to students of Chinese literary culture that the ultimate pursuit of the literati in imperial China was to excel in the genre of *shi*; whereas writing plays and *xiaoshuo* [narrative novel] was considered a secondary concern.

According to the Ming critics and writers in question, it is not only the writing of dramatic lyrics that should be elegantly feminine, but also their musical-theatrical realization, which was staged mostly in the form of Kunqu. Xu Wei, commenting on the Kunshan style of singing then most prevalent, writes in *Nanci xulu* [Account of the southern style of drama], "in terms of *flowing beauty and lingering mellifluousness,* it surpasses all the other three styles. When one hears it, one cannot but be completely captivated by it. *Courtesans are especially good at it*" (242; emphasis added).[2] In regard to this association of Chinese opera with the feminine, it is revealing to note that in the performance aesthetics of this most influential, most highly esteemed, and most elegant and elite form of Kunqu, the controlling concept is one of the circular/rounded [*yuan*]. We can draw on the writings of the performing artists of modern times to explicate this aesthetic concept: Wang Chuansong, the revered Kunju master of the *chuan* generation [*chuanzibei*][3] said in a 1963 speech, "On the stage, everything strives for the circular" (178). Yu Zhenfei, another master Kunju performer has said, "The performance convention of Chinese opera requires 'ascending from the left and descending on the right.' It demands the 'circular'" (283). Every sound, gesture, movement, pattern on costumes, or piece of property should be in the form of a circle or suggest the circular. This is regarded as the ideal aesthetic aspiration of this theatre. Jo Riley has aptly and meticulously illustrated this aesthetic in practice, focusing on the performer's body (295-8). This essence of the performance aesthetics of Chinese opera, "the principle of the rounded body"[4] with its emphasis on the circular, echoes the aesthetic of Chinese calligraphy embodied in the cursive style [*caoshu*].[5] Mainland Chinese scholar Zheng Chuanyin has argued that Western classical theatre is a product of "linear thinking" while Chinese theatre is a reflection of "circular thinking" (*Zhongguo xiqu* 403). Elsewhere, he also discusses in detail "the preference for the circular" [*shangyuan*] and "the aesthetic of complete reunion" [*yuanman zhimei*] in Chinese culture (*Chuantong wenhua* 67-94). The non-linear working implied in this cursive and circular aesthetics can be further discussed from the perspective of the contemporary French feminist cultural politics of the erasure of masculine linearity (Humm 96) and the formulation of "non-linear forms of reading" (Moi 102). Critiquing the "phallic direction" and "phallic line," Irigaray writes of Plato's myth of the cave, which only allows the people inside to look in the straight and forward linear direction:

> One is only to look ahead and stretch forward. Chains, lines, perspectives oriented straight ahead — all maintain the illusion of constant motion in one direction. Forward. The cave cannot be explored in the round, walked around, measured in the round.
>
> (*Speculum of the Other Woman* 245)

In contrast, Chinese operatic performance requires movements in the round, and traditional Chinese audiences expect a reunion at the closure of the opera. From our modern perspective, the aesthetics of Chinese opera appears closer to the feminine than the masculine realm. At this point, we must be aware of cultural and historical differences in juxtaposing modern European feminist theory and imperial Chinese theatre. Let me point out however, that Chinese dramatic lyrics and theatrical performance were already dubbed in a feminized discourse in imperial China's critical tradition.

The last entry in Wang Jide's *Rules of Dramatic Songs* is very interesting in reference to the present argument. Wang talks about the "good fortune" and "bad fortune" of Chinese drama [*qu*] and lists forty items associated with the two situations. Among the "good fortune" items for dramatic lyrics include "pretty women singing," "handsome boys singing," "beautiful-looking *dan* [note: the player can be a woman/girl or man/boy]," and "gorgeous costume." On the "bad fortune" side, he lists, among other things, "old and ugly players," "poor costume," and "low prostitutes" (4: 182-3). Wang does not seem to take this entry seriously in that he states that the lists are there to make fussy people laugh. But it is significant that he repeatedly associates Chinese drama with the notion of (1) "prettiness" and (2) the "feminine" — the prettiness of "handsome boys" is more often perceived as on the side of the feminine; the *dan* role-type can be played by either a man or woman, but the role-type itself is feminine; and the term "prostitutes" refers generically to women. Although "prettiness" can be masculine too, the juxtaposition of "prettiness" with "femininity" by Wang here is obvious.

The performance history of Chinese opera in the past four hundred years that we can reconstruct today has been dominated by the so-called plays of the young male and female [*shengdan xi*]. This is partly because what we rely on for historical reconstruction today are mostly writings by the literati, and what they were mainly interested in recording were plays of the young male and female. Theatre historians have complained about and even protested against this situation (Lu Eting, Zhang Faying). They seem to be suggesting that "real" theatre history was different; as if they expected there to be more documents about the more masculine painted-face and comic role-types, especially the painted-face. However, we are textualizing through written texts, and what we have reconstructed is a performance history dominated not simply by plays of the young male and female, but even more by the *dan* than the *sheng*. In the traditional critical discourse, prettiness-eroticism and artistry have been the two predominant notions shaping Chinese theatre's aesthetics and theory.

This can be seen in many examples. Dramatist You Tong (1618-1704) describes the private female troupe which Li Yu brought to Suzhou as "exquisitely beautiful in both singing and appearance" [*shengse shuangli*] (quoted in Lu Eting 167); and Xu Maoshu, a contemporary of Li Yu, also kept a female troupe which was praised by a contemporary as "especially moving and impressive for their prettiness-eroticism and artistry" [*seyi youwie dongren*] (quoted in Lu Eting 168). The greatest *dan* performer in Kunqu in the late Qing period, Zhou Fenglin, a man, was praised as "equally great in prettiness-eroticism and artistry" [*seyi jujia*] (quoted in Lu Eting 289). The four great Anhui opera troupes which came to Beijing to perform for the celebration of the eightieth birthday of Emperor Qianlong (1790) were extolled by a scholar in the 1820s for "getting all the colors and charm because of their ultimate refinement in prettiness-eroticism and artistry" [*seyi zhijing, zhengyuan duomei*] (quoted in Zhang Faying 138).

The highest attainment of the art was felt to be the fulfillment of the two ideals of prettiness-eroticism and artistry. But these two ideals are oppositional. A young and beautiful player is often considered lacking in artistic sophistication while older players have lost their prettiness-eroticism by the time they attain the highest art in performing. Of the two, however, it is prettiness-eroticism that has often been seen as more appealing. The conflict between prettiness-eroticism and artistry can also be read as a power struggle between established forms and emerging forms, old players and young players. Caught in contending moments of history, established but aging forms and players always resist the threat of being replaced by the emerging and youthful. The rise of Beijing opera since 1790 and the subsequent fall of Kunju opera are the most conspicuous incidents of this in Chinese theatre history. The conflict of power is shown also in the rise and fall of theatrical forms.

We have here on the one hand, a desire for prettiness-eroticism which is associated with youthfulness and fades as time goes by, and on the other hand an appreciation of artistry accumulated through years and years of training and performance. In a book of commentaries on actors belonging to the so-called "manual of flowers" [*huapu*] published in 1806, the author begins by saying :"It is required that one must select the beauty before listening to songs" (*Zhong xiang guo* 1017). From the beginning, there has been an obsession with "prettiness-eroticism." "Delicate prettiness" [*junmei*] is required of the players' stage appearance (this also applies to major *sheng* roles) as a constitutive element toward the ideal of "attaining both the prettiness-eroticism and artistry" [*seyi shuangquan*] of the art. However, ultimate artistry is not easily obtained at a young age. Prettiness-eroticism is desired, but if not accompanied by artistry, it is at once condemned as a cheap and vulgar means of appealing to the lustful desires of the audience. These self-contradictory aesthetics can be clearly seen in traditional critical writings.

Now that we have film and video technology to reproduce visual images, we can easily see that certain performances in which aged "masters" — who are thus "unbeautiful" in appearance — play young damsels and scholars have been canonized as the ultimate models. For instance, available on the latest video technology, DVD, are several performance excerpts from the later years of the legendary male *dan* Han Shichang (1898–1976), hailed as "the King of Kunqu" [*Kunqu dawang*] (see *Beifang Kunqu Juyuan lao yishujia wutai yishu* [The art of the senior artists of the Northern Kunqu Opera Company] [2002]). These aged performers were considered to have achieved the "aesthetic essence" and the "divine inspiration" of the art, despite their faded theatrical feminine prettiness-eroticism. The "unbeautiful" yet critically acclaimed stage representations of young female roles by the old masters is a virtual embodiment of an aesthetic opposition, which results in a dismantling of the art form's own obsessive aestheticism of feminine prettiness-eroticism — especially when the latter-day image of the "master" is contrasted with the impeccable stage prettiness-eroticism of his golden years. Prettiness-eroticism and artistry, the two dominant terms in the critical tradition of this theatre, have interlocked and interplayed to betray the instability of the art form's own aesthetic assumptions. In a way, the gradual displacement of Kunju opera by Beijing opera during the nineteenth century can be read as the triumph of prettiness-eroticism over artistry, a triumph which has been lamented by many traditional scholar-intellectuals as indicating the "fall" of the essentiality of this theatre art.

The several Beijing opera films made by Mei Lanfang in his later years are revered by performers, critics, scholars and fans. His 1960 Kunju opera film *Youyuan jingmeng* [Wandering in the garden, waking up from the dream], is an example par excellence of a canonized performance text by an "aged master." He made the film, in which he portrays a sixteen-year-old maiden, when he was sixty-six years old. In the 1955 film version of the Beijing opera *The Hegemon King Says Farewell to the Concubine,* Mei has naturally lost the essential feminine prettiness that can be seen in his photographs from the 1910s and 20s. Physical limitations also did not allow him to perform the technical virtuosity of *xiayao* (the movement of bending the spine backward and letting the head drop to almost floor level) in the sword dance that he had created to add to this play. Unlike various contemporary performances by "younger and prettier" female performers who either learned from his students or were inescapably influenced by him, Mei's "classic" performance texts reveal a fracture of the aesthetic field of the art form itself, resulting from the art form's own self-questioning of the categories of the feminine and the essence of artistic attainment.

The Body Beneath: Female Scholar and Male Queen

Entangled in the contradictory aesthetics of prettiness-eroticism and artistry, Chinese opera is turned into an unstable site of gender contestations. This aesthetic convention simultaneously reinforces and dismantles the category of "femininity" and bipolar notions of gender, since the very convention of stylization and cross-dressing has rendered the theatrical representation of the female gender a construct. This construct, in Butlerian terms, illustrates the point that physical sex and gender are not one and the same thing. The "pretty woman" on the Chinese operatic stage has almost nothing to do with biological sex: in theory and practice "she" can be convincingly and successfully played by either a female or male performer through a mastery of the artistry. In other words, the performer, either a biological man or woman, "*accumulates the force of authority through the repetition or citation of a prior, authoritative set of practices*" (Butler, *Bodies That Matter* 227; original emphasis). For example, the credibility of a *dan* character depends on the art of fulfilling the time-tested, well-established theatrical practice of the *dan* role-type. The female impersonation on stage is materialized by complex theatrical pacts of gender constructions that are "differentiated citations and approximations called 'feminine'" (15). Configurations of gender are based on these complicated sets of stylized conventions that are artificial and arbitrary and thus far removed from, yet still bear some resemblance to, real men and women. These performance conventions are the result of decades and even hundreds of years of artistic accumulation — a process of sedimentation — and are utterly revered by the practitioners of Chinese opera. Foregrounding this gender performativity in the operation of Chinese opera decodes the gendered body as a construct of the "forcible and reiterative practice of regulatory sexual regimes" (15). The acquisition and perfection of these authoritative skills requires thousands of hours of repetitive practice on the part of the player. When young, pretty players perform they reproduce a socially and artistically desirable representation of the feminine on stage. When old masters perform, they recreate femininity as radically constructed, and at the same time self-expose its constructedness, for their female appearance can no longer be taken for real women and deceive the gaze of the spectator. Yet in the eye of the expert, their *performance* of the female roles is considered incomparable since they have internalized the *artistry* of female impersonation through long years of stage experience. Paradoxically, the ultimate achievement in artistry and the simultaneous disappearance of physical prettiness point to the constructedness of the "woman" on stage.

The stylized conventions, the cross-dressing tradition, the obsession with prettiness-eroticism, and the success of young female impersonators on the Chinese stage have long made conservatives and moralists extremely uneasy about the transgression of gender boundaries in the theatre. As mentioned before (chapter 7), the fifteenth century gentry-scholar Lu Rong warned against the threat of male cross-dressers and urged those of his class who wanted to have a virtuous family to reject female impersonators on stage, because their theatrical representations of women looked too much like real women (112-3). This oscillation of gender is pushed to another level in plays where a cross-dressed player plays a character, female or male, who is further disguised as the opposite sex. This double-twisted cross-dressing greatly intensifies the crossing and blurring of gender lines. There are numerous instances of this kind of gender-crossing in early modern English drama, and Chinese theatre also features ample examples. The cross-dressing theatrical conventions of Chinese theatre themselves expose the instability of conventional gender categories by showing how a dramatic persona can shift back and forth between genders "credibly" just by changing costumes, regardless of the "true sex" of the player. This illustrates that costume and makeup are two of the most powerful theatrical components to define gender on the Chinese stage. At this point let us remind ourselves once again that in Chinese opera role-types are first and foremost divided into two genders, and any role-type can be played by either sex. Therefore, there are three levels of representation in which switching genders is possible: player – role-type – character. The interfacing level of "role-type" makes possible a triple criss-crossing of gender disguise. For a quick illustration of this three-tier relation of gender play, we can draw on today's different practices in various regional operas. For instance, in Yueju opera we have the female lead Meng Lijun of *Zaisheng yuan* [Love of a life reborn] (cited in "The Face, the Hand, and the Foot," chapter 6) played by an actress specialized in the male role-type [*sheng*]; in the Yueju opera Liang-Zhu, it is a female *sheng* playing the male protagonist, whereas in the Beijing opera Liang-Zhu, a straight gender alignment is usually seen in the "player – role-type – chapacter" correlation, i.e., a male *sheng* plays the male lead Liang Shanbo and a female *dan* plays the female lead Zhu Yingtai. Let me draw three plays from classical drama to illustrate how the binary gender system is, to varying degrees, destabilized by this tripartite gender switching.

Xu Wei's *The Female Top Graduate Declines a She-phoenix and Gets a He-phoenix* is the story of Huang Chonggu, a talented young woman disguised as a man who comes in first in the imperial civil service examination and wins the highest honor of "top graduate" [*zhuangyuan*], a term which is gender specific to males. Maintaining her male disguise, for three years she performs excellently as an official, but her female identity is finally unveiled when the prime minister wishes to marry his daughter to her. There is a happy ending, however, with the female top graduate marrying the prime minister's son, the male top graduate.

Dramatizing such a story in the sixteenth century was bold and the play was pioneering in some ways. This is Xu's second play with a cross-dressed heroine, the first being *Maid Mulan*. But Chonggu is a gentry woman, while Mulan is a military woman. Chonggu's story does not compare to Mulan's in terms of popularity, but it has a long circulation history and was already collected in the tenth century compilation *Anthology of Widely Gathered Accounts in the Taiping Era*.

Following the standard convention of matching the gender of role-type and character, Xu's female protagonist is played by the *dan* (334). The play opens with Chonggu's entrance, and the theme of wanting to become a man is overtly expressed in her poem: "I wish Heaven would instantly transform me to a boy" (349). But becoming a man is just to revert to the binary hierarchy, not to collapse this structure of oppositional pairs in which one violently dominates the other. Acting like a man is also just to be admitted membership to be honored as a man, not a woman. Xu's cross-dressed heroines, whose deeds equal that of men and challenge the gender system to a certain degree, are ultimately conservative representations: though both Mulan and Chonggu are men's equals, neither is threatening to men. The structure of *The Female Top Graduate* begins with the girl aspiring to scholarly honor and moves toward the establishment of a beautiful binary balance of a married couple at the closure, as eulogized in the play: "The female top graduate and the male top graduate / Heaven matches a pair of mandarin ducks in the prime minister's mansion" (350). Honor, station, wealth, family, and love constitute a complete and stable reunion of people and things. In the end, the disruption of the existing gender system caused by the *dan*, playing a girl who passes as a boy is stabilized and the gender system is restored. Xu's twin plays of strong cross-dressed heroines construct a design based on binary harmony: two plays, two cross-dressed heroines, the binary of military/civil, and at the end, two marriages.

Inspired by Xu's ground-breaking elevation of woman's status through an inherently transgressive dramatic cross-dressing, a series of similarly cross-dressed heroines emerged in drama through the late Ming and early Qing up to the mid-nineteenth century, with some woman playwrights contributing highly interesting works in this regard. Gentry woman Wu Zao's *Shadow of Disguise* (early nineteenth century) is a short, single-act play for a solo player, and is a more disrupting play than Xu's in many aspects. The heroine Xie Xucai is unhappy with her own sex. In her own words, she is: "Shameful of being female" [*zican jinguo*] (295). She prefers practicing with the sword to putting on make-up and describes her ambition as being as lofty and adventurous as a flying roc, saying, "Changes are up to Heaven; but I am in control" (295). As her name "Xucai" implies, she is multi-talented. In the past she had cross-dressed herself as a scholar and painted a portrait of herself dressed in male garments. She entitled the painting "Drinking Wine, Reading Qu Yuan's *Li Sao*." Returning to woman's dress Xucai wanders into her study one day singing songs full of sadness and grievances, drinking wildly and woefully crying for herself. Full of sound and fury, she recites Qu Yuan's poem while admiring and talking to the "he" in her self-portrait. Her pent-up grief as a talented woman living in an oppressive system and her desire to break out of the limits of femaleness to become a man need no more elaboration.

Subtle references to fictionality and reality, playacting and gender disguise are inscribed in this text. First and foremost is the disruptive move to cross-cast the *sheng* as the heroine. This is a complex issue concerning the casting convention of the role-types, since it is not generally common to bend the gender alignment between the role-type and the dramatis personae. As I point out in chapter 2, there is a long history of male transvestism in Chinese theatricals intended as a travesty of the female gender and a misogynist mockery, and even today the practice of casting the male-gendered *chou* as old women for comic effect is not uncommon in some regional operas. This is part of the convention and is acceptable as not irregular. In chapter 3, I also note that in the Ming play *The Thousand Pieces of Gold*, the minor *dan* is cast as Liu Bang, the rival of the Hegemon King, and examine the effects in the nuanced construction of masculinity in that case.

In *Shadow of Disguise*, the heroine does *not* cross-dress as a man throughout the play, making it unusual for this cross-casting. Although Xucai does appear as a cross-dresser in the portrait, which is an important prop in the performance, and her identity as a cross-dresser is overwhelmingly established through her lyrics and recitation, in stage performance we see a player trained in acting male characters playing a woman. The indeterminacy of the text is that we have stage directions of "*Sheng* enters" and "*Sheng* looks at the portrait" embedded in a text inscribed with a female voice from a female body, radically dislocating the gender stability of the heroine who wishes to become a man all along. This cross-gender casting effects a masculinization of the player's body to emphasize the masculine pursuits of the heroine. This twisting of gender roles in the "player – role-type – character" tripartite layering seriously bends gender roles and imagines the divisions as really flexible. In one of her songs, Xucai herself alludes to her inverted playacting: "You Meng's acting built upon inversion / Turning new deceits and the unexpected" (296) (You Meng is an ancient actor excelled in impersonation; see chapters 2 and 7).

The world in the play is also crossing between reality and self-imagination. The title itself suggests the heroine's "shadow" [*ying*] self in male "disguise" [*qiao*]. The whole play is Xucai's enacting the chasing after a shadow in a dream. She realizes that the "female scholar" is only an "empty phantom" (296) and she is "looking at her shadow" and sighs (297). In the last tune, Xucai asks herself: "When is it to wake up from the butterfly dream?" (300), metaphorizing her action as a dream, with an allusion to Zhuang Zi. The tune continues: "Forever attaching to the person in the scroll / Forever be the bird of Jialing / Undifferentiated shadow and form having dissolved into each other" (300). The boundaries between the identities of Xucai the gentry woman and the cross-dressed female scholar; between reality and self-imagination are all dissolving, if not dissolved, in the process of the enactment of this female play.

Let us go back to Xu Wei again. Xu's student Wang Jide wrote *Chen Zigao Disguises as a Male Queen* as a complement to his mentor's work *The Female Top Graduate*. The "male" and the "female" cross-dressings match neatly as two halves completing the two-way female/male transvestism.

"Chen Zigao" is the literary representation of the historical figure Han Zigao of the Chen Dynasty (557-589). The biography of this man with a pretty feminine appearance who became the favorite of an emperor and rose to military power is recorded in the official histories, *Chen shu* [The book of Chen] (*juan* 20; 2: 269-70) and *Nanshi* [History of the Southern Dynasties] (*juan* 68; 6: 1664). Chen Zigao also appears in a work by Li Yi of the Tang Dynasty, later collected in the seventeenth century compilation of 52 stories (historical, literary, and legendary) of male homosexuality — Wuxia Ameng's *The Cut Sleeve Compendium*.

The Male Queen is set against a background of dynastic chaos. Chen's pretty appearance captures the attention of a homosexual king and Chen is made his "queen," living in disguise as a woman. His peculiar feminine beauty captivates even the king's unmarried younger sister, who does not know that "she" is a "he." After the revelation of a lady-in-waiting who knows the true sex of the "queen," the king is happy to marry his "queen" to his sister and keep him/her as his favorite companion.

At first glance, *The Male Queen*'s narrative structure follows the trajectory of beginning with a disruption of order and ending in its restoration. In most English Renaissance comedies, the male transvestite (and also the female-to-male transvestite) returns to "normal" sex/gender roles, and ends up with a happy heterosexual marriage, signifying the restoration of conventional order. But *The Male Queen*, like the Shakespearean comedies featuring cross-dressing, has a "comic closure [that] is far less closed than it looks" (Solomon, *Re-dressing the Canon* 36). Upon closer reading, *The Male Queen* is a rare *marginal* text in the whole repertoire of classical Chinese drama — Wang's play unquestionably and obviously addresses homosexuality and bisexuality.

The whole play single-mindedly zeros in on the unsettling crisscrossing of sexualities and points to subversive gender issues that were repeatedly repressed, only to return in the margins of the theatre. In contrast with the more conservative *Maid Mulan*, this play constitutes a field of fractures and reveals contentious ideologies at work. For anyone reading Chinese opera queerly, the radical subversiveness embedded in this play carries special meanings.

The entire play is inscribed in an unsettling discourse of sexuality — the pretty young boy Chen Zigao points to his erotic androgynous charm right from the beginning:

> Although I have a male body, I look like a woman. I was born with a great prettiness so charming that one would desire to eat [*xiu'se kancan*].

(1b)

In the opening scene, soon after Chen describes his androgynous appearance which can easily pass as female, he is also described as *yao* [monster] — a person crossing boundaries of gender style, biological sex, and compulsory heterosexuality — by the king's soldiers who capture him. The soldiers immediately reveal that the king is fond of the "southern custom" [*nanfeng*](3a) — homosexuality — and at once turn Chen over to the king , who dresses Chen in female costume and makes him his "queen." Charmed by the new queen's feminine "heavenly appearance and prettiness that enchants a nation" [*tianzi guose*] (15b), the king's younger sister, played by the minor *dan*, expresses her ambiguous sexual desire:

> It is not just my brother — a man — that loves her. I as a girl also crave for swallowing her with a glass of cold water. How could there be such a nice woman in this world!

(15b)

The interconnection between sexuality and food and eating in Chinese culture is important and requires detailed investigation but it is not my focus here. The facts that the representation of sexuality in *The Male Queen* is not regimented by the binary gender system, and is not stable and monolithic concern us most. Sexuality turns out to be highly flexible — the princess is heterosexual and is aware of her own sexuality as prescribed by the binary system, yet she immediately has a crush on a "woman" because of her intense "prettiness-eroticism" [*se*]. And in the end Chen, as an androgynous object of desire, delightfully serves both the unambiguously gay king and the ambiguously heterosexual princess. At the wedding of Chen and his sister the king announces:

> My beauty, I am now letting you get married. Today you are the bridegroom. I should have let you return to your original appearance, but the yarn hat and black boots are ordinary. Therefore, do not change. Keep your female adornments.

(28a)

At the ceremony, Chen is addressed in the capacity of the queen [*niangniang*] by the lady-in-waiting. The text reads, "The queen and the princess please now worship heaven and earth" and the stage direction states, "the *dan* and the minor *dan* perform the act of worship" (28a). Here the textual plane simply breaks into pieces, ruptured by this heightened indeterminacy in gender and sexuality that not only oscillates between genders but also hopelessly frustrates any of the reader's remaining sense of a stable and coherent gender system by a multivalent dislocation of the sign and its referent.

Adding more visible to challenges to the rigid binary gender system, the fluidity of Chen's gender and sexual identity is intensified by the criss-cross of gender assignment between the role-type and the dramatis personae, as it is in Wu Zao's *Shadow of Disguise*, but this time with a male/female inversion. Whereas the virtual cross-dressing gentry woman Xie Xucai is played by a *sheng*, the boy transvestite Chen Zigao is assigned to the *dan*. There is an over-intensification of cross-gendering in the text and verbal indeterminacy of gender because all the time what we read in the stage directions is the *dan* playing and singing the *boy's* part — the *dan is* the boy. The "true sex" of the transvestite character in *The Male Queen* is supposed to be male, but it is a *dan* who is playing the character, and the *dan* can be either a man or a woman player. In this condition of contamination of multilevel twisting of cross-dressing it becomes radically impossible to *straighten* out the "natural" sex/gender relations of the player – role-type – character. A mimetic notion of gender and sex is radically destabilized. The perplexity of "transvestism and the 'body beneath'" in this instance in Chinese theatre stretches further than the "speculating on the boy actor" found by Peter Stallybrass in the English Renaissance stage. He draws our attention to a (con)fusing situation similar to *The Male Queen* and *Shadow of Disguise* in a 1594 version of *The Taming of the Shrew*:

> In the printed text of Shakespeare's *The Shrew* in 1623, the boy is named as "Bartholomew my Page" . . . , in changing into the clothes of a woman, he is entirely subsumed into her role. When in *A Shrew* [the 1594 anon. version], a stage direction reads *"Enter the boy in Woman's attire,"* in *The Shrew* it reads: *"Enter Lady with attendants."* Moreover, the speech prefixes are all for *"Lady"*or *"La."* . . . . In the Folio *The Shrew*, we are thus presented with a wild oscillation between contradictory positions: the plot of the induction demands that we remain aware of Bartholomew *as* Bartholomew, while the language of the text simply cuts Bartholomew, replacing him with "Lady."
>
> ("Transvestism and the 'Body Beneath'" 75)

In the specific context of Chinese opera, the "body beneath" can be a boy's or a girl's, therefore the speculation on the body beneath is not limited to the boy actor; it extends to the girl actress. Embedded between the body beneath and the stage character on the outside is the gendered role-type that can be cross-gendered by either sex.

NINE

"THE LAST FEMALE IMPERSONATOR":
WEN RUHUA AND HIS AESTHETICS OF MALE TRANSVESTISM

The "Last Female Impersonator" in Beijing Opera: Wen Ruhua

The gender and sexual perplexity derived from "the body beneath" draws our attention to the tripartite structure of "player – role-type – character" in the performance practice of the Chinese theatrical tradition. Throughout the history of this theatre, there have been different manifestations of this transgender performance convention, in different historical moments from the Yuan period through the Ming and Qing. In contemporary China, we can see a bifurcated development in cross-dressing; the gradual demise of the male *dan* across all forms of regional opera, and the continual flourishing of the female *sheng*, particularly in Yueju opera. Pei Yanling, a Heibei Clapper opera performing artist officially extolled as a "national treasure" [*guobao*], is an actress whose performances in male military role-type captivated audiences. She has been dubbed a "hero" [*yingxiong*]," not a "heroine" on stage (Yu Zhen). Two renowned female *sheng* players are currently among the top performing artists in the whole profession of Chinese opera — Yue Meiti, of the Shanghai Kunju Company, and Shi Xiaomei, of the Jiangsu Province Kunju Company,[1] and both have been awarded the Plum Blossom Award, the highest national honor in Chinese opera performance. Yue published her autobiography in 1994 and the title

itself juxtaposes interesting ambivalence of the gendered subject: *I —
A Solitary Female Young-Male-Role Actor* [*Wo — yige gudan de
nüxiaosheng*]. Both the female and the male genders are embodied in a
solitary body performing a gendered subject of the "I" in the flamboyant
and boisterous world of Chinese opera.

In view of the contrasting fortunes of male and female cross-
dressing today, it is fascinating to look for the social and cultural reasons
determining their different fates.

There is evidence that the policy of the People's Republic of China
was intended as a *general* policy to straighten out the gender alignment
between the on-stage character and the body beneath, whether it was
man playing woman or woman playing man. In the "Speech Given at
the Seminar on the Festival of Beijing Opera on Modern Themes" of
1964, Premier Zhou Enlai commented on the distinguished male *dan*
Zhang Junqiu (1920–1998):

> For instance, Comrade Zhang Junqiu has been feeling depressed.
> His art was formulated in the old society. His art of singing can be
> taught to students. He can also perform some traditional plays.
> However, are we going to perform plays on modern themes? He
> really intends to do so with a lofty mind. . . . But *man playing woman
> will have to be gradually terminated. It is the same in the case of
> Yueju opera, woman playing man will have to be terminated.* [The
> art of the male *dan*] is allowed to be demonstrated on stage for a
> small number of people, for the purpose of testing out artistic validity.
> But it is not allowed to be carried out extensively. . . . It is allowed to
> be demonstrated for a small number of people in the [drama] school
> and as part of the students' training. But it is certain that this is *not*
> the direction we *encourage.*
>
> ("Zai Jingju xiandaixi" 204; emphasis added)

Zhang first made a name for himself as a teenager in mid-1930s
Beijing. When Zhou pronounced the Party's policy, Zhang, one of the
handful of giant performers, was only in his forties. Judging from Zhou's
speech the policy was stated in no uncertain terms — the Party wanted
to ultimately see the end of male transvestite actors, as well as female
transvestite actresses, in Chinese theatre. A year before, in a 1963 article
entitled "Striving to be a Revolutionary Worker in the Arts," Premier
Zhou had written regarding Yueju opera:

> Ten years ago I already said that Yueju opera had to first solve the problem of men and women performing together on the stage.
>
> ("Yaozuo yige geming de" 170)

All the evidence indicates that the Party's cultural ideology toward transgender performance on stage was made clear to the public soon after the establishment of the PRC. Paradoxically, in his youthful revolutionary days Zhou himself was active in and good at theatrical female impersonation in the new form imported from the West — the spoken drama. Communist revolutionaries in the early decades of the twentieth century were already making good use of the theatre as a means of political propaganda to promote the socialist revolution. When he was studying in Tianjin in the 1910s, Zhou was said to be "playing very well" [*yande henhao*] as a transvestite actor and his female impersonation was called "pioneering" [*kai fengqi zhixian*] ("Zhou Enlai tongzhi qingnian shiqi" 187). In early twentieth century China the long history of male dominance of the public theatre had resulted in a cultural situation where there were no women available to perform female parts at the nascent stage of the development of spoken drama, Zhou and other progressive youths had to take up the roles by themselves. At the same time this male transvestism in spoken drama was not seen as unnatural, and was easily accepted because of the long tradition of this artistic practice in Chinese theatre.

Yueju opera poses an intricate and interesting case history of the problem of mixing men and women, as well as cross-dressing, on stage: it presents both a gender trouble and a musical question. With the rise of the all female Yueju opera troupes in the early 1920s and the gradual displacement of the earlier male troupes, the music of this regional opera was transformed to suit the singing range of the female voice. There had already been experiments in mixing male and female players during this period, but the tunes were basically pitched according to the range of the male voice, thus creating a problem for female singing that had to be contained within a limited low register. More directly related to the present interrogation of gender representation is the fact that the male and female players mixing in performance at this time was an interesting criss-crossing of genders: there were simultaneously male *dan* and female *sheng* players on stage (Qian Facheng 30). This was not the female *dan* with the male *sheng,* and hence not a "natural" alignment of the player's sex and the gender of the character. This "experiment" was not successful and the opera turned all female in the end.

Two decades later, "a historical moment in the history of the development of Yueju" (as described by Qian Facheng, 50) took place when the Zhejiang Yueju Opera Second Troupe "pioneered male-female co-performance" (50) in 1952. By this time Yueju opera music had totally changed to conform to the female singing range, and a "male tune" [*nandiao*] thus had to be created (50) to accommodate the male voice in this all female theatre. The situation was the inversion of the earlier attempt at mixing male and female players in the 1920s, because the female voice had become dominant and the male voice was now trying to adapt and reinvent itself within a ruling feminine musical structure. At first glance, it looked like it was the initial stage of a "male empire strikes back" scenario, and from the late 1950s to the early 1960s, several successful male players were trained. *China's Yueju Opera* (1989) provides short biographies of seven notable actors (Qian Facheng 91-5), and needless to say, all were *sheng* role-type actors. It seems that the Party's gender policy on Chinese opera was gradually taking effect. However, when various Chinese operas were gradually revived from the early 1980s on, after more than a decade of interruption caused by the Cultural Revolution, male *sheng* actors in Yueju opera appeared to have declined compared to the situation in the early 1960s. *China's Yueju Opera* names only one representative actor for the new period since the 1980s (96-100), whereas numerous actresses who are now well-known superstars of this opera emerged during the same period.[2]

Clearly, "the problem of men and women performing together on the stage" raised by Premier Zhou was never solved. Lois Wheeler Snow reported the policy established in the 1950s in her 1973 book *China on Stage:* "Communist policy strove to popularly establish male and female roles played by the respective sexes and sung in natural rather than falsetto (false) voices. Mei Lan-fang and a few other aging exceptions were recognized by the young government" (5). Almost a decade later, Colin Mackerras reported in his 1981 book *The Performing Arts in Contemporary China*:

> Before liberation most troupes were unmixed, mainly exclusively male, and a special art attached to men's acting the parts of women. The only male *dan* left now are those of the old generation, the most famous being the Beijing opera actor Zhang Junqiu, who began performing again in October 1978 as part of the rehabilitation of old actors and of the reputations of dead ones . . . . He told me, when I met him in January 1980, that in 1951 Zhou Enlai had said: "up to Zhang the male *dan*, and that's the end." Except Zhang himself and his wife, who told me they regarded the passing of this art as a great pity, none of the many Chinese with whom I have discussed the matter disagrees with the present policy, which is to encourage the present male *dan*, but not to train any more. He Jingzhi, Deputy Minister of Culture, gave me three reasons for the present view. First, "*People act better if portraying those of their own sex*"; second, *it is unnatural for men to play the roles of women*; and third, the custom of the male *dan* arose in a feudal society and reflects conditions no longer applicable to China.

> (183-4; emphasis added)

The commentaries from Zhou through Snow to Mackerras pose the theatrical issues of "naturalness" in gender representation and the asserted superiority of the practice of playing one's own sex, and these are key issues that I shall return to momentarily. First however, I would like to point out that in Mackerras' post-Cultural Revolution report the emphasis of the Party's concern, as represented by the very left-wing He Jingzhi, is solely on the elimination of male cross-dressing. Does the fact that the cross-dressed actress was left out of the Party's exposition of its gender ideology mean that she was not as disturbing as before? If we historicize the issue, it may well be the case that female cross-dressing was never as disturbing as its male counterpart in the history of Chinese opera.

Earlier on I argued that in classical criticism the aesthetic ideal of *becoming* the real through *performance* underlay the practice of cross-dressing. The records available today mostly concern the "passing" magic of male transvestism; for instance the supreme male *dan* actor noted by the Qing scholar Ji Yun, and the incident of Mei Lanfang's being mistaken as a real woman by a Japanese spectator. In the anecdote of Qing'er, her male disguise almost entirely passes the male gaze, except for that of her true love. Today, the transvestite performance convention of the (almost all) female Yueju opera contrasts with that of the traditional all male Kunju and Beijing (Jing-Kun) operas. The aesthetic demand of the Jing-Kun female impersonator is that he passes as a real woman on stage, whereas the male impersonator of the much younger Yueju opera always looks not so much a man on stage, as a woman dressing in male costume. The construction of gender resulting from cross-dressing in these two instances turns out to be a double movement: while the Jing-Kun transvestite actor *veils his masculine body*, the Yueju transvestite actress *unveils her corporeal femininity*. It seems that it is a necessity of the form of Yueju opera (including the performance conventions) that the transvestite actress, although in male disguise, is to be immediately recognizable as female.

Yueju opera happens to construct through transgender performance an image of the young male roles [*xiaosheng*] analogous to that of the players of men's roles [*otokoyaku*] of the Takarazuka Revue, another female musical theatre which emerged in the early decades of the twentieth century. The Yueju female *xiaosheng* and the Takarazuka *otokoyaku* almost surely do not pass as men on stage in the eyes of the spectators, even though there are excessive markers of masculinity on the surface of their constructed "male body." In her study of the Takarazuka Revue, Jennifer Robertson argues that "a female who passes successfully as a man does not appear androgynous" and that "successful passing was a great source of anxiety on the part of conservative pundits committed to retaining a polarized sexual hierarchy, which they equated with social stability" (87). On the level of form, the Yueju opera cross-dressers share such an appearance of androgyny, whereas the ultimate achievement in representation for the male transvestites in the Jing-Kun tradition is a total appropriation of femininity through the appearance of female prettiness. This realization that male *dan* actors could successfully pass as women must indeed have been disturbing to hierarchal power. However female *sheng* actresses, to borrow Robertson's words, let "the woman" permeate "the man," and draw attention to "the facticity of their female bodies," thus ensuring that their primary "female gender" keeps in check their secondary "male gender" on stage (78). The degree of subversion (collapsing "polarized sexual hierarchy") of this female body in male disguise is more contained ("kept in check") than that of the male body in female disguise. While the complex processes of social negotiation and cultural operation of form (in the case of Yueju opera) transgressed the limits of power and bolstered the female *sheng*, this relatively less threatening androgynous body may have caused the Chinese Communist Party less anxiety, thus escaping prohibition. Male homophobic anxiety in modern China must also have a great deal to do with the fact that the tradition of theatrical male transvestism was stopped, while female transvestism has been, and continues to be, tolerated (or perhaps in a twisted way, "endorsed"). The anxiety of non-heterosexuality seems to divide along gender lines: with male homophobia more visible than female homophobia.

The original government policy to eradicate both male and female cross-dressing unfolded contrary to what Premier Zhou and the Party intended — today female cross-dressing is thriving, and while the suppression of the male transvestite has been more clear-cut and almost complete, the death knell has yet to be struck. The staging of this "Götterdämmerung" seems to linger on like a Becketian endgame without a conclusion. As the millenium approached, the older generations of famed male *dan* players were retiring (for instance, Mei Lanfang's son Mei Baojiu [1934-], Song Changrong [1935-]) and one by one passing away, (for instance, Zhao Rongchen [1916-1996], Zhang Junqiu, and the tradition of male theatrical transvestism seemed to be dying with them, when, in the mid-1980s, a tactfully deployed, disturbing young body of a "last female impersonator" in Beijing opera popped up.

Wen Ruhua, born in 1947, emerged as an actor in the post-Cultural Revolution period and successfully reinvented himself in the ambiguously tabooed role-type of the male *dan* in Beijing opera during the 1980s.[3] More accurately, the official designation of his self-fashioning of identity should read "the last male *dan* actor in professional Beijing opera troupes nationwide" [*quanguo zhuanye Jingju tuan zhong zuihou yiwei nandan yanyuan*] as publicized in a promotional leaflet entitled "Jingju *Qiunü zhuan* jianjie" [A brief introduction to the story of Damsel Qiu] released by the Beijing Opera Company of the City of Beijing, dated August 1996 and attached with the company's red seal. Wen Ruhua studied with the male *dan* master Zhang Junqiu and excelled in performing works in the style of both the Zhang school and the Mei school. Outside mainland China, he has performed on various occasions in Japan and Taiwan, and has lectured in Hong Kong. He sang behind-the-scenes for the male *dan* lead played by Leslie Cheung in the film *Farewell My Concubine*, and participated in the making of a mainland China television serial drama entitled *Mei Lanfang* (Figure 2). Wen is regarded as one of the great successors of Zhang Junqiu (Figure 3).

Figure 2   Wen Ruhua, 'the last female impersonator in Beijing opera' cross-dresses as Concubine Yu of the Hegemon King. Courtesy of Mr Wen Ruhua.

Figure 3   Wen Ruhua and his mentor, Zhang Junqiu. Courtesy of Mr Wen Ruhua.

However, when Wen entered the National Chinese Opera School [Zhonguo xiqu xuexiao] at the age of eleven in 1958, he started as a student of the *sheng* role-type. At the age of eighteen (1965), he began taking private lessons from Zhang on male *dan* performance (perhaps secretly?), because the school did not allow the training of the male *dan* at all. Wen graduated in 1966 at the age of nineteen as a *sheng* player. Unfortunately for Chinese opera performing artists of any role-type, fresh graduates and veterans alike, it was the beginning of the Cultural Revolution. For a decade Wen, and many others, did not have the chance to practice the art they acquired through years of hard training, except for those recruited to perform, willingly or unwillingly, and in a modernized style, in the Revolutionary Model Beijing opera. In any case, Wen's "formal" training in Beijing opera is in the *sheng* role, not *dan*. His subsequent successful self-fashioning as a *dan* actor and his tactics of survival as a male *dan* in an adverse cultural condition in which non-heterosexuality is regarded as not "natural" is instructive. The significance of the phenomenon of Wen, "the last female impersonator," lies in its demonstration of some of the ways cultural transgression can defy power, though still be far from subverting it.

Wen belongs to the generation of Chinese which grew up after the establishment of the PRC. He received his Beijing opera training in the "new" society that has claimed to "change ghosts into human beings"; whereas the "old" society did the opposite, "oppressing human beings into ghosts" — in the words of a household couplet originally from the "new music drama" [*xin geju*] *Baimao nü* [The white-haired girl] (1950).[4] The embarrassment that this disciplined yet undisciplined body causes the power machinery is that unlike Mei, Zhang and the many other male *dan* actors who surviving from the "old" society, Wen is a product of the "new" era under the power of one party and the dictatorship of the proletariat. But Wen's artistic self-fashioning implies the stubborn persistence of an artistic tradition whose nature [*dingxing*] the Party has determined to be an "unnatural" legacy of the old feudal society and which it has tried to eradicate since coming to power in 1949, simply by *not* allowing the training of any more actors in this vein. The erasure of the formal training of the male *dan* at opera school made it invisible, but failed to annihilate the phantom that lurked behind the routine of daily classes. The long shadows of Freud and Nietzsche might be overseeing this repressed un/disciplined body of "the last female impersonator" which has returned to haunt that which cannot kill it. Highly disciplined in the art of Beijing opera, this body is at the same time undisciplined — it refuses to be erased by the Communist regime. The political meaning of "the last female impersonator" becomes more ironic when we realize that this *last* female impersonator inherited the artistic practice from a previous *last* who had been named the *last* in the line, according to the policy set down during the 1950s and 60s and made explicit by Premier Zhou. Just when the power machinery thought that the hour had struck long past the last "last," the figure of the male *dan* returned just like the figures on a Chinese revolving lantern.

When Wen first launched his acting career in post-Cultural Revolution China, his *identity* as a Beijing opera performer was initially positioned as a *sheng* doubling the *dan*. He gradually transformed his artistic image into a Beijing opera male *dan* [*jingju nandan*]. In 1980 Wen gave his first performance in the capacity of the male *dan*, staging a traditional play from the repertoire of the Zhang school (*Chunqiu pei* [The matching of spring and autumn]). He immediately received admiration and commendation from the audience in Beijing and from master performers of Beijing opera, including the great Li Hongchun (1898-1990) (who specialized in the old and military male role-types). Wen later regarded this occasion as the real beginning of his artistic career (Liu Yang 43). At the time he was a member of the Comrades-in-Arms Beijing Opera Troupe of the Beijing Military Region [Beijing junqu zhanyou Jingjutuan]. In 1982 he was transferred to the Beijing Opera Company of the City of Beijing. In the meantime, the renowned and revered playwright Weng Ouhong tailor-made a play for him. This Beijing opera, entitled *Baimian langjun* [The fair-faced gentleman], takes its protagonist Zheng Tianshou from one of the one hundred and eight heroes in the classic long narrative *Shuihuzhuan* [Water margin]. In chapter 32 of this fourteenth century work, Zheng is described as "born with a fair complexion and is delicately handsome" [*shengde baijing junqiao*] (Shi Nai'an 517). This description, which borders on androgyny, partially explains why this figure was chosen by Weng, who turned this minor *Water Margin* character into the cross-dressed hero(ine) in the new play (Figure 4).

Figure 4   Wen Ruhua as the "delicately
handsome" hero Zheng Tianshou in
Baimian langjun [The fair-faced
gentleman]. Beijing, 1983. Courtesy of
Mr Wen Ruhua.

Figure 5   Wen Ruhua plays Zheng
Tianshou disguising as a woman. Beijing,
1984. Courtesy of Mr Wen Ruhua.

In the new play, Zheng, with the help of other *Water Margin* heroes,
disguises himself as a pretty woman, then sneaks into the villain's
mansion and saves his wife who has been held captive (Figure 5). In
playing out gender subversion in its specific cultural context, the play's
trick is that the leading character is formally assigned to the *sheng*
role-type. In performance, this *sheng* performer plays a male character
who most of the time passes as a woman and performs in the style of
the *dan* role-type. Zheng, the "hero," appears in his "natural" sex
only briefly, in the opening and closing moments of the play. The "male
dan," through a twist of *naming*, does not officially exist in this play.
In praxis, however, the body beneath the character is the male *dan*.
The specific male *dan* player in this case must also be able to do the
sheng role-type.

Around this time, Wen's identity as a Beijing opera actor was aptly represented in the title of a write-up in *Beijing wanbao* [Beijing Evening News] of February 11, 1984: "Wenwu xiaosheng jian qingyi" [The military and civil young male doubling the blue-robe female]. The "blue-robe," also called the "principal female" [*zhengdan*], is the central role-type among the variety of female role-types for the *dan* player. This deliberate appropriation of the cardinal female role-type by a male player during a time of anti-male transvestism required highly sophisticated semiotic mobilizations: the meaning of *jian* — doubling — is the key. A jazz saxophonist doubling as a flute player *is* a saxophonist. The part of the identity that is a doubling flute player is so minor that it has no defining power toward the primary identity: the jazz *saxophonist*. When a *sheng* doubles as the male *dan*, he is supposed to be, first and foremost, a *sheng*. In an article focusing on Wen in a 1985 issue of one of the leading Chinese publications on the theatre, *Xijubao* [Drama journal], the writer begins his discussion with an identification of Wen's role-type specialization as the young male:

> In early winter last year, the *xiaosheng* actor of the Beijing Opera Company of the City of Beijing Wen Ruhua staged Mr Weng Ouhong's new work *The Fair-faced Gentleman*. In less than a year, this play had run for more than forty shows.
>
> (Yi Ping 40)

Yet the article is devoted to analyzing and praising Wen as an excellent and creative successor of the Zhang school of "blue-robe" performance. It is implied that his success in this style of performance contributed to this Chinese opera running for over forty shows, on and off, within a year (in a time of the rapid decline of traditional arts in the flux of modern media cultural domination, this was more than impressive by any standard, if not somewhat miraculous). Wen's art as a *xiaosheng* is not referred to in the article. All in all, in Wen's career trajectory, the male gendered sign of *xiaosheng* is emptied of its referential function. It is rendered an empty sign to rename and hence legitimize the "natural" existence of a male performing body that ironically did not at all substantiate the name attached to it.

"*Xiaosheng*" existed in name only and was a necessity as a semiotic protection shield. We see here an operation of an inverted form of Confucius' "rectification of names." The male transvestite body is "rectified" fundamentally in the name of *xiaosheng* (with a potentially transgressive variation of *xiaosheng jian qingyi*) in order for it to survive the compulsory heterosexist-homophobic matrix of "natural" alignment of biological sex and gender role. The actor was a *sheng* in name, but his *dan* "doubling" was put into practice more often in reality. The realization of the performing body (male *dan*) never substantiated the name (*sheng*). Furthermore, the "doubling" in question operated as a double-crossing. Wen was not merely crossing role-types, something which is not uncommon between related role-types of the same gender; he was simultaneously crossing gender boundaries. Toward the end of the 1980s the disjuncture between the sign and the referent was gradually readjusted and cultural pages from newspapers and magazines began publishing articles carrying titles such as "Famous Male *dan*, Beijing Opera Actor Wen Ruhua" ["Zhuming nan danjiao Jingju yanyuan Wen Ruhua"] (*Anshan ribao* [Anshan Daily] July 22, 1989). In the 1990s, the "male *dan*" was gradually transformed into "the last male *dan*." For instance an English caption reading "Shen [*sic*] Ruhua being the last male actor playing female role" and an accompanying Chinese one reading "China's last male *dan* Wen Ruhua" appeared underneath a photograph of Wen in a 1990 Chinese-English bilingual inflight magazine of Shanghai Airlines (Li Zhiyan 47). The May 30, 1997 edition of *Beijing ribao* [Beijing Daily] featured an article focusing on Wen being "the last male *dan* in China" ["Zhongguo zuihou yiwen nandan"] (Liu Liren). Some time later in 1999 *Beijing gongrenbao* [Beijing Worker's Daily] entitled a report "Wen Ruhua: China's Last 'Male *Dan*'" ["Wen Ruhua: Zhongguo zuihou de 'nandan'"] (Yi Hong). More recently, Hong Kong's *Ming Pao Daily* (December 2, 2001: D7) devoted a half-page, including four-color photographs, to reporting Wen's two special performances in Beijing. The headline was simple and direct: "The Last Male *Dan*" ["Zuihou de nandan"].

An Aesthetic of Male Transvestism

Since the opening of China to the world in the late 1970s, the grip of
Party ideology has gradually lost its power to contain the male *dan*
specifically, and on sexual discourse and practice in society on the whole.
The time had thus come for supporters of the male *dan* role-type to
"rectify" the name once more. This time the pendulum swung away
from the *sheng* to the opposite direction, the "male *dan.*" The name
and the substance, the sign and the referent now befitted each other,
but there is more here than the appropriation and reappropriation of
names. The determination in contemporary China that the ideology of
theatrical transvestism as "unnatural" by nature had to be reverted as
well.

By the late 1990s, and in tandem with the fashioning of the (last)
male *dan*, some writers on Chinese opera began raising the issue of
rehabilitating the status of the male *dan* by arguing for this *artistic*
practice. This issue was clearly incited by Wen's launching of another
new work — *Qiunü zhuan* [Story of Damsel Qiu], based on a story in
Pu Songling's *Liaozhai's Records of the Strange* set in imperial times.
Coincidentally, in 1915 the same story was staged in the form of spoken
drama in modern costume by progressive students of Nankai College
in Tianjin, with Zhou Enlai cross-dressed to play a supporting female
character.[5] In December 1996, almost a century later, in the Beijing
opera version produced by the Beijing Opera Company of the City of
Beijing, ostensibly paying homage to the early revolutionary theatrical
activity of the CCP, Wen played the title character Damsel Qiu. Damsel
Qiu is a courageous woman with a strong sense of good and evil and
fears no authority, who revives her declining family and then retires
from the leadership of the house. The social and political implications
of using the past to criticize the present is not the focus of my analysis
here; instead, I would like to point out that the voices incited by this
production on the question of the legitimacy of the male *dan*
demonstrate another revealing moment in the process of cultural
negotiation with official censure and power.

In a review of *Story of Damsel Qiu* published in the widely
circulated *Xiju dianying bao* [Theatre and film journal] (March 6,

1997), the critic Zhou Chuanjia concludes his article by highlighting the question of the male *dan*:

> In my opinion, the male *dan* occupies a significant position among the role-types in Beijing opera. It has contributed enormously to the development of the art of Beijing opera. The male *dan* is an inevitable question in reality and a theoretical question of important value. On the occasion of the centenary celebration of Mei Lanfang and Zhou Xinfang, I wrote an article entitled "Some Free Thoughts on the Male *Dan*" ["*Nandan cihuang*"] calling attention to take the male *dan* seriously, that we study it and appropriately develop it. My intention was to provoke controversies and to learn from the experts. *Story of Damsel Qiu* has now demonstrated the charm and vigor of the male *dan* through a lively stage image. It has convincingly accounted for the rationality and necessity of the existence of the male *dan*. This is delightful.

Zhou Chuanjia uses the opportunity of reviewing *Story of Damsel Qiu* to lay out his assertion about the male *dan* clearly and firmly, in an undaunted tone. Although it is in a short passage at the end of the review, the idea expressed is diametrically opposed to Premier Zhou's statement in the early 1960s and He Jingzhi's in the late 1970s on the status of the male *dan*. This critic also tells us in his review that he had written in support of reviving the male *dan* back in 1994 (the year the centenary celebration of Mei and Zhou was held). After Wen staged *Story of Damsel Qiu* in Beijing, a critic from Qingdao, Shandong published a newspaper article intended to dismantle the bias against the male *dan* with more fully elaborated arguments:

> In fact, the "forbidden zone" of the male *dan* in Beijing opera is totally man-made [*renwei*]. It has been said that some people deemed that the male *dan* was a product of feudalism, a dusted remnant of history, and a sick, abnormal aesthetic. I humbly think that this viewpoint is too extreme. It is not the least realistic. Beijing opera is a high and graceful art. The Thai transvestite entertainers [*renyao*] and the like are trash "art." There is an enormous difference between the two. They should not be compared on the same plane. The male *dan* is a role-type in Chinese opera. It is a performing art to practice it. One should absolutely not use obsolete moral and aesthetic values to evaluate the male *dan* and its art. Mei Lanfang's artistic

achievement is everlasting and no one can defame him. As Mei's lifelong career, the male *dan* was his self-realization. We can say that without the male *dan* role-type, there would have been no Mei. Therefore I hold that we should treat the Beijing opera male *dan* the same as female old *sheng*, female painted-face, female military *sheng*, etc. Anyone who has the quality to do so should be offered training and chances to perform. We should truly practice "let a hundred flowers bloom, let a hundred schools of thought contend" to further enliven our garden of Beijing opera. Why should we not go ahead with it?

(Lü Mingkang)

Regardless of the crude sexual politics presented (the demonizing of the Thai transvestite entertainers) and its theoretical limitation of being trapped within the humanist, binary framework, the significance of this article lies in the full-scale articulation of the repressed civil voice to completely repudiate the Party's policy. The central argument builds upon the presumed given, the universal value of "art" — more accurately "high art" as opposed to "low art," which is considered vulgar and sick. By this logic Beijing opera, as a high art, transcends the perversion of transvestism. Low art can be abnormal, but not high art. Thus the male *dan* is not abnormal, whereas the Thai transvestite entertainers are "sick." The Chinese term *renyao* [human prodigy] used to label the Thai transvestites nakedly demonstrates the heterosexist ideology behind the argument. Arguing for the validity of the male *dan* as high art does not challenge the constructed concept of "the natural" in a compulsory heterosexist matrix, rather that (male) transvestism in Beijing opera is "not unnatural."

Wen himself voiced the arguments for preserving the practice of the male *dan* in various interviews. In a magazine under the jurisdiction of the PRC's Ministry of Culture, *Wenhua yuekan* [Cultural monthly] (Vol. 55 [July 1997]), Wen asserted that in Beijing opera "the male *dan* uses external things to express the characters [,] . . . to vividly represent the classical woman. This has nothing to do with abnormality in life [*shenghuo zhong de biantai*]" (Wu and Xu 9). In an article in *Beijing Evening News* (May 30, 1997), Wen is quoted as saying:

Nowadays there are people who slight the male *dan*, despise the male *dan* as an art. This is contradictory to objective principles, at least unreasonable. . . . There are female *sheng* as well as female painted-face players in Beijing opera. Why is it regarded not honorable when a man plays a woman? How could we assert that since Cao Xueqin vividly portrayed Black Jade, and Tolstoy Anna Karenina that they were unnatural [*bu zhengchang*] and abnormal [*biantai*]? The male *dan* is an artistic creation. We should treat it with an ordinary attitude.

(Liu Liren)

This assertion still follows the discursive strategy of distancing the male *dan* from "abnormality." Wen's allusions to Cao Xueqin and Tolstoy are more interesting. His logic is that he is like these male authors, in that they are all *representing* women via various artistic practices. So why should one be celebrated and the other scorned? To respond to Wen's question, one could argue that a male novelist's writing women characters does not belong to the same category as a male *dan* playing women on stage in terms of the materiality of representation, not to mention the proximity of the physicality of the gendered bodies in the two different modes of expression of the textual and the corporeal. Looking at it in another vein, the body and the text are often intricately intertwined as well.

The analogy will not seem too far-fetched and will reveal more to us if we look at the issue in the light of Madeleine Kahn's "narrative transvestism." From this perspective we see, contrary (ironically) to meaning intended by Wen and the critics sympathetic to him, that the male *dan* and narrative transvestism in eighteenth century English novels (Kahn's object of study) such as Defoe's *Roxana* and Richardson's *Clarissa* do in fact share the same position as transgressive gender(ed) practices.

Looking at the first (English) canonic novels that "were written by men in the person of women" (2), Kahn developed the concept of narrative transvestism — "th[e] use by a male author of a first-person female narrator" (2) — and has argued that "the transgression of the boundaries between genders in narrative transvestism extends to the transgression of an entire binary epistemological structure" (159). The novel, which appeared in the modern era is, in this perspective, a destabilizing genre:

> In a period that longed for the balance and stability that binary structures seemed to offer, the novel emerged as a form designed for the exploration of the undefined realm between the poles.
>
> (159)

Theatrical and narrative transvestism do have common features in gender politics. The male *dan* as a cultural product and form of practice of a pre- and non-European, modern, capitalistic mode of social process, posed a greater threat to modern China than it did to the imperial past, for (European) modernity in China brought along with it much modern European cultural logic. From a postmodern perspective, the ambiguous and unstable body of the male *dan* embodies an "undefined realm" between binary genders and prickles the male homophobic nerves of the modern Chinese patriarchy. This is the radical aspect of the gender politics that the pro-male *dan* discourse in the Mainland does not address. Instead, its strategy is to recuperate the male *dan* as part of the heterosexual structure — more specifically the masculine aesthetic structure that I shall examine below. As Wen said in an interview in 1999, "The male *dan* actor in real life is still a dignified, loud and clear, and audacious masculine man [*nanzihan*]" (Yi Hong).

From the identity politics of the insinuation of the "male *dan*" into the "*sheng,*" to the reappropriation of the name of the "male *dan,*" and an open proclamation of the legitimacy of this theatrical transvestite practice, it has taken the repressed decades to return with a certain visibility. But so far the repressed has only returned as the last of its kind. It has been reported that Mei Baojiu considered training one or more male *dan* to succeed him, and that "the government departments concerned expressed that they understood the matter" (Xu Chengbei, *Zhongguo Jingju* 158). But nothing concrete has been realized so far. It would be a very bitter irony to see the *glorification* of the last male *dan* serve as a tribute to the demise of the practice. Wen has said more than once that he would not want to turn out to be the real "last" (Liu Liren; Lü Mingkang). As far as it goes, the practice of the male *dan* survives fragilely in this very "last" individual figure who aspires to hand down the art to the next generation. Wen, consciously or unconsciously, intentionally or unintentionally, calculatingly or indistinctively, has used a marginal tactic to cope with the oppressive situation. He has been playing as the "exception," the "last," hence supposedly not extensive, nor continuous. He was able to cross the boundary line by playing on the margins: first he assumed the positioning of the male role-type doubling the female role-type, then the "double" (the *dan*) displaced the "primary" and "original" (the *sheng*), and then deployed the rule of the exception as "the last" for survival.

The performing body of the male *dan* is a site of complex ideological contention. While it challenges the heterosexist patriarchy, the body of the male *dan* also reinstates the ideology of "woman" as a masculine construct. It is illuminating to compare and contrast European theories of theatrical cross-dressing with the aesthetics of male cross-dressing in Beijing opera with reference to Wen's formulation of his own views of the uniqueness of the male *dan* as a performing art.

Goethe, in the treatise "Women's Parts Played by Men in the Roman Theater" explicates the art of the male transvestite in these words:

> . . . he does not portray himself but a third nature actually foreign to him. We come to know this nature even better because someone has observed it, reflected on it, and presents us not with the thing itself but with the result of the thing. . . . We applauded the young man [on the Roman stage] lightheartedly and were delighted that he was so well acquainted with the ensnaring wiles of the fair sex that through his successful imitation of feminine behavior he had avenged us for every such offense women had made us suffer. I repeat what I said already: what we found here was the enjoyment of seeing not the thing itself but its imitation, to be entertained not through nature but through art, to contemplate not an individuality but a result.

(49-50)

Lesley Ferris' reading of Goethe is that in Goethe's view, the cross-dressed actor is "the epitome of the male artistry" ("The Legacy of

Goethe's Mimetic Stance" 53). "Femininity" is a construct, a representation — one that is best played by men. What is being admired on stage is not a real woman, but a form of femininity *performed*. Wen has made the following theoretical exposition on the art of the male *dan* which in some major ways echoes that of Goethe's:

> The male *dan* role demonstrates the woman image of the ancient times through a series of vocal utterances and gestures. The male *dan* on stage is a woman played by man and also a man playing woman. . . . The male *dan* is not imitating woman in a simple way. It is acting woman — a recreation of the tenderness, loyalty, courage, and elegance of Chinese women. A male *dan* actor does not rigidly play a character; instead, he is to translate across the characteristics of the character.
>
> (Wu Gang 10)

It is now a common argument in the discussion of the art of *dan* in Chinese opera that it is exactly because a male actor is not female, compared with the female *dan*, that he excessively observes, reflects upon, and studies femininity, resulting in the most meticulous *performance* of the particularities of "woman" on stage. While a female actor, on the contrary, so takes femininity for granted as part of her nature that her performance of the *dan* role on stage tends to be relaxed and less meticulous. Sharing this view, Wen rates the male *dan* over the female *dan* performers who are now the dominant norm on principle.

Volpp's study of late imperial Chinese theatre helps us further understand this connection. In interrogating the politics of the construction of femininity, she argues, by way of a close and insightful analysis of *The Male Queen*, that the play demonstrates "the most extended and complex seventeenth-century argument for the superior femininity of the cross-dressed actor" (139). Linking Volpp and Wen's arguments, we see a long history of this male-oriented assertion of the supremacy of the transvestite actor. All in all, these discourses constitute the grounds for the powerful argument that the "woman" on the stage of Chinese opera is a male construction. Volpp further elaborates the logic of gender representation in *The Male Queen*:

> The basic paradigm in the cross-dressed boy's relation to the female sex is an aversion of the normal relation between original and copy. The simulacrum becomes more highly valued than the original — in fact it becomes an original.
>
> (145)

Wen's aesthetic assumption differentiates itself by a self-awareness of the male *dan* as not the original — this male copy of woman is more highly valued than the female copy, but not the original woman. Perhaps in Wen's framework the original does not exist anymore. Wen is subtle in delimiting his theory to the representation of the "classical woman" in Beijing opera. He believes that "the male *dan* actor can understand woman deeper and act the role better to sublimate *classical beauty*" (Yi Hong; emphasis added). He does not seem to generalize his theory of the male *dan* as universally encompassing all realms of the representation of the female gender in the theatre for all ages. Within this cultural and historical boundary, he considers the male *dan* a mode of artistic expression built upon the male body,

> . . . because from its inception the exploration of the artistic theory of Beijing opera was based on the characteristics of the masculine. From vocalization to make-up, it all takes the masculine as the standard. . . . Men [doing the *dan*] primarily have the advantageous position in terms of stature and vocal range.
>
> (Yi Hong)

Wen's historicization lends force to his argument. From the time of Beijing opera's emergence in the late eighteenth century up to the early decades of the twentieth century, it was exclusively a male theatre. Wen further boldly argues that the practice of the male *dan* created "the four great *dan*" performing artists in the history of Beijing opera and elevated the art of the opera to the summit (Liu Liren). It is historically accurate that the period between the 1910s and the 1930s, generally considered the heyday of the opera, coincided with the rise and dominance of the great male *dan* actors. Wen further argues that Beijing opera declined with the fall of the male *dan* caused by the discouragement of man playing woman on stage after the establishment of the PRC (Yi Hong). At this point, Wen's assertion turn too arbitrary in that he shuns many other cultural, social, political, and economic factors contributing to the decline of Chinese opera in contemporary times and implies that the dismissal of the male *dan* was a fatal cause. Wen's aesthetic assertions on Beijing opera seamlessly echo Lesley Ferris's critical characterization of the European theatre as an "art form whose very impetus and invention arise from an entirely masculine pursuit of aesthetic representation" (*Acting Women* xiv).

In sum, Wen emphasizes three related aspects in the artistic performance of the *dan* in his argument: the physical form of the male body is more powerful; as a result the male *dan* has a larger voice; and thus he can reserve [*shou*] and open up [*fang*] at ease in performance. According to him, the female voice on the contrary is smaller and less dynamic. I tend to think that this is ultimately a question of the dynamic range of the voice: for instance, in European classical music, achieving the greatest dynamics of tone from *fff* to *ppp* and the largest possible range of tone colors is a general ideal and goal pursued by every singer and instrumentalist. It may be correct to assert that on the average men have a larger physique than women, but the quest for dynamic range need not be a gendered issue.

The key to the link between gender and the *dan* role-type lies in the notion that Beijing opera (or for that matter, Kunju opera) represents the "classical woman" on stage. And this is argued as a male conception of feminine beauty from the past (it seems that there is no place for modernity in traditional Beijing opera). The assertion of the superiority of men performing the *dan* rests on sexual differences, while the Beijing opera *dan* is also simultaneously considered first and foremost an art independent of *natural* sex. While turning the female-male gender difference in physicality to his advantage, Wen also gears the whole issue toward a performing artist's point of view, focusing on the artistry of the *dan* role-type itself. Wen, as a man, is thus able to play woman on stage better than his female colleagues. In this regard *The Fair-faced Gentleman* may have served as a showcase for Wen to prove his point since the staging of this Beijing opera juxtaposes a male *dan* and a female *dan* playing enemies in long exchanges of singing and dialogue. In effect it virtually highlights moments of rivalry between the two modes of acting woman in this theatre: the male *dan* and the female *dan*. The female *dan* performers today are not unaware of the controlling influence of the long aesthetic tradition of the "male *dan*" as a performance practice, i.e., a system of man playing woman. The renowned female *dan* Du Jinfang (1932–), one of the greatest successors to Mei Lanfang, realized at 50 years of age that she had followed "a crooked path" in following the footsteps of the male *dan* actors. She has consciously begun "searching for a system of method of woman playing woman" and that "she is a woman playing woman in the capacity of a woman" (Xu Chengbei, *Zhongguo Jingju* 153). The ultimate question is, from the perspective of cultural studies, one of the politics of "representation." Whether Wen had successfully demonstrated the superiority of the male *dan* was, and will always be, subject to the judgment of individual critics and spectators.

In the case of Wen, the aesthetics of the male *dan* serve as a theoretical reflection and a tactic for survival at the same time. It is a means for a male *dan* living in the era of the "natural" female *dan* to delineate a space for himself. This brings the argument back to the Party's first gender ideology of the "naturalness" of playing one's own sex on stage. He Jingzhi's idea that "people act better if portraying those of their own sex" is diametrically opposed to the male transvestite aesthetic of Wen. The underlying assumption informing Wen's aesthetical tactic of survival is a contradictory one: art transcends gender, yet man is superior to woman in playing the *dan*.

In *M. Butterfly*, David Henry Hwang has Song Liling reveal to us the constructive nature of femininity under a patriarchal ideology: "Because only a man knows how a woman is supposed to act" (63). The defiant gesture of "the last female impersonator" against patriarchal, homophobic institutional power is, at the same time, a reinforcement of male dominance materialized through an aesthetics of performing gender predicated upon the superiority of the male body.

EPILOGUE

Cross-dressed plays such as the various Liang-Zhu operas, *The Male Queen,* and *Shadow of Disguise,* constitute texts mirroring and complementing each other in disturbing the rigid categories that support gender hierarchy and compulsory heterosexuality. The radical indeterminacy of the boundaries between fiction and reality, and between the male and female gender categories in the Chinese theatrical and literary tradition has absurdly and ironically been put into practice in contemporary real life, most conspicuously in the "Butterfly Scandal" of Shi Pei-pu and Bernard Boursicot. The relevance of traditional Chinese theatre to contemporary society lies significantly in the self-(un)masking of this art form effected by its multilevel cross-dressing traditions and its self-dismantling aesthetics of prettiness-eroticism and artistry. In the long-standing prevalence of transvestism on the public stage, the male *dan* player is perhaps the most perplexing entity throughout the history of Chinese opera. The ultimate icon of Chinese opera in modern times is unquestionably Mei Lanfang. Lu Xun in his critique of culture and politics bitingly refers to the ambiguous and unsettling transvestite figure of the *dan*, and the transnational film *Farewell My Concubine* again centers on a male *dan*. Hwang relies on this same figure to construct his "deconstructive" *M. Butterfly*. This role-type virtually embodies boundless ambiguity and anxiety concerning the transgression of gender and sexual boundary and the attempt to eradicate this subversive body in mainland China is symbolic of repressive anxiety. Cheng Dieyi, the transvestite *dan* in *Farewell My Concubine* is characterized by his foremost admirer, the Chinese opera aficionado Yuan the Fourth Master in an eight-character couplet:

Undifferentiating human reality and theatrical illusion [*renxi bufen*]

Coexistence of the female and the male [*cixiong tongzai*]

My reading of this remark — appropriating it to my critical project — is that it is a metaphor for the subversive functioning of Chinese opera in collapsing rigid hierarchal boundaries.[1] The subversive and unsettling body of the male *dan* is what the film text of *Farewell* tries to annihilate in order to restabilize the heterosexual matrix built upon the "normal" relationship of a "real" man (Duan Xiaolou) and a "real" woman (Juxian). A prime effect of the cultural operations of Chinese opera is a forever unsettling self-inquiry into the question posed by Foucault in the English introduction to his *Herculine Barbin dite Alexina B.*: "Do we *truly* need a *true* sex?" (original emphasis). To assign any text, form or human agency to any fixed position in the continuum of transgression and containment does not address effectively the operation of cultural practices as we perceive them today. While putting into question established social and cultural values, Chinese opera itself is being produced by and producing values, defined by and redefining reality. Theatrical cross-dressing is participating simultaneously in the cultural construction and transgression of desires and meanings in the perpetual struggle for the power to define truth and reality.

In analyzing the cultural politics played out on the unstable site of Chinese opera, I wish to demonstrate that such a critique of traditional culture can be made to speak to the concerns of today's ideological resistance to political hegemony and cultural dominants in the "Chinese" context, where we find a totalizing force in the discursive field that can loosely be termed "Chinese culture." Destabilizing differences in this discursive field are constantly being neutralized by a master "Chinese"cultural narrative that strives for a monolithic "grand unity" [*dayitong*] — an idea that has been equally forcibly at work in the numerous enterprises for geographical "unification" in the history of China. Ironically, we see more moments of multiple divisions than singular unification in the history of this empire. I have tried to look for fissures in this supposedly coherent plane to demonstrate the possibility of a resistance to a totalitarian and totalizing discourse by exposing its incoherences — polyvalent meanings of gendering and gendered differences that are constructed, reproduced, dismantled, and contested in a particular site of Chinese culture. An inquiry into how the subversiveness of Chinese opera is at once suppressed yet emergent in ancient and modern (con)texts is instructive for attempts at a broader remaking of a history that refuses unjust hierarchies perpetrated by the present configurations of power.

The theory of "uninterrupted revolution" [*buduan geminglun*] advanced by Mao Zedong, which at first glance sounded like a call for continuous renewal of society, was ironically frozen into a definitive answer to history and turned against *revolution* (read "change") itself to reinforce one man's ideology and perpetuate one single power machinery. It is of great urgency to resist oppression through and with a practice of unceasing problematization of all hegemonic discourses in order to resist the closure of the questioning of existing ideologies and institutions in the name of "home-truths." Therefore, in my critical investigation of Chinese opera as a cultural artifact, I aim at opening up discursive spaces for a polyphony of contrapuntal voice-parts, by questioning ideological assumptions of gender and sexuality that posed as "natural" tonal harmonies backing a single dominant melodic line of cultural dogma on top of the established power hierarchy.

NOTES

1   See Chao Tsung's *Zhongguo dalu di xiqu gaige: 1942–1967* [Traditional music drama reform in mainland China: 1942–1967] (1968) for a critical account of censorship and prohibition of Chinese opera in the period. See Gao Yilong and Li Xiao's *Zhongguo xiqu xiandaixi shi* [History of Chinese music drama in modern themes] (1999) for a comprehensive account of contemporary Chinese opera "reform" from a mainland Chinese perspective. Wang Xiaochuan's *Yuan Ming Qing sandai jinhui xiaoshuo xiqu shiliao* [Historical materials on the censorship and destruction of fiction and drama in Yuan, Ming and Qing periods] (1958) collects invaluable historical sources on the policing of Chinese drama during the last three imperial dynasties.

2   Michael Shapiro lists 79 plays of this kind which appeared between the late sixteenth and the mid-seventeenth century ("Chronological List of Plays with Heroines in Male Disguise" 221–3).

3   The currently known woman writers and their works featuring cross-dressed heroines include: Liang Xiaoyu (late Ming), *Heyuanji* [The reunion] (lost); Liang Mengzhao (late Ming), *Xiangsiyan* [The inkstone of mutual love] (lost); Zhang Lingyi (1669–1747), *Qiankunquan* [The circle of male and female] (lost); Wang Yun (1749–1819), *Fanhuameng* [The flourishing dream] (1768), *Quanfuji* [Story of total blessing] (1772); Wu Zao (1799–1863), *Qiaoying* [Shadow of disguise]; He Peizhu (c. 1814–?), *Lihuameng* [Dream of the pear flower] (written between c. 1839–

1847). Altogether we now know of 23 woman playwrights in imperial China from the sixteenth to the nineteenth century, most of whom were gentry women, though some were courtesans (Ye Changhai, *Quxue yu xijuxue* 80–1).

4 Male writers produced a larger number of plays of this theme. For instance, Xu Wei, *Maid Mulan, The Female Top Graduate*; Anonymous, *Zengshuji* [Story of the complimentary book] (late Ming); Li Yu (1611–1680), *Yizhongyuan* [The love you want]; Wang Fuzhi (1619–1692), *Longzhouhui* [The dragon boat fair]; Long Xie (1640–1697), *Jianghuameng* [Dream of the river flower]; Zhang Jian (1681–1763), *Mengzhongyuan* [Predestined love in a dream]; Shen Qifeng (1741–1802), *Hongxin cike sizhong* [Four plays by the red-heart poet]; *Bao'enyuan* [A predestined love of repaying a favor]; *Cairenfu* [The good fortune of a talent]; *Wenxingbang* [The honor roll of the Big Dipper]; *Fuhutao* [Strategy of taming the tiger]); Zhou Gao (Qing), *Yu yuanyang* [The jade mandarin ducks]. In addition, Ruan Dacheng (c. 1587–c. 1646) briefly employed female cross-dressing as a minor device in his play of "ten mistaken identity/identification" *Chundengmi* [The riddle of the spring festival lantern] (1633).

CHAPTER ONE

1 Lu Xun's cultural status in modern China needs no further qualification. This brief comment of his on theatrical female impersonation in connection with politics has been well remembered and quoted in recent sexology studies in China (see following text). In the English-speaking academic world, Lu Xun's "fame" was catapulted to a new international height in the 1980s by Fredric Jameson's "marvellously erudite reading" (Ahmad 95) of him (along with several other "Third-World" writers) in the controversial article "Third World Literature in the Era of Multinational Capitalism" (1986). Aijaz Ahmad's criticism of Jameson ("Jameson's Rhetoric of Otherness and the 'National Allegory'" [1987]) serves to remind us that Lu Xun may have been "valorized beyond measure" and "elevated to the lonely splendour of a representative — of a race, a continent, a civilization, even the 'Third World'" (98). My reference to Lu Xun here once more reinforces the paradox of the "overflow" of Lu Xun's radical signification in contemporary critical discourses.

2 Cultural essentialism is often at odds with historical contingency. The various Chinese operatic forms enjoyed a period of resurgence after the opening of China in 1978. Witnessing the gradual decline of Chinese opera among public audiences since the mid-1980s, the revival of this

traditional art has become an obsessive topic, almost a mission, to all kinds of people surrounding it: workers in the theatre, scholars, government officials, theatergoers, and intellectuals. It is assumed that there are essential values inherent in Chinese opera, and that it is a moral mission to "reform and save rapidly" [*gaige he qiangjiu*] the art. The dominant discourse on Chinese opera in contemporary China since the advent of Euro-American cultural imperialism is underscored by a sense of constant crisis. Meanwhile, in the international frame, the United Nations Educational Scientific and Cultural Organization (UNESCO) honored Kunju opera as a "Masterpiece of the Oral and Intangible Heritage of Humanity" in May 2001.

3 A frequently quoted explication of *xing* by Zhu Xi (1130–1200) from his *Shi ji zhuan* [A comprehensive annotation of *The Classic of Poetry*].

4 Character role-types in Chinese operas are elaborate and vary to some extent from one opera to the other. For the sake of convenience they can be reduced to four major types: *sheng*, the male; *dan*, the female; *jing*, the painted-face; and *chou*, the comedians. For more explanation on this topic in English, see Hsü 43–50, 341–50; Riley 14; and Zung 37–58. Judging from the context, Lu Xun is probably using the term *huadan*, which in more specific theatrical usage denotes one variety of female role-type, as a substitute for the more inclusive term *dan* (or *danjiao*) to refer to young female role-types in general. This interchangeable usage is common in daily linguistic exchanges.

5 It is for rhetorical purposes that the adjective "male" is added to "transvestism," which is itself a term *normatively male*, as Marjorie Garber comments, " . . . the terms 'transsexual' and 'transvestite' are themselves normatively male in general usage; recent work on the early-modern period, for example, has begun to speak of the visibility of 'female' transvestites in London, while 'transvestite' without a gender qualification is usually taken to refer to men in women's clothing" (102). *The American Heritage Dictionary* (2nd college edition, 1991) defines "transvestite" as "A person especially a male who dresses in the clothing of the opposite sex for psychological reasons." A later edition (3rd ed., PC version 3.0A, 1993) gives a non-gender-biased definition of the word as "A person who dresses and acts in a style or manner traditionally associated with the opposite sex."

6 Biographical works and commentaries on Mei in Chinese are voluminous to date, and an English biography of him was written as early as 1957, by A. C. Scott. A useful reference is the meticulous *Mei Lanfang nienpu* [The Mei Lanfang chronology] (1994). The massive, extravagant, English-Chinese bilingual pictorial album *Mei Langfang* (Beijing: Beijing chubanshe, 1997) provides a most detailed pictorial biographical history

of Mei to date. Each copy of this limited-edition publication carries a serial number.

7　John Willett, in his translation of Brecht's *"Verfremdungseffekte in der chinesischen Schauspielkunst,"* draws our attention to a penciled note on the article's typescript: "This essay arose out of a performance by Mei Lan-fang's company in Moscow in spring 1935" (99).

8　The deification of Lu Xun began in the 1940s. His "infallibility" was first questioned in the early 1980s with the eradication of the extreme leftist party line. Wong Wang-chi's gripping article "Gei zhengzhi niuqu liao de Lu Xun yanjiu" [A kind of Lu Xun studies that has been distorted by politics] (1994) gives a revealing historical critique of this issue. Wong points out that Lu Xun's words were taken as "golden rule and precious precept" [*jinke yulü*] because Mao's words had been taken as infallible law (64): "Everything is very clear. After Mao's conclusive appraisal . . . , who would dare or be willing to stand up and contradict Mao's assertion?" (74).

9　For instance, Jiang Xingyu in his "Lu Xun xiansheng lun Mei Lanfang — lüelun 'Lüelun Mei Lanfang ji qita'" [Mr Lu Xun on Mei Lanfang — brief comments on "Brief comments on Mei Lanfang and other topics"] (1988) takes Lu Xun to task by rebutting his various adverse criticisms collected in *Huabian wenxue* [Literature of floral margins] (1934).

10　Mei Lanfang was touring Japan in 1956 on the invitation of the *Asahi Shimbun* and other organizations. He gave 23 shows to more than 70,000 spectators. In response to this cultural exchange between China and Japan, Yoshikawa wrote a series of commentaries, including "Bai Ranhō no chi'i" [Mei Lanfang's status], "Bai Ranhō so no ta" [About Mei Lanfang], "Kabuki to kyogeki" [Kabuki and Beijing opera], "Kyogeki zakkan" [Miscellaneous thoughts on Beijing opera], "Minamiza kangeki zekku" [Poetic quatrains written after watching drama]. In "About Mei Lanfang," Yoshikawa relates an interesting story which shows that Mei Lanfang was an irresistible performing artist: a housewife wrote a letter to a newspaper telling the readers that she was poor and had never even been able to pay for a Kabuki show; yet she made the effort to buy a ticket and watch Mei Lanfang (597).

11　Literally, *sizen denai* means "the unnatural." It is a positive aesthetic judgment in this context. A direct English rendition would be "artificial." An obsolete meaning of "artificial" is "artful."

12　The geographical permeation of Beijing opera in mainland China today is a result more of political maneuver than autonomous cultural operation. Beijing opera troupes have been set up in locations as culturally different and geographically distant as Inner Mongolia, Xinjiang, and Ningxia.

13　See, for instance, Jonathan Goldberg's critique of Jean Howard, Laura

Levine, Stephen Orgel and Lisa Jardine in his *Sodometries* (1990) (chapter 4, "The Transvestite Stage: More on the Case of Christopher Marlowe"); and also Valerie Traub's critique of Marguerite Waller's critique of Stephen Greenblatt, and Lisa Jardine in her *Desire and Anxiety* (1992), the chapter entitled "Desire and the Differences It Makes."

14 Feng Menglong (1574–1646), *Taiping guangji chao* [Selections from *Anthology of Widely Gathered Accounts in the Taiping Era*], *juan* 72 has a section entitled "*Renyao*" [Human prodigies], consisting of tales of female and male cross-dressers and people with paranormal sex transformation. Feng's anthology is a short re-edition of the 500-volume *Taiping guangji*, compiled in 977. See also Judith Zeitlin's "Dislocations in Gender" in her *Historian of the Strange: Pu Songling and the Chinese Classical Tale* (1993) for an account of the records and commentaries on "the human prodigy" in Ming-Qing times. See R. H. Van Gulik, *Sexual Life in Ancient China* (158–160) for an account of the transformation of woman into man and hermaphrodites as *yao*.

15 Another translation came out in Taiwan in 1994, entitled *Zhongguo yanqing: Zhongguo gudai de xing yu shehui*. The 1990 Mainland translation is called *Zhongguo gudai fangnei kao*, which is van Gulik's original Chinese title.

16 Only 12 of the original illustrations are reproduced in this translation due to censorship considerations. But *all* the original erotic plates with the Chinese translation are reproduced in Taiwan's lavish, gigantic volume *Mixi tu da guan* [Grand view of paintings of the clandestine game] (1994), which also collects a plethora of other pre-modern erotic paintings from China and Japan. Another extravagant album of illustrations of erotica (paintings and artifacts included) by leading mainland Chinese sexologist Liu Dalin (see n17) was published in Hong Kong in 2000. The point of interest about this bilingual publication, *Chinese Sex Artifacts Over 5000 Years*, apart from its informative sexual content, is that it was self-censored shortly before its originally scheduled date of release. In a letter dated February 28, 2000 with the heading "The Progress of Editorial Work of *Chinese Sex Artifacts Over 5000 Years*" [Guanyu *Zhongguo wuqiannian xingwenwu daguan* de bianji jinzhan] addressed to the pre-publication subscribers, the publisher explains that the book has been reduced from its original length of two volumes with a total of 600 pages to a single volume of 300 plus pages due to the cutting away of "sensitive parts" that touch upon "sensitive topics such as religion, etc." The listed price was cut from HK$998 (US$128) to $698 ($89). The book was finally published in August 2000.

17 Geographical *mainland* China's second "Western exposure" in this century, if we take the May Fourth Movement as the first exposure. The

other two major communities of ethnic Chinese, Hong Kong and Taiwan, have not been "shuttered" from the West since modern times, ironically because of Euro-American imperialisms — military and cultural.

18 Liu Dalin, author of the aforementioned *Chinese Sex Artifacts Over 5000 Years*, among his publications are also *Zhongguo dangdai xing wenhua* [The sex culture of contemporary China] (1991), *Zhongguo gudai xingwenhua* [The sex culture of ancient China] (1993), and, as chief editor, *Zhonghua xingxue cidian* [A Chinese sexology dictionary] (1993). His popularity is demonstrated by his appearance in one of the most popular "tabloid" weekly magazines in Hong Kong and Taiwan, *Next Magazine/ Yizhoukan* 223 (June 17, 1994): 80–4. He was recently dubbed the "Chinese Dr Comfort" by *Ming Pao Daily* (September 3, 1999):F3.

19 Van Gulik, reading a handbook of sex from the Ming Dynasty, points out that "sapphism [lesbianism] among the womenfolk of a household was not only viewed tolerantly, but on occasion even encouraged" (*Sexual Life* 274). See also "Appendix: Lesbianism in Imperial China" in Hinsch (1990) and "*Nü tongxingai*" [Lesbian love] in Xiaomingxiong (1997).

CHAPTER TWO

1 Public troupes composed solely of young female players first appeared in several big cities in the last decades of the nineteenth century (e.g., Shanghai, Hangzhou and other cities in Jiangsu and Zhejiang). These troupes performed in regional operas as well as Beijing and Kunju operas. This was labelled *mao'er xi* ["female" theatre/"kitten" theatre]. Xu Ke's *Qing bai lei chao* [Categorized anecdotes from the Qing period] (1917) contains four entries on *mao'er xi* (53–5). For historical accounts of the emergence of female players in this period, see *Zhongguo Jingju shi* 1: 280–91; Zhang Faying 389–92; Xu Muyun 201–4; Lu Eting 247; for the rise of the female Zhejiang Yueju, see Shengxian wenhuaju, ed., *Zaoqi Yueju fazhan shi* [The early history of Yueju opera] and Gao Yilong.

2 "The boy actress" was used by Harley Granville-Barker in *Prefaces to Shakespeare*, Vol. 3 (Princeton: Princeton University Press, 1946), 12; quoted in Kelly (81). "Play-boy" was used by Lisa Jardine and Shapiro.

3 The "four great Anhui theatre troupes" were hired to perform in the imperial capital of Beijing on the occasion of the eightieth birthday of the Emperor Qianlong (reign 1736–1796) in 1790. Afterwards these troupes stayed in the capital and played a major role in the development of Beijing opera. A Bejing opera festival in celebration of the bicentennial anniversary of the four great Anhui opera troupes coming to Beijing was held from December 20, 1990 through January 12, 1991. The largest-scale activity

of the kind ever held in the People's Republic of China, the festival staged 166 shows of various regional operas, held symposiums and a large exhibition. For information, see Wang Wenzhang, ed., *Two Hundredth Anniversary of Anhui Opera Coming to Beijing* (1991). A series of Chinese opera performances were also held in Hong Kong in October 1990. For an account in English of actors and boy actors in the Qing period, see Mackerras, *The Rise of the Peking Opera* 40–8, 145–53.

4   The source of this incident is the notation book *Yinhualu* [Records of chats] by Zhao Lin, who was active in the time of the Tang emperor Xuanzong (reign 837–860). A full quotation is given in Zhang Faying 32–3.

5   Other versions of this story are found in Liu Shu's *Jiu Tang shu* [Old Tang history] *juan* 29, and Duan Anjie's *Yuefu zalu* [Miscellaneous notes on *yuefu* songs] 44–5. For a detailed historical and ethnological study of the mask of Lan Ling, see Zhou Huabin, "*Lan Ling Wang* jiameng yanjiu" [A study of the mask of *Prince Lang Ling*].

6   Based on Chung-wen Shih's translation (5) with a number of places altered to render the translation closer to the original.

7   The following two quotes are also from Cui 18.

       Versions of "The Stomping-Swaying Wife" are also found in *Jiu Tang shu* [Old Tang history] *juan* 9, and *Yuefu zalu* [Miscellaneous notes on *yuefu* songs] 45. Written about a century and a half after Cui, Duan's account is shorter and does not mention the female impersonation in the performance of this theatrical act.

8   This "select-scene play" is taken from act 17 of the Ming drama *Jinsuo ji* [The golden casket], in which the corresponding act title is "Wushang" [Mistaken injury]. This Ming play is an adaptation of arguably the greatest Yuan tragic drama *Dou'e yuan* [Injustice to Dou'e]. In the Yuan plot it is the father of Zhang the Donkey who is poisoned to death.

9   According to Lu Eting, Ding Jizhi was born in 1585 and lived for more than 90 years (154 n1). Eighteenth century critic Jiao Xun also includes an anecdote of Ding acting at the age of 80 in *juan* 6 of his *Jushuo* [Discourse on drama] (8: 216).

10   Wang Guowei in his *Song Yuan xiqu kao* (1915) already suggests the connection between shamanism and the beginnings of Chinese theatre. For comprehensive accounts of the various theses, see Zheng Chuanyin, *Zhongguo xiqu* 4–44; T'ang Wen-piao 1–42; 215–33.

11   These boisterous military plays, which mainly exhibit acrobatic fighting and dance, are frequently performed in Chinese opera troupes' overseas tours. The plays featuring the Monkey King are particularly "representative" in this sense. Obviously this has something to do with Arthur Waley's *Monkey* (1942) (Harmondsworth: Penguin, 1961) — his

popular (abridged) translation of the sixteenth century classic fiction
Xiyouji [Journey to the west]. There are two complete translations:
Anthony C. Yu's *The Journey to the West* (Chicago : University of Chicago
Press, 1977–1983), and W. J. F. Jenner's *Journey to the West* (Beijing :
Foreign Languages Press, 1982–1986).
      The "roc" is a mythic bird of great size and strength.

12 Roger Baker in his book *Drag: A History of Female Impersonation on
the Stage* (1968) gives one chapter to the Chinese *tan* — i.e. the *dan* and
the Japanese *onnagata* ("Onnagata and Tan" 149–56). He also includes a
full-page picture of Mei Lanfang in a young *dan* disguise. Majorie Garber's
1992 *Vested Interests* (234–51; 411 n11) and the Bulloughs' 1993 *Cross
Dressing, Sex, and Gender* (243), also make several references to Chinese
theatrical cross-dressing to further illustrate their arguments. Interestingly
enough, the Bulloughs even cite "Shaoxing opera" (i.e., Yueju opera of
Zhejiang), which is little known among Westerners, as an example of an
"all-female theatre," "wherein all the roles were played by women (a
conscious reversal of the Beijing Opera, whose roles were performed by
men)" (231). The Chinese female theatre is much more complicated than
"a conscious reversal" of a male-dominated theatre in its historical-cultural
context, and, to be exact, "Shaoxing opera" is an *almost* all-female theatre
in which there are few male performers, though hardly occupying a
significant position in this theatre.

13 Also writing in commendation of Mei as a great artist, Yoshikawa Kōjirō
instead of making him an example par excellence of the allegedly privileged
status of the female impersonator in Chinese society, attributes to him
the contribution of raising the status of Chinese actors in modern times:
"Actors in old China had low status and people despised them. With his
great art and high accomplishment, [Mei Lanfang] made people change
their understanding of the Chinese theatre" ("Bai Ranhō no chi'i" 590).
This is more in accord with what happened in history.

14 According to the account in *Zhongguo da baike quanshu: xiqu, quyi*
[The great Chinese encyclopedia: traditional music drama, folk musical
art forms], Beijing opera as we see it today came into being during the
reign of the emperor Guangxu (1875–1908) and the designation *jingxi*
[Beijing opera] was created after 1911 in Shanghai (158).

15 The film adaptation of *M. Butterfly* with the same title (Geffen Pictures
1993), directed by David Cronenberg, screenplay written by Hwang
himself, and starring Jeremy Irons and John Lone, was not as successful
as Chen's *Farewell My Concubine* in the international cinema world.
Chen's film was based on an original novel by Hong Kong writer Lilian
Lee which was published in English translation by Andrea Lingenfelter
(Penguin, 1993). John Lone was at first cast as the Beijing opera female

impersonator in *Farewell My Concubine*. He quit soon after shooting began. The production company Tomson (HK) Films then signed top Hong Kong pop singer-actor Leslie Cheung, who ended up giving an acclaimed performance. Cheung's ambiguously closet queer identity perhaps also added to the film's appeal. In the film *M. Butterfly*, the play's radical edges of postcolonial politico-cultural intervention were domesticated and transformed into, in the motion picture's own publicity language, a melodrama which "boldly portrayed" the "mysteries of love and the sting of betrayal" (words in quotation marks taken from the back cover of the US video release of the film).

16 "The beginning of the activity and literature known as theatre is traditionally assigned to the plays and practices of the Athenian festivals of Dionysus in the sixth and fifth century B.C.E. . . . In the sixth century, both women and men participated in these ceremonies, but by the fifth century, when the ceremonies were becoming what is known as theatre, women disappeared from the practice" (Case 318). Based on the authoritative work by Margarete Bieber (*The History of the Greek and Roman Theatre* [Princeton: Princeton University Press, 1939]), Case says, "Scholars do not record any evidence for specific laws or codes forbidding women to appear in songs and dances" (319).

17 Some historians insist that it was composed exclusively of men, yet there is a tale about Aeschylus's *The Eumenides* relating that the Furies represented by the chorus appeared so frightening that women in the audience miscarried on the spot (Arnott 25–6). Sue-Ellen Case in her feminist investigation of drag in Greek theatre mentions that "[j]udging from the gender-specific quality of Athenian practice and Aristotle's thoughts on tragedy, it would seem appropriate that women were not in the audience. Or, in the context of chapter 4 [of *Poetics*], that they would be inferior members of the audience" (326).

18 Some of the well-known examples are: the great emperor Han Wudi (reign 140–187 B.C.E.) and the musician-entertainer Li Yannian (Sima Qian, *Shiji* [Records of the historian], *juan* 125 "Lingxing liechuan" [Biographies of the male favorites], 10: 3194–5); the late Tang emperor Yizong (reign 860–873) and his favorite entertainer Li Keji (Ouyang Xiu and Song Qi, *Xin Tang shu* [New Tang history], *juan* 181 "Cao Que liechuan" [Biography of Cao Que], 17: 5351–2). Jiao Xun in his *Discourse on drama* records an anecdote of Li entertaining the emperor with a humorous reference to the Buddha, Laozi and Emperor Wenxuan as *women*, (8: 100–1); the late Ming politician Yan Shifan (son of Yan Song [d. 1568], a corrupt statesman whose power even overshadowed the emperor Jiajing [reign 1522–1566] for 20 years) and the transvestite actor Jin Feng (Jiao Xun 201; also Yang Enshou *Xu ciyu conghua* [Sequel to *Collected Chats on Music Drama*], 321–2).

Yoshikawa, in his account of the relation between the Mongolian court and Yuan drama, also brings our attention to the many instances of emperors assigning high offices to actors during the Yuan Dynasty (*Yuan zaju yanju* 58; 60–2). According to Yoshikawa, actors in the Yuan Dynasty were frequently appointed to high offices because of many emperors' great enthusiasm for drama.

19   In a footnote to her article "The Saint Play in Medieval France" (1986), Lynette R. Muir cites another incident of women on stage: "A tantalizingly brief entry in the account books of Lorraine mentions a woman (*femme*) who played the *Vie de Sainte Barbe* before the duke in 1505 in Nancy" (176), taken from vol. 2 of *Les Mystères* edited by L. Petit de Julleville (Paris 1880). She also gives another three pieces of evidence in "Women on the Medieval Stage: The Evidence from France" (1985) of women performers in religious plays at Mons in 1501, Romans in 1509, and Valenciennes in 1547 (107–19).

20   Although theatrical activities in the Song periods (960–1279) were already flourishing, there has never been any dispute that Yuan *zaju* drama was the earliest *mature* form of Chinese theatre. Wang Guowei says, "To talk about real music drama, one has to begin with Yuan *zaju* drama" (*Song Yuan* 82). Yoshikawa shares the same view (*Yuan zaju yanjiu* 3, 224). He further suggests that Yuan drama reached maturity during the years 1264–1294 at the latest, adding that the first center of literary output and performance was the Yuan capital Dadu (Beijing), which gradually shifted to the southern city Hangzhou in the later years of the Yuan Dynasty (18–9). Chung-wen Shih begins her *Golden Age of Chinese Drama: Yüan Tsa-chü* (1976), the first full-length study of this genre in English, with these words: "Chinese theatre first began to flourish during the Yüan period . . . " (ix). Yuan drama scripts are also the earliest entire playscripts of Chinese drama extant today. (Shih's work was translated into Chinese recently: *Zhongguo xiju de huangjin shidai* [Trans. Xiao Shanyin and Wang Hongxiao. Taiyuan: Shanxi renmin chubanshe, 1991].)

21   This and other Yuan imperial prohibitions are quoted in detail in 3–10 in Wang's work.

22   There were many occasions of prohibitions of mixing men and women during imperial times. For quotations from Qing edicts, see Wang, *Yuan Ming Qing* 18, 23, 24, 33, 74, 94, 100, 101, 110, 120.

23   During the Qing Dynasty, numerous provincial and central edicts were issued to ban women audiences and players, see Wang, *Yuan Ming Qing* 78, 110–111, 120, 133 (prohibiting women from attending public performances); 18, 20, 23, 44 (prohibiting female players), 26 (prohibiting female troupes from entering the capital city).

24   There are more references to female players in Wang Yun's writings, and Yoshikawa gives some detailed accounts (*Yuan zaju yanjiu* 67–9).

25 *Juan* 4 and 19 together record three anecdotes about another actress, Shun Shi Xiu (351, 559), whose biography is also found in *The Green Bower Collection* (20).

26 That is *sanqu*, following James J. Y. Liu's translation of this Chinese poetic genre (*The Art of Chinese Poetry* 32). He translates *qu* as "dramatic verse"; Victor H. Mair once rendered it as "cantos" (4).

27 Ye Yuhua first made this suggestion and received retorts from Hu Ji, Qi Gong and Zhou Miaozhong. See Ye Yuhua, "Shuo beiqu zaju xiyou nüxing yanchang" [Northern music drama was sung by females] (1954); Hu Ji, "Beiqu zaju yanchang ren xingbie de taolun" [On the sex of the singers in Yuan *zaju* drama] (1955) and Qi Gong's "Lun Yuan dai zaju de banyan wenti" [A discussion of the question of impersonation in Yuan theatre] (1955); Zhou Miaozhong, "Guanyu Yuan qu de sange wenti" [Three questions concerning Yuan music drama] (1955).

28 Zhou Yibai explains this point in detail in his *Zhongguo xiju shi* [History of Chinese drama] (1953), 3: 280–3.

29 Apart from the several contending articles of the 1950s, we have more evidence through anthropological and historical studies. For instance, Zhang Faying in his *Zhongguo xiban shi* [History of Chinese theatre troupes] (1991) reconstructs a general picture of Yuan traveling troupes which were individually built upon members of a family, centering around *either* a woman *or* a man performer (65–94).

30 A long time ago, the sinologist Herbert Giles once mistook the Yuan playwright Zhang Guobin as a woman: "Just as there have always been poetesses in China, so women are to be found in the ranks of Chinese playwrights. A four-act drama, entitled 'Joining the Shirt,' was written by one CHANG KUO-PIN [sic] [Zhang Guobin], an educated courtesan of the day, the chief interest of which play lies perhaps in the sex of the writer" (274). Liu Wu-chi has already pointed out this error in a short note. We have records of, and extant works by, female playwrights from the Ming and Qing periods, but not the Yuan Dynasty. See n32 and n33 below.

31 Zhang Faying (1–26) gives a concise history of this institution.

32 For instance, Li Zhaogan's brief article "Zhejiang gudai de nü zuojia" ["Women playwrights from Zhejiang in ancient times"]; Ye Changhai's paper entitled "Preliminary Reflections on the Mind-Set of Female Dramatists" given at the conference "Women and Literature in Ming-Qing China" held at Yale University, June 22–26, 1993; and his *Quxue yu xijuxue* [Theory and criticism of music drama and theatre], part 2, chapter 5. Tao Qiuying's *Zhongguo funü yu wenxue* [Chinese women and literature], an early historical work of its kind written in the 1930s, did not mention women playwrights.

33 Although Hu Wenkai's initial research work on Chinese women writers lists more than four thousand women writers in the past, there was only one traditional lyrical genre which was the domain of women, the *tanci*. Apart from one or two women poets, such as Li Qingzhao (1084–1155), whom Julia Kristeva appropriates for her feminist agenda as the one woman whose name "dominates Chinese literature" (90), female *tanci* writers like Chen Duansheng (1751–96), Liang Desheng (1771–1847), and Tao Huaizhen (17 c.) have also appeared in Chinese literary histories published in recent times.

34 It is interesting to note that in the English language there is no formal term for "customer for prostitutes," although prostitutes call them "johns." In this binary structure between the male consumer of sex and the female prostitute, only the female pole is formally named — the first and male term is missing from negative designation. In the Chinese term, the male is also named in formal usage: *piaoke*.

35 Adapted from Stephen Orgel's reading of the theatre of early modern England: " . . . there are lots of *others* in this theatre; in fact, Elizabethan drama is often dependent on otherness. Comedies are Italian, French, or provincial, tragedies Spanish or Scandinavian or ancient, pastorals take place somewhere else. Dekker, Jonson, and Middleton placing comedies in contemporary London are doing something new. The Other, for this theatre, is as much foreign as female — Othello is the Other. And in the largest sense, the Other is theatre itself, both a threat and a refuge" ("Nobody's Perfect" 9).

36 Quoted in Yoshikawa, *Yuan zaju yanjiu* 49. The original sources quoted are *Tongzhi tiaoge* [Yuan laws] (*juan* 3) and *Yuan dianzhang* [Yuan documents] (*juan* 18).

37 T'ien Ju-k'ang in his *Male Anxiety and Female Chastity: A Comparative Study of Chinese Ethical Values in Ming-Ch'ing Times* (1987) also states that "[t]he Mongol empire was the first nomad dynasty to conquer the whole of China, shattering the native traditional ethical code which had constrained Chinese society for more than a thousand years previously" (2).

38 It is instructive to note that Chinese opera performers are officially called performing artists [*biaoyan yishujia*] or theatrical performers [*yanyuan*] in mainland China today, in contrast with the old insulting labels of *xizi* ["player" with a sense of contempt] or *changxi de* [literally "one who sings drama"]. But traditional theatre has been censored as it was in the past.

39 Their names are: Mary Pix, Catharine Trotter, Delariviere Manley, Susanna Centlivre, Jane Wiseman, and Mary Davys. Quoted by Lesley Ferris based on Kathryn Kendall's "Theatre, Society and Women Playwrights in

London from 1695 through the Queen Anne Era" (Ph.D. Diss., U of Texas 1986) (*Acting Women* 155).

40 Used in the sense that Jonathan Dollimore defines as signifying "reversal of position and/or reversal of direction, both being inimical to effective government and social control. . . . it is in this sense that the female cross-dresser of the early seventeenth century could be described as an 'invert' or 'pervert,' and hardly at all in the sense of those words as coined and popularized by the nineteenth century sexologists and, later, psychoanalysis" (*Sexual Dissidence* 287–8).

41 Charlotte Chark's dual cross-dressing made her a scandalous invert. Many breeches role actresses cross-dressed only on stage. Her unsettled sexuality made her further at odds with normative social ideology of gender and sex: "she went from playing men's roles on the stage to living as a man, even for a time . . . living with a young widow. At least two other women, mistaking her for a man, allegedly fell in love with her, ultimately 'forcing' her to reveal her true sex . . . . It was probably the threat posed by her putative lesbianism that made her less popular than some of the other women who played what came to be called 'breeches' roles" (Bullough 86). Kristina Straub in her *Sexual Suspects* (1992) devotes one whole chapter to Charlotte Chark, illustrating the difficulties, dangers as well as virtues "of reading the ambiguities of past sexualities from the perspective of resistance to the social oppression that goes by the name of normative sexuality" (147).

42 There is similar evidence from Turkish and Egyptian harems in the nineteenth century.

43 The two terms *nüxi* and *nüyue*, depending on the context, can refer to either "female performers" or "female troupes."

44 One or two rare exceptions of men acting together with women on private and informal occasions can be found. Based on a Ming source, Lu Eting notes that the amateur [*chuanke*] painted-face actor Wang Yian (active in the reign of Wanli 1573–1620) occasionally acted with courtesan-entertainers in the city of Changan (83) ("In the city of Changan, Wang visited the brothels and joined in the courtesans' drama performance. He played the character of Zhang Ming the Board Secretary and was extolled by the connoisseurs." From Zhang Yuanchang's *Meihua caotang qutan* [Chats on drama from the thatched cottage of peach blossoms] 11; also quoted in Lu Eting 82). Another exception is recorded in an eighteenth century notation book. The son of the teacher of a female troupe called Double Purity [*Shuangqing ban*] occasionally cross-dressed to play the young female role, pairing with the girl player who cross-dressed in reverse to play the young male role. People called it "the shifting game of the male and female roles" [*shengdan bianju*] (Lu Eting 241).

45 They quote from the information given in *Records of Dreams* on Qian Dai's female troupe and another notation book, Xiang Gu Shi, *Canlu gushi* [Stories from the broken bamboo box]. Following the common academic practice in mainland China, Hu and Liu do not give a full citation of their source. Based on the edition of *Records of Dreams* that I have in hand, of the singing-girls in Qian Dai's private troupe whose age is recorded, three were of the age of 12 and one 11 (3235). According to Lu Eting, the singing-girls in the Qing period were also usually around eleven or twelve years of age (241).

CHAPTER THREE

1   English translation *Opera, or the Undoing of Women* (1988).
2   *I Puritani di Scozia*, libretto by C. Pepoli, first produced in Paris and London in 1835.
3   The story of the Hegemon King and his concubine has been made famous to moviegoers worldwide through Chen Kaige's film *Farewell My Concubine* (1993) (see chapter 2 n15) in which the two male leads are Beijing opera masters who excel in staging this play.
4   *Qianjin ji*, one of the most popular plays from the traditional canon/ repertoire. The play, based on a historical incident, is well known for its episode of the Hegemon King Xiang Yu and his concubine Yu Ji who died for him. A detailed analysis of this play is given in the following text.
5   *An Extensive Collection of Writings on Music Drama* is collected in and makes up one-quarter of Ren's edition of the 12-volume *Xinquyuan* [The new collection of critical writings on drama]. Ren's work as a compiler has been severely criticized by Ye Dejun (462–77) from a conventional literary historian's point of view. The value of this collection is given a positive evaluation in *Zhongguo da baike quanshu: xiqu, quyi* (331).
6   Zhuang Yifu gives an entry of this play in his exhaustive *Gudian xiqu cunmu huikao* [A comprehensive catalogue of existing traditional music drama titles] (1982) (3: 1356). Wang Yongjian 645–52 gives a detailed biography of Shen.
7   Zhuang Yifu explains about the title: "This is about Xiangting's first encounter with Qing'er, thus the title of *A Smile of Thousand Pieces of Gold*" (3: 1356). It is common for playwrights after the Yuan period to give happy endings to existing plays, histories, and stories "to rectify the regrettable" [*buhen*].
8   This record is not quoted in major works in related fields; for instance, Lu Eting, *Performance History of Kunju Opera*, Gu Duhuang, *Kunju shi bulun* [Supplementary discussions on the history of Kunju] (1987), Hu Ji and Liu Zhizhong, *History of Kunju Opera* (1989).

9   For instance, see Lu 160.

10 Adapted from Teresa de Lauretis, *Technologies* 25–6.

11 I consulted the videos of two recent different performances of the Northern
    Kunqu Opera Company's (see bibliography for details). I have also
    compared two performance scripts by the company: a later version entitled
    Bawang bieji starring the current leading *dan* actress Yang Fengyi and a
    traditional version entitled *Bieji* (in according with the Ming play's act
    title) passed on orally by the great painted-face actor Hou Yushan (1893–
    1998). The latter of these two stencil scripts bears the date of July 29,
    1986. The older text is very close to the Ming play *The Thousand Pieces
    of Gold*. It represents the legacy of the old tradition. This script was later
    included in *Hou Yushan Kunqu pu* [The Kunqu music and script as passed
    on by Hou Yushan] (1994), 53–7. The company's leaders told me that
    they considered this old version not effective theatrically today and that
    they had therefore attempted the new versions. I am grateful for the
    assistance provided by them.

12 Mei Lanfang provides more details of his creation of this play in his
    Wutai shenghuo sishinian [Forty years' performing on the stage] (1987),
    664–76.

CHAPTER FOUR

1   Since Maxine Hong Kingston was born into a family of Cantonese origin,
    she remembers Hua Mulan (spelling following the convention of the pinyin
    system) in its Cantonese romanization: Fa Mu Lan.

2   Thus the presence of the Cantonese romanization "Fa Mu Lan" instead
    of the more official PRC putonghua/pinyin or ROC *guoyu*/Wade-Giles
    "Hua Mu(-)lan" in Hong Kingston's text can be read with significant
    semiotic meaning: the denial of monolithic authority and the celebration
    of marginality.

3   The narrator recounts, "'We are going to carve revenge on your back,'
    my father said" (34).

4   Chang-tai Hung's *War and Popular Culture* (1994) carries a section on
    the figure of the woman warrior in spoken dramas: "Female Symbols of
    Resistance: Patriotic Courtesans and Women Warriors." See especially
    72–8 for a discussion of the Hua Mulan plays during the Sino-Japanese
    War.

5   There are many plays from the Yuan Dynasty onward that dramatize the
    military adventures of the Yang family generals and their widows. An
    often mentioned early play is *Yangliulang diaobing po tianzhen* [Yang
    the sixth son deploys troops to destroy the Heaven's Gate battle
    formation], in *Quanyuan zaju waibian* [Sequel to complete works of Yuan

drama]. *Yangjiafu shidai zhongyong yanyizhuan* [Chivalric stories of several generations of the Yang family generals], prefaced in 1606 by Qinhuai moke [pseud.] (Ming) is one of the popular versions of the saga in long narrative form.

6   Among the four major role-types in Chinese opera (*sheng*, *dan*, *jing*, and *chou*) (chapter 1, n4), the *daomadan* role-type can be considered a subdivision of a category of *dan*, the *wudan* ["military female"]. The *daomadan* in general specializes in playing woman generals and wears military armor while the *wudan* plays civil women who excel in martial arts, or bandits, or demons, etc.

7   Catherine Clément's psychoanalytic-feminist reading of *The Ring* and Brünnhilde and opera in general is inspiring toward a rereading of women representations in Chinese opera.

8   According to Huang Wenyang, *Quhai zongmu tiyao* [Synopses for *A Bibliography of Plays*], Vol. 1, 650 and Zhuang Yifu, Vol. 2, 948. Zhuang states that the Beijing Library's collection has an edition of *Xianglin xian* dated 1736, the first year of the reign of Emperor Qianlong. Other sources state that this play has been lost.

9   For a brief biography of Ma, see *Zhongguo xiquzhi: Tianjin juan* [Annals of Chinese music drama: Tianjin volume], 432.

10   I am indebted to Ms Yang Fengyi, winner of the Plum Blossom Award and Deputy Director of the Beijing Northern Kunqu Company for making the script and video of the play available to me and for her explication of her stage interpretation of the dramatic character. I first watched the performance of the play at the Hong Kong Cultural Center on November 17, 1989 on an occasion in which all six Kunqu troupes from China were, for the first time, gathered together to celebrate this traditional theatre. In December 1994, I attended another staging of this play at Ms Yang's "special performance" [*zhuanchang*] in Beijing. The most recent performance by Ms Yang with the company took place in Taipei on March 18, 2002, presented by the New Aspect Cultural Foundation [Xinxiang wenhua jijinhui].

11   "Battle formation" is a translation of the Chinese term *zhen*, which in this context refers to a kind of magic warfare with the formation of troops in the form of mazes in preparation for battle. It appears often in the military adventure novels (also referred to as "military romance" by some critics) in traditional Chinese literature. See Hsia 352–7 for more details of *zhen* and its use in Chinese novels. *Zhen* is also frequently seen in traditional theatres; for instance, the Beijing opera play *Tianmen zhen* [The Heaven's Gate battle formation] is another popular piece that dramatizes an episode of the Yang family woman warrior Mu Guiying who is also one of the leading roles in *Yangmen nüjiang*.

12 Lois Wheeler Snow uses the word "pause" to translate *liangxiang* (31) and "Bright Appearance" (glossary) for a literal translation. This is not accurate. *Liang* in the compound *liangxiang* is a verb, meaning "to show" (as in "to disclose"). However, her brief English description of this term is useful to further illustrate this performance convention: "A convention of Peking opera. It is a still, statuesque pose assumed for a brief moment by the principals and others while entering or leaving the stage, sometimes after a dance or an acrobatic feat, in order to bring out sharply and concentratedly the spiritual outlook of the characters" (glossary).

13 Translations of this play are based on a stencil-print script dated July 16, 1989.

14 The term "tune" is used instead of "aria" to denote a *qupai* [literally "tune-title"] because the concept of "aria" in European opera is not exactly the same as that of a *qupai*. The word "tune" is relatively more neutral in referring to an organized structure of musical sounds.

15 Interestingly, the performance convention of *qiba* originated in the imperial past from the Kunqu performance of *The Hegemon King Says Farewell to the Concubine*. "The lord rises up" is Jo Riley's translation (*Chinese Theatre and the Actor in Performance* 296).

16 As Simon Shepherd points out in *Amazon and Warrior Women*, "The business of needlework is a stock emblem of femininity, and of woman's social place: modest, passive, ornamental. Its rejection by female fighters is commonly insisted on: Tasso's Clorinda finds it necessary to abjure these attributes in order to fulfill herself as a woman" (7). But cultural processes are full of exceptions. Dorothy Ko has pointed out that in seventeenth century China, embroidery was for a time turning into a respectable art form practiced even by some scholar-officials. This was one of the "playful transgressions" that Ko uses to argue that "the Ming-Qing gender system was more flexible in practice than what the official ideology would have one believe" (175).

17 This is the term used by revered ethnomusicologist Rulan Chao Pian in her study of Beijing opera "arias" [*banqiang*] (Pian 1975).

18 The synopsis given in Chen Weiyu's *Kunju zhezixi chutan* [A preliminary survey of the select scene plays in Kunju opera] (1991) describes this earlier version, not the current one.

19 The main architects in the making of the new version were Shi Hongtu, then Company Director of the Beijing Opera Company of the City of Beijing [Beijing Jingjuyuan] and An Rongqing, a noted Beijing opera *daomadan* actress.

20 The two terms are used after Teresa de Lauretis, see "Feminist Studies/ Critical Studies" 1.

21 Mark Elvin in his study of the Chinese "body-person and heart-mind"

states that "the Chinese body (*shen*) is a peg-doll whose role is to be a carrier of corporeal and/or sartorial attributes" (267).

22 The other three were Cheng Yanqiu (1904–1958), Shang Xiaoyun (1900–1976), Xun Huisheng (1900–1968).

23 "[T]he facade of sexual equality in contemporary Chinese society" (Li Ziyun 306) has been unmasked by writers and critics. For critical reflections on various aspects of the failure of women's emancipation in China and critiques of the marginalization of women's voices as signifiers of high-sounding political causes, see Tonglin Lu (ed.), *Gender and Sexuality in Twentieth-Century Chinese Literature and Society* (1993), and the section "Becoming Women in the Post-Mao Era" in Christina Gilmartin, et al. (eds), *Engendering China: Women, Culture, and the State* (1994).

CHAPTER FIVE

1 This well-known concerto for violin and orchestra was composed by He Zhanho and Chen Gang in 1959. As a footnote, it is instructive to notice that this piece of programmatic music has not represented, or is unable to represent the transgender dimension.

2 The lyrics are collected in Qian Nanyang, *Liang-Zhu xiju jicun* 1.

3 Collected in Lu Gong, Zhou Jingshu and Qian Nanyang, *Liang-Zhu xiju jicun*.

4 The romanization of this regional opera is the same as that of the Guangdong province — "Yueju" in both cases. I shall use "Yueju opera" to refer to the Zhejiang opera and "Cantonese opera" to refer to the Yueju of Guangdong.

5 It should be pointed out that in terms of musical rendition, this Huangmeidiao opera film is more modernized and hybrid (Yu Siu-wah 122–5) than the other Liang-Zhu Chinese opera films which more closely follow their own individual regional operatic musical styles. This film is modern cinema supplemented with modernized Huangmeidiao opera music. We can say that in the Yueju and Cantonese opera film versions, Chinese opera comes before cinema. It is just the opposite in this Huangmeidiao film. The cinematic quality must have contributed greatly to this film's phenomenal success.

6 Yuan Xuefen, arguably the most important actress in the recent history of Yueju opera, relates her own story and the early history of the opera in chapter 15, "The Girl in the Butterfly Opera" of Dymphna Cusack's *Chinese Women Speak*. Her named is romanized as "Yuan Sui-feng" in this 1958 book.

7　See Lu Gong 1–2 for the original Tang and Song texts.

8　Zhou Jingshu, Vol. 1: 286–92, reprints many of these records.

9　Huang Shang's 1953 reading of these two plays is a good example of this "critique of feudalism" approach ("Liang Zhu zaji").

10　Fong was voted "queen of the *huadan*" in 1952 by the magazine *Yule zhiyin* [The sound of entertainment].

11　*Tongzhi* — a term originally used by Dr Sun Yat-sen meaning "comrades" in his nationalist revolution was later widely adopted in Chinese communist rhetoric. In 1989, Hong Kong avant-garde theatre director-writer Edward Lam started the city's first annual *Tongzhi dianying jie* [Lesbian and Gay Film Festival] and by historical contingency reappropriated the term *tongzhi* into another context for the cause of queer people. This Chinese term has now been commonly adopted across Hong Kong, Taiwan and the Mainland in referring to queer matters. "*Tongzhi*" should not be understood as a translation of "lesbian and gay," "homosexuals," or "queer." These terms have their various Chinese translations. The significance of *tongzhi* is that it is a locally invented sign for a local context. "The appropriation of the term '*tongzhi*' is so appropriate to its own cultural space and temporality. It implies a sense of revolutionary subversion and goes beyond the self-limitation and also repudiates the unequal power relation involved in the translation of an equivalent foreign term. The term 'fully grasps the local cultural context'" (Li Siu Leung 38). Chou Wah-shan has written extensively in Chinese on *tongzhi* issues. For an English reference, see his *Tongzhi: Politics of Same-Sex Eroticism in Chinese Societies* (2000). For a comprehensive collection of works by Edward Lam and writings about him, see his *Lin Yihua de xiju shijie* [The theatre world of Edward Lam] (2000). Rozanna Lilley's *Staging Hong Kong* (1998) includes a chapter on Edward Lam.

12　The two novels are collected in Zhou Jingshu, 483–665 and 666–750 respectively. For Zhao's use of male pronouns, see 726 passim; for Zhang's switching to female forms of address, see 605 passim.

13　For a detailed analysis of the construction of masculinity in China with special reference to the representation of the "scholar," see Song Geng's dissertation "The Fragile Scholar."

14　This is a transcription from the English audio track of the documentary film. I consulted the version aired on TVB (Television Broadcasts Ltd) which is bilingual. There is also a Cantonese audio track. Both Chinese and English subtitles are provided. The Chinese subtitles are transcriptions of the Cantonese track put in standard written Chinese. The English subtitles are translations of the Chinese subtitles. There are slight differences among all these renditions of the voice-over narrative of the documentary.

15 It should be pointed out here that the imposition of the modern notion of "gay and straight" and "homosexuality" on traditional Chinese culture is problematic. Put simply (after Foucault and the scholarship on sexuality that followed), these notions did not exist in imperial China, nor did they even exist in, for instance, early modern England. In focus here are modern reinterpretations and remakes of a traditional Chinese story, not what same-sex love really was in a certain historical moment in imperial China. In a different historical, cultural context, the Chinese did have other terms to refer to men whose sexual orientation was same-sex love: *duanxiu* [cut sleeve], *fentao* [shared peach], *longyang* [the Lord of Longyang], *nanse* [male color], *nanfeng* [southern custom], *tuzi* [rabbit], etc. But there were no terms on the opposite pole to form binaries. For recent discussions on the construction of same-sex love in imperial China in English, see Hinsch (chapter 1), Vitiello (chapter 1), Song Geng (chapter 5).

16 This featurette entitled *The Making of the Lovers* strangely misspelled the official English title of the musical play which should read "The Lover" without an "s," as seen in its press releases, advertisements and the house program. This significance of the omission of the "s" is discussed in the following text. This English featurette was aired on TVB (Television Broadcasts Ltd) Pearl on January 1, 1999.

17 See Kei Lo, "Dang Qu Yuan yushang tongzhi" [When Qu Yuan meets tongzhi] (*Xinbao* [Hong Kong Economic Journal] June 17, 1999: 32); Poon Kwok-sum, "Mozai feibang Qu Yuan" [Stop slandering Qu Yuan] (*Ming Pao* June 21, 1999: E4); Xiaomingxiong, "Tongzhi kan lishi tongzhi" [Tongzhi looking at historical tongzhi] (*Ming Pao* June 26, 1999: E4).

CHAPTER SIX

1 A color photograph is included in *Zhongguo da baike quanshu: xiqu, quyi* [The great Chinese encyclopedia: traditional music drama, folk musical art forms] (1983), illustrations p. 8; see also *Zhongguo xiquzhi: Shanxi juan* [Annals of Chinese music drama: Shanxi volume] (1990), color plate (not paginated). Shen Congwen's monumental *Zhongguo gudai fushi yanjiu* [Study of ancient Chinese costumes] (1981, 1992) contains a reconstructed color illustration (illustration 206, p. 434). Further photographic reprints of varied quality are found in Liao Ben's *Song Yuan xiqu wenwu yu minsu* [Cultural relics and folk custom of the music drama of Song and Yuan dynasties] (1989), color plate 31, and in Shih's *The Golden Age of Chinese Drama* — the frontispiece, a black and white reprint with some portion of the right margin cut off.

2   The wording of the two entries are almost identical. The one in *The Great Chinese Encyclopedia: Traditional Music Drama, Folk Musical Art Forms* was written by Liu Nianzi who also authored one of the first articles referring to the Yuan mural, "Yuan zaju yanchu xingshi de jidian chubu kanfa" [Some preliminary reflections on the performance practice in Yuan *zaju* theatre] in *Xiqu yanjiu* [Study in Chinese music drama] 2 (1957). Liu was also one of the contributing editors to *Annals of Chinese Music Drama: Shanxi Volume* (797). The entry in *Annals* is very likely adapted from the one in *The Great Chinese Encyclopedia*.

3   The bound feet, as a unique cultural sign in imperial China, were transformed onto the male transvestite stage through the nineteenth century and into the early twentieth century in the fetishistic prop of the *qiao*, a pair of tiny wooden shoes "put on" by some of the male *dan* role-types to emphasize the femininity of Chinese women. For a detailed study of the *qiao*, see Huang Yufu's *Jingju, qiao he Zhongguo de xingbie guanxie 1920–1937* [Chinese gender relations as seen through *qiao* in Peking opera (1902–1937)] (1998).

4   See Shen Congwen, illustration 137.2. For Khitan men with earrings, see also Shen Congwen, illustrations 121.1, 121.4, 121.5.

5   For instance, the Javanese *ludruk* plays in which the transvestite actor "deliberately reminds the audience that he is a man displaying the illusion of a woman" by clearing his throat "in a deep bass" (Peacock 212). In the traditional Iranian theatre called *ta'ziyeh*, "women are portrayed by males dressed in black cloaks similar to the green and red cloaks worn by men. . . . they also wear male trousers and shoes. . . . the 'women' are dressed in virtually the same type of costume as the males, with one exception: They also wear a thin facial veil. Their veil is translucent, allowing anyone to see that the actor is male and not a female. Moreover, the persons depicting women chant in their normal, identifiably male voices" (Beeman 18). In Balinese *Parwa* dance drama, apart from the inversions and reversals of the gender of the role and the gender of the role player, "[r]arely is the gender of the performer completely disguised" (Emigh and Hunt 196).

6   The role-types of *fujing* (or *jing*) and *fumo* played a major part in the theatrical performance of the Song *zaju* and Jin *yuanben*. They constituted an interdependent pair of comic roles. The *fujing* (*jing*) role-type of the Song-Jin times is said to be the forerunner of the *jing* (the painted face role-type) in later regional operas.

7   The two photographic reproductions are of approximately the size of 7.25"x 8.75" and the reconstructed picture 7.8" x 10". The original mural measures 4.11m x 3.11m (Liao 217).

CHAPTER SEVEN

1   Charlotte Furth's "Androgynous Men and Deficient Females: Biology
    and Gender Boundaries in Sixteenth- and Seventeenth-Century China"
    (1988) gives an account of the treatment of gender in important medical
    writings and notation books in Ming-Qing China. See also her *A
    Flourishing Yin* (1999). Judith Zeitlin draws on various notation books
    to illustrate attitudes toward gender ambiguity in these periods
    ("Dislocations in Gender," *Historian of the Strange: Pu Songling and the
    Chinese Classical Tale* [1993]).
2   There are many explications of *xing* in classical criticism. But my
    formulation here is indebted to a comparative study by Chou Ying-hsiung,
    "The Linguistic and Mythical Structure of *hsing* [*xing*] as a Combinational
    Model" (1980).
3   Quoted in Orgel, *The Illusion of Power* 42.
4   In their epoch-making study on Chinese history entitled *Xingsheng yu
    weiji* [Prosperity and crisis] (1984), Jin Guantao and Liu Qingfeng give
    insightful analyses of the interrelational functioning of imperial power
    and the bureaucratic system in the larger context of a social-economic-
    political system of subsystems in the Chinese feudal society, which they
    theorize as an ultra-stable system with a marvelous capacity for self-
    recovery and self-restoration.
5   For instance, Emperor Qianlong. One of the major entertainments in his
    several imperial inspection tours across the empire was Kunqu opera. In
    general, late Qing emperors and the Empress Dowager (who controlled
    the court from 1861 to her death in 1908) were very fond of watching
    Bejing opera.
6   I have an uneasy feeling about this statement by Earl Miner: "It is a very
    Chinese assumption, often shared by foreign students of China, that if
    something exists anywhere else it necessarily and thrivingly exists also in
    China" (60).
7   From the famous Ming play *Xiuru ji* [The embroidered shirt] written by
    Xu Lin (1462–1538). Some acts are retained and still performed in today's
    Kunju opera.
8   The first record is probably Jiao Xun's own, while the other three records
    are quoted from existing works.
9   Qin Hui lived at the turn of the Northern and Southern Song periods
    when the imperial dynasty of Han rule was under severe threat from
    foreign races. As minister, he set up and then executed the righteous and
    loyal general Yue Fei who had fought bravely against the Jin Dynasty, a
    foreign people who had taken over the northern part of China. In
    traditional Chinese culture, Yue Fei and Qin Hui have become the ultimate
    symbols of good and evil.

In Yuan drama, their story was told in *Qin taishi dongchuang shifan* [Minister Qin's conspiracy leaked out under the east window], a *zaju* which was lost and has been attributed to the playwright Jin Renjie (?– 1329) (Zhuang Yifu 1: 316–8) and also in an extant Ming edition of a *xiwen* play, also known as *nanxi* [southern drama] of the same title (1:51– 2). An extant Yuan *zaju* play on the same theme, entitled *Dizang wang zheng dongchuang shifan* [The Buddhist deity of salvation bears witness to the conspiracy under the east window] by Kong Wenqing of early Yuan, is collected in Xu Shusen's *Yuanqu xuan waibian* [Supplementary volumes to *Selected Yuan Plays*], vol. 2, and in *Yuan kan zaju sanshi zhong* [The Yuan dynasty edition of thirty *zaju* plays] (Xu Qinjun 2: 530–60; Ning Xiyuan 2: 82–97). The early Ming playwright Yao Maoliang's *Jingzhong ji* [Story of the loyal] is the play referred to in Jiao Xun's records. The most popular novel version of this story is the 80-chapter *Shuo Yue quanchuan* [The complete saga of Yue Fei] by the early Qing writer Qian Cai.

10 "The judge pitied him for his righteousness and reduced his penalty" (Jiao 203).

11 At the same time, the role of spectator in the production of meaning has been relatively neglected in theatre semiotics: "It is precisely this exclusion of 'audience passion' from studies of theatre semiotics that has generated a suspicion of its mode of inquiry as reductive, scientific, or somehow inappropriate to the nature of theatre . . . a semiotics of theatre needs to make space for its inclusion and write the spectator into the frame as an engaged, active receiver" (Aston and Savona 121–2).

12 "Once Chuang Chou dreamt he was a butterfly, a butterfly flitting and fluttering around, happy with himself and doing as he pleased. He didn't know he was Chuang Chou. Suddenly he woke up and there he was, solid and unmistakable Chuang Chou. But he didn't know if he was Chuang Chou who had dreamt he was a butterfly, or a butterfly dreaming he was Chuang Chou. Between Chuang Chou and a butterfly there must be *some* distinction! This is called the Transformation of Things" (Burton Watson's translation; *Chuang Tzu* 45; original emphasis). The passage is from the chapter "Qiwulun" [Discussion on making things equal].

13 These incidents of representations of reality relating to Chinese opera are perhaps more multivalent than our latest imaginations of the postmodern, Baudrillardian virtual reality in American popular culture. In the 1999 hit movie *The Matrix*, for instance, a "Welcome to the real world" is extended to Neo (Keanu Reeves) early in the narrative. Regardless of the dizzying CG effects and the innovative "bullet-time" editing, the real world and the simulated world of the "Matrix" in the film are nevertheless clearly distinguished.

14   This is taken from Wang Chi-chen's translation, entitled *Dream of the Red Chamber* (11). I chose this translation because it is literally closer to the original than the others. (David Hawkes and John Minford's acclaimed translation is entitled *The Story of the Stone* [New York: Penguin Books, 1973–86]. Yang Xianyi and Gladys Yang rendered it *A Dream of Red Mansions* [Beijing: Foreign Language Press, 1978–80].)

15   Xia Xieshi in his *Lun Zhongguo xiju piping* [On Chinese dramatic criticism] (1988) follows an "allegorical" reading of this incident of playacting and interprets it as a political comment (13–4).

16   Tang's most famous play *The Peony Pavilion* became the focus of an international controversy when in 1998 the scheduled performances of a modernized production of the play — which was a co-production of the Lincoln Center Festival, Festival d'Automne à Paris with Parc de la Villette and Théâtre de Caen, the Sydney Festival and the Hong Kong Arts Festival and performed by the Shanghai Kunju Opera Company — was blocked by Chinese cultural officials. The production was recast and finally had its premiere at the Lincoln Center Festival in New York, July 7–25, 1999.

17   See Xia Xieshi 31–124, especially 87–96. With regard to this concept of capturing the essence/psyche, let me draw on a piece of commentary comparing two of the most important Chinese opera performing artists who excelled in playing the Monkey King for further illustration. Yang Xiaolou (1878–1938), a Beijing opera military-male-role performer and Hao Zhenji (1870–1945), a Kunju opera painted-face player were the greatest Monkey King actors of their time. In 1933, an essay of theatre criticism in the newspaper *Yishi bao* compared the two in this way: "Xiaolou's monkey is still a human disguising as a monkey; Hao's is virtually a monkey disguising as a human" (Hou Yushan 214).

18   In classical Chinese writings on acting, there are plenty of statements that sound similar to Stanislavski's theory. The expression "putting oneself in the other's position" [*sheshen chudi*] is prevalent in the discussion of acting in traditional writings. To give another example, the eighteenth century critic Xu Dachun discusses singing/acting in these terms: "It is a must that the singer puts himself/herself in the position of what s/he is playing. Imitate that person's emotions and action, as if that person is speaking himself/herself. In this way, the verisimilitude in appearance will capture the audience's heart and mind, making the audience feel like facing that real person, forgetting that it is only a performance" (14). There is no doubt that Chinese acting theories also emphasize the performer's putting himself/herself in the position of whomever or whatever s/he is going to play. But this is where the similarity ends. The

epistemological conceptions and theatrical concerns are very different. We should also note that it is often the general types of characters with corresponding types of people-referents in the real world, not the specific individual characters in a play (the subject of Stanislavski's theory), that is being referred to. Further evidence for this argument is found in traditional writings about performers. They were always represented as good at playing certain role-types rather than individual characters (see *The Green Bower Collection*). This has undergone some changes nowadays. Inevitably influenced by Western culture in modern times, Chinese theatre criticism today does also identify a Chinese opera performer by the several dramatic characters s/he plays the best, in addition to focusing on her/his role-type's specialization. However, one should still bear in mind that on the traditional Chinese stage, individual characters tend to represent more of a type than an individual; for instance, the heroine Dou'e in the Yuan play *Injustice to Dou'e* has been read by some critics as an impersonation of morality more than a round individual character in the Western sense. For more discussion in English on the "psychological preparation" of the performer in Ming times, see Grant Shen 77–81.

19   In her analysis of the Takarazuka Revue using the concept of androgyny, Jennifer Robertson traces a similar concept in Japanese culture back to the classical theory of the Kabuki onnagata which "was a twist on the Buddhist concept of *henshin*, or bodily transformation or metamorphosis" (53). There are some common grounds for comparison between the Chinese and Japanese notions of "androgyny." This will require another full-length study.

20   There are records of incidents of sex transformation found in various classical Chinese writings from *Soushen ji* [Seeking the spirits] (from the fourth century) through official historical records to informal writings by the literati. For accounts in English, see Furth, "Androgynous Men and Deficient Females" and Zeitlin.

21   There are a number of contemporary critiques of the anti-theatrical debates in early modern England constituted by the writings of John Calvin, Stephen Gosson, the two treatises *Haec-Vir; or The Womanish Man* (1620) and *Hic Mulier; or The Man-Woman* (1620), John Rainoldes, William Prynnes, and Phillip Stubbes. See, for instance, Barish; Bray; Digangi; Goldberg; Jean Howard; Lisa Jardin; Kelly; Levine; Orgel; Rose; Shapiro; Shepherd; Bruce Smith; Stallybrass; Traub.

CHAPTER EIGHT

1   In the sense of Timothy J. Wiles. ". . . I refer to the creative interaction of literary text, actor's art, and spectator's participation as 'the theater event' " (3).

2   K . C. Leung's English translation (69). It is useful to note that it has been argued that "One of the primary themes in late-imperial Chinese representations of the actor is the rivalry between actor and *courtesan* for the ground of femininity. . . . As the appropriation of feminine names, feminine kinship terms, and allusions commonly used to describe *courtesans* implies, the discourse on male actors in late-imperial China is largely shaped by cultural icons of the feminine, and, in particular, the representation of *courtesans*" (Sophie Volpp 139; emphasis added).

3   "*Chuan*" literally means "to pass on and to spread." This generation of Kunqu performers, which totaled around 40 members at the beginning, were trained in the 1920s in Suzhou when the art form was dying in southern cities. They sustained the existence of the art form and have taught subsequent generations of Kunqu artists. Many students of the *chuan* generation masters are core and active performers today. For a quick overview, see Hu Ji and Liu Zhizhong 649-66, 684-711.

4   Jo Riley's expression (298). She also structured her book *Chinese Theatre and the Actor in Performance* (1997) following this principle of *yuan*: ". . . the eight chapters of this work could be read in any direction. All routes pass the central, unifying figure of Mei Lanfang. The passage across the work is not intended to be linear, but multi-layered, interconnected, like a spider's web" (11).

5   To translate the qualities of *caoshu* into musical terms, the renowned composer Chou Wen-chung wrote an avant-garde piece for flute and piano entitled "Cursive" (New York: C. F. Peters, 1965) which makes use of microtones and key-tapping on the flute and prepared piano to express the cursive concept.

CHAPTER NINE

1   Both of them have often been invited to perform outside China. Hong Kong Chinese opera-goers are familiar with their art. Not limiting herself to the traditional form, Shi Xiaomei recently participated in a multi-media music theatrical production by the avant-garde Hong Kong theater company Zuni Icosahedron, "Sigmund Freud in Search of Chinese Matter and Mind", which ran from February 1 to 3, 2002 at the Hong Kong City Hall Theatre.

2   Some of these actresses have ventured into film roles. For instance, He Saifei of the Zhejiang Xiaobaihua Yueju Opera Troupe starred in Zhang

Yimou's film *Raise the Red Lantern* (1991) as the third wife of the master of the House of Chen.

3   I am indebted to Mr Wen Ruhua for granting me interviews with him and providing various materials about his career for my present discussion. For quick reference, I provide a brief chronology of Mr Wen here:

1958/11 years: Entered the National Chinese Opera School, graduated in 1966 (19 years old), specializing in the *sheng* role-type.

1959/12 years: Captivated by a performance by Zhang Junqiu, began privately imitating his *dan* style.

1965/18 years: Learning the performance of the male *dan* from Zhang as a private student, since the School did not allow the male *dan* to be taught or learned.

1968-1972:   The Cultural Revolution, "re-education" at a military farm [*junqu nongchang*].

1972/25 years: Assigned to the Comrades-in-Arms Beijing Opera Troupe of the Beijing Military Region [*Zhanyou jingju tuan*], turned to composing, scripting and producing, mainly working on model dramas.

1979/32 years: Performed *Wangjiang ting*, a Zhang school play.

1980/33 years: Performed *Chunqiu pei*, another Zhang school play, "officially" began his artistic career. Renowned Chinese opera personality and playwright Weng Ouhong regarded him highly and supported him.

1982/35 years: Reassigned to the Beijing Opera Company of the City of Beijing. Weng Ouhong wrote the play *Baimian langjun* [The fair-faced gentleman] for him, the story of a man who disguises himself as a woman to save his wife from villains. The role-type of the leading actor of this play is assigned to the *sheng*, Wen's "official" role-type specialization. But the male lead appears as a woman and performs in the *dan* style for most of the play.

1984/37 years: More than forty shows of *The Fair-faced Gentleman* were staged, signifying the revival of the male *dan*. Received a certificate of merit in the capacity of a *sheng* performer from the Cultural Bureau of the City of Beijing.

1985/38 years: National tour from Urumqi in the West to Harbin in the East.

1988/41 years: Invited to perform in Japan. Acclaimed as "a third generation Mei Lanfang" by *Asahi Shimbun*.

1991/44 years: On stage in Japan together with Kabuki actors. Recorded the Chinese opera tunes for the film *Farewell My Concubine*.

1993/45 years: Performed in Japan.

1994/46 years: Performed in Taiwan. In Beijing doubled for the male lead in the television serial *Mei Lanfang* as the on stage Mei Lanfang.

1995/48 years: *The Fair-faced Gentleman* was produced for CCTV television.

1996/49 years: Premiered a new play *Qiunü zhuan* [Story of Damsel Qiu] on December 8, 1996, publicly promoted as "the last male *dan* actor in professional Beijing opera troupes nationwide."

1998/51: Participated in performances in memorial of Zhang Junqiu.

1999/52: An article in *Beijing gongren bao* [Beijing Workers' Daily] (June 3) was entitled "Wen Ruhua: China's Last Female Impersonator." *Story of Damsel Qiu* was produced for television by CCTV.

2001/54 years: Released *Wen Ruhua changqiangji* [The Wen Ruhua aria collection] on CD and cassette on the CRC label. Gave three lectures at the City University of Hong Kong, hosted by the University's Centre of Chinese Culture. Staged two special performances [*zhuanchang*] at Changan Theatre in Beijing. A report (attributed to a Wang Yao) in Hong Kong's *Ming Pao Daily* carried the title "The Last Male Impersonator."

4   The original couplet comes from the finale chorus of Scene 2, Act 5 of the play (*Baimao nü* 467), written by He Jingzhi and Ding Yi, music by Ma Ke, et al.

5   See *Zhou Enlai tongzhi qingnian shiqi zai Tianjin de xiju huodong ziliao huibian* [A collection of information on comrade Zhou Enlai's theatre activities in Tianjin in his youthful years] (1981), 76–102, for the synopsis and stage photos. Zhou Enlai is identified in three of the photos, dressed in female dramatic costume.

EPILOGUE

1   We can compare this to what Greenblatt says about representation and "self-fashioning": " . . . self-fashioning derives its interest precisely from the fact that it functions without regard for a sharp distinction between literature and social life. It invariably crosses the boundaries between the creation of literary characters, the shaping of one's own identity, the experience of being molded by forces outside one's control, the attempt to fashion other selves" (3).

BIBLIOGRAPHY

Chinese and Japanese Sources

An'le Shanqiao 安樂山樵 (pseud.) (Qing). *Yanlan xiaopu* 燕蘭小譜 [Manual of orchids. 1786. *Qing dai yandu liyuan shiliao zhengxubian*. Ed. Zhang Cixi. Vol. 1. Bejing: Zhongguo xiju chubanshe, 1988.1–52.

Aoki Masaru 青木正兒. *Zhongguo jinshi xiqu shi* 中國近世戲曲史 [History of Chinese music drama in recent centuries]. 2 vols. 1931. Trans. Wang Jilu 王吉廬. Taipei: Commercial Press, 1965.

Bawang bieji 霸王別姬 [Hegemon king says farewell to the concubine]. *Xikao daquan* 戲考大全 [Great collection of plays]. 1915–25. Shanghai: Shanghai shudian, 1990. Vol. 3: 591–6. [Beijing opera script; a version of Mei Lanfang's]

——. Ed. Wei Lianfang. Transcribed by Li Junfang. Musical notation by Shen Yanxi and Gu Yongxiang. Shanghai: Shanghai wenyi chubanshe, 1987. [Beijing opera score; a version of Mei Lanfang's]

——. Performance script. Beijing beifang Kunqu juyuan [Beijing Northern Kunqu Opera Company]. Stencil print. c. 1987.

Beijing shi yishu yanjiusuo 北京市藝術研究所 and Shanghai yishu yanjiusuo 上海藝術研究所, eds. *Zhongguo Jingju shi* 中國京劇史 [History of China's Beijing opera]. Vols. 1 and 2. Beijing: Zhongguo xiju chubanshe, 1991.

Bieji 別姬. Performance script. Beijing beifang Kunqu juyuan [Beijing Northern Kunqu Opera Company]. Stencil print. Dated July 29, 1987. [A version passed on by Hou Yushan]

Bimeng xu 筆夢敘 [Records of dreams] (Ming). *Biji xiaoshuo daguan* 筆記小說大觀 [Grand collection of notation books and fiction]. Ser. 5, Vol. 6. Taipei: Xinxing shuju, 1974. 3231–48.

Cai Yi 蔡毅, ed. *Zhongguo gudian xiqu xuba huibian* 中國古典戲曲序跋匯編 [Collection of prefaces and afterwords to classical Chinese music drama]. 4 vols. Jinan: Qilu shushe, 1989.

Chao Tsung 趙聰. *Zhongguo dalu de xiqu gaige: 1942–1967* 中國大陸的戲曲改革1942–1967 [Traditional music drama reform in mainland China: 1942–1967]. Hong Kong: The Chinese University of Hong Kong Press, 1969.

Chen Duansheng 陳端生 (1751–1796). *Zaisheng yuan* 再生緣 [Love of a life reborn]. 3 vols. Ed. Liu Chongyi. Henan: Zhongzhou shuhuashe, 1982.

Chen Sen 陳森 (Qing). *Pinhua baojian* 品花寶鑑 [Precious mirror of ranking flowers]. 2 vols. 1837–49. Beijing: Baowen tang shudian, 1989.

Chen Weiyu 陳為瑀. *Kunju zhezixi chutan* 崑劇折子戲初探 [A preliminary survey of the select-scene plays in Kunju opera]. Zhengzhou: Zhongzhou guji chubanshe, 1991.

Cheng Fuwang 成复旺, Cai Zhongxiang 蔡鐘翔, and Huang Baozhen 黃保真. *Zhongguo wenxue lilunshi* 中國文學理論史 [History of Chinese literary theory]. 3 vols. Beijing: Beijing chubanshe, 1987.

Cui Lingqin 崔令欽 (Tang). *Jiaofang ji* 教坊記 [An account of the Music Academy]. *Zhongguo gudian xiqu lunzhu jicheng*. Vol. 1. Beijing: Zhongguo xiju chubanshe, 1959. 3–30.

Dai Zheng 戴爭. *Zhongguo gudai fushi jianshi* 中國古代服飾簡史 [A short history of ancient Chinese costumes]. Taipei: Nantian shuju, 1992.

Du Mu 都穆 (1458–1525). *Du gong tan cuan* 都公談纂 [Chats by Master Du]. Changsha: Commercial Press, 1937.

Duan Anjie 段安節 (Tang). *Yuefu zalu* 樂府雜錄 [Miscellaneous notes on *yuefu* songs]. *Zhongguo gudian xiqu lunzhu jicheng*. Vol. 1. Beijing: Zhongguo xiju chubanshe, 1959. 33–89.

Feng Menglong 馮夢龍 (1574–1646). *Taiping guangji chao* 太平廣記鈔 [Selections from *Anthology of Widely Gathered Accounts in the Taiping Era*]. Prefaced 1626. *Juan* 72, "Renyao" 人妖 [Human prodigies]. Henan: Zhongzhou shuhuashe, 1982. Vol. 3: 1910–32.

Feng Yuanjun 馮沅君. "Guju sikao" 古劇四考 [Four investigations on ancient drama]. *Song Yuan Ming Qing xiqu yanjiu luncong* 宋元明清戲曲研究論叢 [Collection of studies on Song Yuan Ming Qing music drama]. Vol. 2. 1936. Ed. Cuncui xueshe. Hong Kong: Dadong tushu gongsi, 1979. 79–90.

Fung Tze 馮梓. *Fang Yenfen zhuan ji qi xiqu yishu* 芳艷芬傳及其戲曲藝術 [The biography of Fong Yim-fan and her art of Chinese opera]. Hong Kong: Holdery Publishing Enterprises, 1998.

Gao Yilong 高義龍. *Yueju shihua* 越劇史話 [An informal history of Yueju]. Shanghai: Shanghai wenyi chubanshe, 1991.

Gao Yilong and Li Xiao 李曉. *Zhongguo xiqu xiandaixi shi* 中國戲曲現代戲史 [History of Chinese music drama in modern themes]. Shanghai: Shanghai wenhua chubanshe, 1999.

Gu Duhuang 顧篤璜. *Kunju shi bulun* 崑劇史補論 [Supplementary discussions on the history of Kunju]. Jiangsu: Jiangsu guji chubanshe, 1987.

Gu Qiyuan 顧起元(Ming). *Kezuo quyu* 客坐曲語 [Words on music drama with guests]. *Xinquyuan*. Vol. 2. Ed. Ren Zhongmin. Shanghai: Zhonghua shuju, 1940.

Hang Kan 杭侃. *Liao, Xia, Jin, Yuan: caoyuan diguo de rongyao* 遼夏金元：草原帝國的榮耀 [Liao, Xia, Jin, Yuan: glory of the empires of the steppes]. Hong Kong: Commercial Press, 2001.

Hatano Kan'ichi 波多野乾一. *Jingju erbai nian zhi lishi* 京劇二百年之歷史 [Two hundred years of history of Beijing opera]. 1926. Trans. Luyuan Xueren 鹿原學人. *Pingju shiliao congkan* 平劇史料叢刊 [Beijing opera historical material series]. Eds. Liu Shaotang and Shen Weichuang. 1933. Taipei: Zhuanji wenxue chubanshe, 1974.

He Jingzhi 賀敬芝 and Ding Yi 丁毅. *Baimao nü* 白毛女. Music by Ma Ke 馬可, et al. *Yan'an wenyi congshu diba juan: geju juan* 延安文藝叢書第八卷：歌劇卷 [The Yan'an literature and art series, vol. 8: music drama]. Changsha: Hunan wenyi chubanshe, 1987.

"Hongdong Mingyingwangdian Yuan zaju bihua" 洪洞明應王殿元雜
劇壁畫 [The Yuan drama mural of the Hall of Mingyingwang in
Hongdong county]. *Zhongguo da baike quanshu: xiqu, quyi.*
Shanghai: Zhongguo da baike quanshu chubanshe, 1983. 117.

"Hongdong Mingyingwangdian Yuan zaju bihua" 洪洞明應王殿元雜
劇壁畫 [The Yuan drama mural of the Hall of Mingyingwang in
Hongdong county]. *Zhongguo xiquzhi: Shanxi juan.* Beijing:
Wenhua yishu chubanshe, 1990. 583–4.

Hou Yushan 侯玉山 (1893–1998). *Hou Yushan Kunqu pu* 侯玉山崑
曲譜 [The Kunqu music and script as passed on by Hou Yushan].
Beijing: Zhongguo xiju chubanshe, 1994.

——. *Youmeng yiguan bashinian* 優孟衣冠八十年 [An acting career of
eighty years]. Ed. Liu Dongsheng. Beijing: Baowen tong shudian,
1988.

Hu Ji 胡忌. "Beiqu zaju yanchangren xingbie de taolun" 北曲雜劇演
唱人性別的討論 [On the gender of the singers in northern *zaju*
drama]. *Wenxue yichan zengkan* 文學遺產增刊 [Literary heritage
supplementary series]. Vol. 1. Beijing: Zuojia chubanshe, 1955.
297–303.

Hu Ji 胡忌 and Liu Zhizhong 劉致中. *Kunju fazhanshi* 崑劇發展史
[History of Kunju opera]. Beijing: Zhongguo xiju chubanshe, 1989.

Hu Wenkai 胡文楷. *Lidai funü zhuzuokao* 歷代婦女著作考 [Study
of women's writings in past eras]. Shanghai: Shanghai Commercial
Press, 1957.

Hu Yinglin 胡應麟 (1551–1602). *Shaoxishanfang qukao* 少室山房曲
考 [Jottings on music drama from the Mountain Study with Few
Rooms]. *Xinquyuan.* Vol. 2. Ed. Ren Zhongmin. Shanghai:
Zhonghua shuju, 1940.

Hu Zhiyu 胡祇遹 (1227–1293). *Zishan daquan ji* 紫山大全集
[Complete works of Hu Zhiyu]. *Juan 8. Wenyuan ge siku quanshu
jibu 135 biji lei* 文淵閣四庫全書集部135筆記類. Taipei: Taiwan
Commercial Press. Vol. 1196.

Huang Shang 黃裳. "Liang Zhu zaji" 梁祝雜記 [Miscellaneous notes
on the Liang-Zhu dramas]. *Xixiang ji yu Baishe zhuan* 西廂記與
白蛇傳 [*West Wing* and *White Snake*]. Shanghai: Pingming
chubanshe, 1953. 64–103.

—— . "Lu Xun xiansheng dui xiqu de yixie yijian" 魯迅先生對戲曲的
一些意見 [Mr Lu Xun's comments on Chinese music drama].
Xixiang ji yu Baishe zhuan [*West Wing* and *White Snake*].
Shanghai: Pingming chubanshe, 1953. 127–33.

Huang Shilong 黃士龍. *Zhongguo fushi shilüe* 中國服飾史略 [A brief
history of Chinese costumes]. Shanghai: Shanghai wenhua
chubanshe, 1994.

Huang Wenyang 黃文暘 (Qing). *Quhai zongmu tiyao* 曲海總目提要
[Synopses for *The Comprehensive Bibliography of Plays*]. 3 vols.
Ed. Tong Kang. Taipei: Xinxing shuju, 1967.

Huang Yufu 黃育馥. *Jingju, qiao he Zhongguo de xingbie guanxie
1902–1937* 京劇，蹺和中國的性別關係 1902–1937 [Chinese
gender relations as seen through *qiao* in Peking opera (1902–
1937)]. Beijing: Sanlian shudian, 1998.

Huanmen zidi cuo lishen 宦門子弟錯立身 [The wrong career of an
official's son]. *Yongle dadian xiwen sanzhong jiaozhu* 永樂大典戲
文三種校注 [An annotation of three *xiwen* plays from the *Yongle
Canon*]. Ed. Qian Nanyang. Beijing: Zhonghua shuju, 1979. 219–
55.

Hujiazhuang 扈家莊 [Hu's manor]. *Jingju huibian* 京劇匯編 [A corpus
of Beijing operas]. Compiled by Beijing shi xiqu biandao
weiyuanhui. Vol. 19. Beijing: Beijing chubanshe, 1957. 21–30.

Ji Yun 紀昀 (1724–1805). *Yuewei caotang biji* 閱微草堂筆記 [Notes
from the Thatched Cottage of Careful Reading]. *Biji xiaoshuo
daguan bupian* 筆記小説大觀補篇 [Grand collection of notation
books and fiction, the supplementary series]. Vol. 10. Taipei:
Xinxing shuju, 1973. 5782–937.

Jiang Ruizao 蔣瑞藻. *Xiaoshuo kaozheng* 小説考証 [Studies on fiction
and drama]. Shanghai: Commercial Press, 1919.

Jiang Xingyu 蔣星煜. "Lu Xun xiansheng lun Mei Lanfang — lüelun
'Lüelun Mei Lanfang ji qita'" 魯迅先生論梅蘭芳 —— 略論〈略
論梅蘭芳及其他〉 [Mr Lu Xun on Mei Lanfang — brief comments
on 'Brief comments on Mei Lanfang and other topics']. *Zhongguo
xiqushi suoyin* 中國戲曲史索隱 [Investigations in history of Chinese
music drama]. Jinan: Qilu shushe, 1988. 227–234.

Jiao Xun 焦循(1763–1820). *Jushuo* 劇説 [Discourse on drama]. *Zhongguo gudian xiqu lunzhu jicheng*. Vol. 8. Beijing: Zhongguo xiju chubanshe, 1959. 73–220.

Jin Guantao 金觀濤, and Liu Qingfeng 劉青峰. *Xingsheng yu weiji* 興盛與危機 [Prosperity and crisis]. 1984. Taipei: Fengyu shidai chuban gongsi, 1989.

Lam Yik-wah, Edward 林奕華, *Lin Yihua de xiju shijie* 林奕華的戲劇世界 [The theatre world of Edward Lam]. Hong Kong: Chen Mi Ji, 2000.

Li Diaoyuan 李調元 (Qing). *Juhua* 劇話 [Discourse on drama]. c. 1775. *Zhongguo gudian xiqu lunzhu jicheng*. Vol. 8. Beijing: Zhongguo xiju chubanshe, 1959. 31–72.

Li Dou 李斗 (Qing). *Aitang qulu* 艾塘曲錄 [Aitang's records of drama] (from *Yangzhou huafang lu* 揚州畫舫錄 [Records from the decorated pleasure-boat of Yangzhou]). 1792. *Xinquyuan*. Vol. 5. Ed. Ren Zhongmin. Shanghai: Zhonghua shuju, 1940.

Li Siu Leung 李小良. "'Tongzhi' huayu yu shenfen zhengzhi" "同志" 話語與身份政治 ["Queer" discourse and identity politics]. *Hong Kong Cultural Studies Bulletin* 香港文化研究 2 (April 1995): 38–40.

Li Yanshou 李延壽 (Tang). *Nanshi* 南史 [History of the Southern Dynasties]. 6 vols. Beijing: Zhonghua shuju, 1975.

Li Yu 李漁 (1611–1680). *Xianqing ouji* 閑情偶寄 [Casual notes jotted in leisure times]. *Zhongguo gudian xiqu lunzhu jicheng*. Vol. 7. Beijing: Zhongguo xiju chubanshe, 1959. 1–114.

Li Zhaogan 李兆淦. "Zhejiang gudai de nüjuzuojia" 浙江古代的女劇作家 [Women playwrights from Zhejiang in ancient times]. *Zhejiang xiquzhi ziliao huibian* 浙江戲曲誌資料匯編. Vol. 2. Ed. *Zhongguo xiqu zhi Zhejiang juan bianjibu*. 1985. 152–5.

Li Zhiyan 李之言. "Zhonguo Jingju nandan yishu" 中國京劇男旦藝術 ("Chinese Actors Playing Female Role in Beijing Opera"). *Shanghai hangkong hangji zazhi* 上海航空航機雜誌 (*SAL Inflight Magazine*) 7 (July 1990): 46–7.

Liang Shanbo yu Zhu Yingtai 梁山伯與祝英台 [Liang Shanbo and Zhu Yingtai]. Adapted by Xu Jin, et al. Beijing: Zuojia chubanshe, 1954. [Zhejiang Yueju opera script]

——. Adapted by Xu Jin, et al. Shanghai: Shanghai wenyi chubanshe, 1962. [Zhejiang Yueju opera script]

Liao Ben 廖奔. *Song Yuan xiqu wenwu yu minsu* 宋元戲曲文物與民俗 [Cultural relics and folk custom of the music drama of Song and Yuan dynasties]. Beijing: Wenhua yishu chubanshe, 1989.

Liji: yueji 禮記：樂記 (Han). *Liji Zheng zhu* 禮記鄭注 [Book of ritual with Zheng's annotations]. *Juan* 11. Annotated by Zheng Xuan (127–200). Taipei: Xinxing shuju, 1964.

Liu Dalin 劉達臨. *Zhongguo gudai xingwenhua* 中國古代性文化 [The sex culture of ancient China]. 2 vols. Yinchuan: Ningxia renmin chubanshe, 1993.

——. *Zhonghua xingxue cidian* 中華性學辭典 [A Chinese sexology dictionary]. Harbin: Heilongjiang renmin chubanshe, 1993.

——. *Zhongguo wuqiannian xingwenwu daguan* 中國五千年性文物大觀 (*Chinese Sex Artifacts Over 5000 Years*). Hong Kong: Ming Pao Publications, 2000. [A Chinese-English bilingual publication]

Liu Nianzi. 劉念茲 "Yuan zaju yanchu xingshi de jidian chubu kanfa — Mingyingwangdian Yuandai xiju bihua diaocha zhaji" 元雜劇演出形式的幾點初步看法 —— 明應王殿元代戲劇壁畫調查札記 [Some preliminary reflections on the performance practice in Yuan *zaju* theatre — notes on the investigation of the Hall of Mingyingwan wall paintings]. *Xiqu yanjiu* [Music drama studies] 2 (1957): 66–85.

Liu Liren 劉立仁. "Yishi xiongsheng qing qunfang: ji Wen Ruhua" 一試雄聲擎群芳：記溫如華 [An utterance of the male voice props up all flowers: notes on Wen Ruhua]. *Beijing ribao* 北京日報 [Beijing Daily] May 30, 1997. 7.

Liu Shu 劉昫 (Later Jin), et al. *Jiu Tang shu* 舊唐書 [Old Tang history]. 941–5. 16 vols. Shanghai: Zhonghua shuju, 1975.

Liu Wu-chi 柳無忌. "Guanyu yige yuandai juzuojia de xingbie wenti" 關于一個元代劇作家的性別問題 [Concerning the gender of a Yuan playwright]. 1957. *Song Yuan Ming Qing xiqu yanjiu luncong* 宋元明清戲曲研究論叢 [Collection of studies on Song Yuan Ming Qing music drama]. Vol. 2. 1936. Ed. Cuncui xueshe. Hong Kong: Dadong tushu gongsi, 1979. 246–7.

Liu Yang 劉陽. "Dangjin nandan diyiren: caixie Wen Ruhua" 當今男旦第一人：采寫溫如華 [The number one male *dan* today: an interview with Wen Ruhua]. *Kuashiji* 跨世紀 [Across centuries] 37 (May 1996): 42–3. [Zhengzhou, Henan]

Liuyin ji 柳蔭記 [In the shade of willows]. *Diyijie quanguo xiqu guanmo yanchu dahui xiqu jubanxuan* 第一屆全國戲曲觀摩演出大會戲曲劇本選 [Selected plays from the first national festival of traditional music drama]. 2 vols. Ed. Zhongguo xiju jia xiehui. Beijing: Renmin wenxue chubanshe, 1953. Vol. 1: 251–310. [Chuanju opera script]

Lu Can 陸燦 (1494–1551). *Gengsi bian* 庚巳編 [The Gengsi compendium]. *Biji xiaoshuo daguan* 筆記小說大觀 [Grand collection of notation books and fiction]. Ser. 16, Vol. 5. Taipei: Xinxing shuju, 1977. 2545–656.

Lu Eting 陸萼庭. *Kunju yanchu shigao* 崑劇演出史稿 [Performance history of Kunju opera]. Shanghai: Shanghai wenyi chubanshe, 1980.

Lu Gong 路工. *Liang Zhu gushi shuochangji* 梁祝故事說唱集 [A collection of musical-narratives on the Liang-Zhu story]. Shanghai: Shanghai chuban gongsi, 1955.

Lu Rong 陸容 (1436–1494). *Shuyuan zaji* 菽園雜記 [The Shu garden miscellany]. 2 vols. Taipei: Commercial Press, 1965.

Lü Mingkang. 呂銘康. "Jingju nandan chuyi" 京劇男旦芻議 [My humble opinion on the male *dan*]. *Qingdao ribao* 青島日報 [Qingdao Daily] January 31, 1997. 10.

Lü Tiancheng 呂天成 (Ming). *Qupin* 曲品 [Criticism of music drama]. Prefaced 1610. *Zhongguo gudian xiqu lunzhu jicheng*. Vol. 6. Beijing: Zhongguo xiju chubanshe, 1959. 202–63.

Lu Xun 魯迅 (1881–1936). "Lüelun Mei Lanfang ji qita" 略論梅蘭芳及其他 [Brief comments on Mei Lanfang and other topics]. 2 parts. *Lu Xun quanji* 魯迅全集 [Complete works of Lu Xun]. Vol. 5. Beijing: Renmin wenxu chubanshe, 1973. 637–41.

——. "Zui yishu de guojia" 最藝術的國家 [The most artistic country]. 1933. *Lu Xun quanji* 魯迅全集. Vol. 4. Beijing: Renmin wenxu chubanshe, 1973. 503–5.

Ma Shaobo 馬少波. See *Mulan congjun*.

Mei Lanfang 梅蘭芳 (1894–1961). *Mei Lanfang wenji* 梅蘭芳文集 [Writings by Mei Lanfang]. Ed. Zhongguo xiju jia xiehui. Beijing: Zhongguo xiju chubanshe, 1962.

——. *Wutai shenghuo sishinian* 舞台生活四十年 [A stage career of forty years]. Beijing: Zhongguo xiju chubanshe, 1987.

Menghua suobu 夢華瑣簿 [Trivial records of reverie]. 1842. *Qingdai yandu liyuan shiliao zhengxubian* Ed. Zhang Cixi. Vol. 1. Beijing: Zhongguo xiju chubanshe, 1988. 347–81.

Mixitu daguan 秘戲圖大觀 [Grand view of paintings of the clandestine game]. Taipei: Jinfeng chuban youxian gongsi, 1994.

Mulan congjun 木蘭從軍 [Mulan joins the army]. *Xikao daquan* 戲考 大全 [Great collection of plays]. 1915–25. Vol. 4. Shanghai: Shanghai shudian, 1990. Vol. 4. 571–94. [Beijing opera script; a version of Mei Lanfang's]

——. Adapted by Ma Shaobo. Rev. ed. Shanghai: Shangza chubanshe, 1952. [Beijing opera script]

Ning Xiyuan 寧希元, ed. *Yuankan zaju sanshizhong xinjiao* 元刊雜劇 三十種新校 [The Yuan dynasty edition of thirty *zaju* plays: a newly revised edition]. 2 vols. Lanzhou: Lanzhou University Press, 1988.

Ouyang Xiu 歐陽修 (1007–1072) and Song Qi 宋祁 (998–1061), eds. *Xin Tang shu* 新唐書 [New Tang history]. 20 vols. Shanghai: Zhonghua shuju, 1975.

Pan Zhiheng 潘之恒(1556–1622). *Pan Zhiheng quhua* 潘之恒曲話 [Discourses on music drama by Pan Zhiheng]. Beijing: Zhongguo xiju chubanshe, 1988.

Qi Gong 啟功. "Lun Yuandai zaju de banyan wenti" 論元代雜劇的扮 演問題 [A discussion of the question of impersonation in Yuan theatre]. *Wenxue yichan zengkan* 文學遺產增刊 [Literary heritage supplementary series]. Vol. 1. Beijing: Zuojia chubanshe, 1955. 286–96.

Qian Facheng 錢發成, ed. *Zhongguo Yueju* 中國越劇 [China's Yueju opera]. Zhejiang: Zhejiang renmin chubanshe, 1989.

Qian Nanyang 錢南揚, ed. *Liang-Zhu xiju jicun* 梁祝戲劇輯存 [A collection of extant Liang-Zhu dramas]. Shanghai: Shanghai gudian wenxue chuban she, 1956.

——. "Song Jin Yuan xiju banyin kao" 宋金元戲劇搬演考 [Study of theatrical staging in the Song, Jin and Yuan dynasties]. 1936. *Song Yuan Ming Qing xiqu yanjiu luncong* 宋元明清戲曲研究論叢 [Collection of studies on Song Yuan Ming Qing music drama]. Vol. 2. Ed. Cuncui xueshe. Hong Kong: Dadong tushu gongsi, 1979. 49–66.

Qian Yong 錢泳(Qing). *Lüyuan conghua* 履園叢話 [Collected chats of Lüyuan]. *Biji xiaoshuo daguan* 筆記小説大觀 [Grand collection of notation books and fiction]. Ser. 1, Vol. 7. Taipei: Xinxing shuju, 1973. 2541–3270.

Qinhuai moke 秦淮墨客 (pseud.) (Ming). *Yangjiafu yanyi* 楊家府演義 (*Yangjia fu shidai zhongyong yanyi zhuan* 楊家府世代忠勇演義 傳) [Chivalric stories of several generations of the Yang family generals]. Prefaced 1606. Shanghai: Shanghai guji chubanshe, 1980.

Ren Zhongmin 任中敏, ed. *Quhai yangbo* 曲海揚波 [An extensive collection of writings on music drama]. *Xinquyuan* 新曲苑. Vol. 10–12. Shanghai: Zhonghua shuju, 1940.

Shen Cai 沈采 (Ming). *Qianjin ji* 千金記 [The thousand pieces of gold]. *Liushizhong qu* 六十種曲 [Sixty plays]. Vol. 2. Ed. Mao Jin (Ming). Beijing: Zhonghua shuju, 1958. 1–154.

——. *Qianjin ji* 千金記. *Jicheng qupu (yuji)* 集成曲譜（玉集）[A collection of Kunqu opera music: jade volume]. 1925. Vol. 5. Eds. Wang Jilie and Liu Fuliang. Taipei: Jixue shuju, 1969. 583–615.

Shen Congwen 沈從文, ed. *Zhongguo gudai fushi yanjiu* 中國古代服 飾研究 [Study of ancient Chinese costumes]. 1981. Revised edition. Hong Kong: Commercial Press, 1992.

Shengxian wenhuaju 嵊縣文化局, ed. *Zaoqi Yueju fazhanshi* 早期越 劇發展史 [The early history of Yueju]. Zhejiang: Zhejiang renmin chubanshe, 1983.

Shi Fang 石方. *Zhongguo xingwenhua shi* 中國性文化史 [History of Chinese sex culture]. Harbin: Heilongjiang renmin chubanshe, 1993.

Shi Nai'an 施耐庵 (c. 1296-c. 1370). *Yibai ershi hui de shuihu* 一百二 十回的水滸 [Water margin: the 120-chapter version]. 3 vols. Hong Kong: Commercial Press, 1969.

Shi Weimin 史衞民. *Yuandai shehui shenghuo shi* 元代社會生活史 [History of social life in the Yuan dynasty]. Beijing: Zhongguo shehui kexue chubanshe, 1996.

Sima Qian 司馬遷 (c. 145–c. 85 B.C.E.). *Shiji* 史記 [Records of the historian]. 10 vols. Hong Kong: Zhonghua shuju, 1969.

Tan Fan 譚帆 and Lu Wei 陸煒. *Zhongguo gudian xiju lilunshi* 中國古典戲劇理論史 [History of classical Chinese dramatic theory]. Beijing: Zhongguo shehui kexue chubanshe, 1993.

Tang Laihe 湯來賀 (Ming). "Liyuan shuo" 梨園説 [Chats on the theatre]. *Gujin tushu jicheng* 古今圖書集成 [The comprehensive collection of books past and present]. 1726. Vol. 48. *Juan* 816. "Youling bu" [Section on stage players]. Taipei: Dingwen shuju, 1977. 8531.

T'ang Wen-piao 唐文標. *Zhongguo gudai xiju shigao* 中國古代戲劇史稿 [History of ancient Chinese theatre]. Taipei: Lianjing chuban shiye gongsi, 1984.

Tang Xianzu 湯顯祖 (1550–1617). "Yihuangxian xishen Qingyuanshi miaoji" 宜黃縣戲神清源師廟記 [The record of theatre-god master Qingyuan's temple in Yihuang county]. *Tang Xianzu shiwen ji* 湯顯祖詩文集 [Collected poetry and prose of Tang Xianzu]. Vol. 2. Ed. Xu Shuofang. Shanghai: Shanghai guji chubanshe, 1982. 1127–8.

Tao Qiuying 陶秋英. *Zhongguo funü yu wenxue* 中國婦女與文學 [Chinese women and literature]. c. 1931. Taipei: Landeng chubanshe, 1980.

Tao Zongyi 陶宗儀 (1316–1403). *Chuogeng lu* 輟耕錄 [Records after ceasing to plow]. *Biji xiaoshuo daguan* 筆記小説大觀 [Grand collection of notation books and fiction]. Ser. 7, Vol. 1. Taipei: Xinxing shuju, 1975. 257–752.

Tiangang zhen 天罡陣 [The Big Dipper battle formation]. Performance script, Beijing beifang Kunqu juyuan [Beijing Northern Kunqu Opera Company]. Stencil print. Dated July 16, 1989.

To Kwok-wai, Raymond 杜國威. *Liang Zhu* 梁祝 [The story of Liang Shanbo and Zhu Yingtai]. Hong Kong: Wenlin she, 1999.

Tseng Yung-i 曾永義. "Nan ban nüzhuang yu nü ban nanzhuang" 男扮女裝與女扮男裝 [Male to female and female to male impersonation]. *Shuo xiqu* 説戲曲 [On Chinese music drama]. Taipei: Lianjing chubanshe, 1976. 31–47.

Van Gulik, Robert Hans 高羅佩, *Mixi tukao* 秘戲圖考 (*Erotic Colour Prints of the Ming Period, with an Essay on Chinese Sex Life from the Han to the Ch'ing Dynasty, B.C. 206–A.D. 1644*). 1951. Trans. Yang Quan 楊權. Guangzhou: Guangdong renmin chubanshe, 1992.

——. *Zhongguo gudai fangneikao* 中國古代房內考 (*Sexual Life in Ancient China: A Preliminary Survey of Chinese Sex and Society from ca. 1500 B.C. till 1644 A.D.*). 1961. Trans. Li Ling 李零, Guo Xiaohui 郭曉惠, et al. Shanghai: Shanghai renmin chubanshe, 1990.

——. *Zhonguo yanqing: Zhongguo gudai de xing yu shehui.* 中國艷情：中國古代的性與社會 (*Sexual Life in Ancient China: A Preliminary Survey of Chinese Sex and Society from ca. 1500 B.C. till 1644 A.D.*). 1961. Trans. Wu Yuëh-t'ien. 吳岳添. Taipei: Fengyun shidai, 1994.

Wang Changfa 王長發, and Liu Hau 劉華. *Mei Lanfang nienpu* 梅蘭芳年譜 [The Mei Lanfang chronology]. Nanjing: Hehai University Press, 1994.

Wang Changyou 王長友. "Song zaju Yanyousuan tu xinshuo" 宋雜劇眼藥酸圖新説 [New views on the Song *zaju* painting "The Eye Doctor"]. *Xiqu luncong* 戲曲論叢 [Chinese theatrical forum] 2 (1989): 23–7. Lanzhou: Lanzhou University Press.

Wang Chuansong 王傳淞. *Chou zhong mei: Wang Chuansong tanyilu* 丑中美：王傳淞談藝錄 [The beauty in the clown: Wang Chuansong on the art of Kunju opera]. Eds. Shen Zu'an and Wang Deliang. Shanghai: Shanghai wenyi chubanshe, 1987.

Wang Guowei 王國維 (1877–1927). *Guju jiaose kao* 古劇角色考 [Study of role-types used in ancient drama]. 1911. *Wang Guowei xiqu lunwenji* 王國維戲曲論文集 [Essays on Chinese music drama by Wang Guowei]. Beijing: Zhongguo xiju chubanshe, 1984. 183–99.

——. *Song Yuan xiqu kao* 宋元戲曲考 [Study of Song and Yuan drama]. 1912. Taipei: Yiwen yinshuguan, 1969.

Wang Jide 王驥德 (?–1623). *Chen Zigao gaizhuang nanhou ji* 陳子高 改裝男后記 [Chen Zigao disguises as a male queen]. *Sheng Ming zaju* 盛明雜劇 [*Zaju* drama of high Ming]. Vol. 9. Taipei: Wenguang, 1963.

——. *Qulü* 曲律 [Principles of dramatic songs]. *Zhongguo gudian xiqu lunzhu jicheng*. Vol. 4. Beijing: Zhongguo xiju chubanshe, 1959. 45–191.

Wang Shoutai 王守泰. *Kunqu gelü* 崑曲格律 [Prosody of Kunqu opera]. Jiangsu: Jiangsu renmin chubanshe, 1982.

Wang Wenzhang 王文章, ed. *Huiban jinjing erbai zhounian zhenxing Jingju guanmo yantu dahui jinianche* 徽班晉京二百周年振興京劇 觀摩研討大會紀念冊 [*Two Hundredth Anniversary of Anhui Opera Coming to Beijing*]. Beijing: Wenhua yishu chubanshe, 1991. [A Chinese-English bilingual publication]

Wang Xiaochuan 王曉傳. *Yuan Ming Qing sandai jinhui xiaoshuo xiqu shiliao* 元明清三代禁毀小說戲曲史料 [Historical materials on the censorship and destruction of fiction and music drama in Yuan, Ming and Qing periods]. Beijing: Zuojia chubanshe, 1958.

Wang Yongjian 王永建. "Shen Qifeng" 沈起鳳 [Shen Qifeng]. *Zhongguo gudai xiqujia pingzhuan* 中國古代戲曲家評傳 [Critical biographies of ancient writers of music drama]. Eds. Hu Shihou and Liu Shaoji. Zhengzhou: Zhongzhou guji chubanshe, 1992. 645–52.

Wang Zhuo 王灼 (Southern Song). *Biji manzhi* 碧雞漫誌 [Discursive notes from Biji alley]. 1149. *Zhongguo gudian xiqu lunzhu jicheng.* Vol. 1. Beijing: Zhongguo xiju chubanshe, 1959. 91–152.

Wei Fei 隗芾and Wu Yuhua 吳毓華, eds. *Gudian xiqu meixue ziliaoji* 古典戲曲美學資料集 [Collection of material on aesthetics of classical music drama]. Beijing: Wenhua yishu chubanshe, 1992.

Wong Wang-chi 王宏志. "Gei zhengzhi niuqu liao de Lu Xun yanjiu" 給政治扭曲了的魯迅研究 [The kind of Lu Xun studies that has been distorted by politics]. *Wenxue yu zhengzhi zhijian — Lu Xun, Xinyue, wenxueshi* 文學與政治之間 — 魯迅，新月，文學史 [Between literature and politics — Lu Xun, New Moon, literary history]. Taipei: Dongda tushu gongsi, 1994. 57–116.

Wu Gang 武剛, and Xu Jingya 徐京涯. "Zhuhou yongbao ji Mei-Zhang" 珠喉永葆繼梅張 [Forever thriving the voice of pearl, carrying forward the art of Mei and Zhang]. *Wenhua yuekan* 文化月刊 [Cultural monthy] 55 (July 1997): 9–10.

Wu Junda 武俊達. *Kunqu changqiang yanjiu* 崑曲唱腔研究 [Study of Kunqu opera music]. Beijing: Renmin yinyue chubanshe, 1987.

Wu Yuhua 吳毓華, ed. *Zhongguo gudai xiqu xubaji* 中國古典戲曲序跋集[Collection of prefaces and afterwords to ancient Chinese music drama]. Beijing: Zhongguo xiju chubanshe, 1990.

Wu Zao 吳藻 (1799–1863). *Qiaoying* 喬影 [Shadow of disguise]. *Qingren zaju* 清人雜劇 [Qing *zaju* plays]. 1931 (Vol. 1), 1934 (Vol.2). One-vol. ed. Ed. Zheng Zhenduo. Hong Kong: Longmen shudian, 1969. 295–301.

Wu Zimu 吳自牧 (Southern Song). *Mengliang lu* 夢梁錄 [Records of millet dreams]. *Biji xiaoshuo daguan* 筆記小說大觀 [Grand collection of notation books and fiction]. Ser. 21, Vol. 2. Taipei: Xinxing shuju, 1982. 925–1184.

Wuxia Ameng 吳下阿蒙 (17 c.), ed. *Duanxiu pian* 段袖篇 [The cut sleeve compendium]. *Biji xiaoshuo daguan* 筆記小說大觀 [Grand collection of notation books and fiction]. Ser. 5, Vol. 7. Taipei: Xinxing shuju, 1974. 4279–321.

Xia Tingzhi 夏庭芝 (c. 1316–post 1368). *Qinglou ji* 青樓集 [The green bower collection]. 1355. *Zhongguo gudian xiqu lunzhu jicheng.* Vol. 1. Beijing: Zhongguo xiju chubanshe, 1959. 3–84.

——. "Qinglou ji zhi"青樓集誌 [On *Green Bower Collection*]. 1355. *Zhongguo gudian xiqu lunzhu jicheng.* Vol. 1. Beijing: Zhongguo xiju chubanshe, 1959. 7–8.

Xia Xieshi 夏寫時. *Lun Zhongguo xiju piping* 論中國戲劇批評 [On Chinese dramatic criticism]. Jinan: Qilu shushe, 1988.

Xiaomingxiong 小明雄 (Samshasha). *Zhongguo tongxingai shilu* 中國同性愛史錄 [History of homosexuality in China]. 1984. Revised edition. Hong Kong: Rosa Winkel Press, 1997.

Xinqishi 辛其氏. *Xianbi xixie* 閒筆戲寫 [Leisurely pen, playful writing]. Hong Kong: Suye chubanshe, 1998.

Xiong Damu 熊大木 (Ming). *Yangjia jiang zhuan* 楊家將傳 [Stories of the Yang family generals]. Changsha: Yuelu shushe, 1980.

Xu Chengbei 徐城北. *Mei Langfang yu ershi shiji* 梅蘭芳與二十世紀 [Mei Lanfang and the twentieth century]. Beijing: Sanlian shudian, 1990.

——. *Zhongguo Jingju* 中國京劇 [China's Beijing opera]. Guangzhou: Guangzhou luyou chubanshe, 1996.

Xu Dachun 徐大椿 (?-c. 1778). *Yuefu chuansheng* 樂府傳聲 [The sound of musical ballad]. *Xinquyuan*. Vol. 4. Ed. Ren Zhongmin. Shanghai: Zhonghua shuju, 1940.

Xu Ke 徐珂 (1869–1928). *Qing bai lei chao* 清稗類鈔 [Categorized anecdotes from the Qing period]. 48 vols. 1917. *Xijulei, bai 78.* Taipei: Commercial Press, 1966.

Xu Muyun 徐慕雲. *Zhongguo xijushi* 中國戲劇史 [History of Chinese theatre]. 1938. Taipei: Shijie shuju, 1977.

Xu Qinjun 徐沁君, ed. *Xinjiao Yuankan zaju sanshi zhong* 新校元刊雜劇三十種 [A newly revised Yuan dynasty edition of thirty *zaju* plays]. 2 vols. Beijing: Zhonghua shuju, 1980.

Xu Shusen 徐樹森, ed. *Yuanqu xuan waibian* 元曲選外篇 [Supplementary volumes to *Selected Yuan Plays*]. 3 vols. Beijing: Zhonghua shuju, 1959.

Xu Wei 徐渭 (1521–1593). *Ci Mulan tifu congjun* 雌木蘭替父從軍 [Maid Mulan joins the army in her father's stead]. *Mingren zaju xuan* 明人雜劇選 [Selection of Ming *zaju* drama]. Ed. Zhou Yibai. Beijing: Renmin wenxue chubanshe, 1962. 351–63.

——. *Nanci xulu* 南詞敘錄 [Account of the southern style of drama]. *Zhongguo gudian xiqu lunzhu jicheng.* Vol. 3. Beijing: Zhongguo xiju chubanshe, 1959. 233–56.

——. *Nü zhuangyuan cihuang de feng* 女狀元辭凰得鳳 [The female top graduate declines a she-phoenix and gets a he-phoenix]. *Xu Wei de wenxue yu yishu* 徐渭的文學與藝術 [Xu Wei's literature and art]. Ed. Liang Yicheng. Taipei: Yiwen chubanshe, 1977. 334–69.

Yan Huizhu 言慧珠. "Qianyan" 前言 [Foreword]. *Hua Mulan* 花木蘭. Adapted by Yan Huizhu. Musical notation by Lu Wenqin. Shanghai: Shanghai wenyi chubanshe, 1961. i–iii.

Yan Qi 研齊. "Wenwu xiaosheng jian qingyi" 文武小生兼青衣 [The military and civil young male doubling the blue-robe female].

Beijing wanbao 北京晚報 [Beijing Evening News] February 11, 1984.

Yang Enshou 楊恩壽 (1834–1858). *Xu ciyu conghua* 續詞餘叢話 [Sequel to *Collected Chats on Music Drama*]. *Zhongguo gudian xiqu lunzhu jicheng*. Vol. 9. Beijing: Zhongguo xiju chubanshe, 1959. 287–327.

Yang Liulang diaobing po tianzhen 楊六郎調兵破天陣 [Yang the sixth son deploys troops to destroy the Heaven's Gate battle formation]. *Quanyuan zaju waibian* 全元雜劇外篇 [Supplementary volumes to *Complete Works of Yuan Drama*]. Vol. 6. Taipei: Shijie shuju, 1974. 4.2541– 4.2637.

Yangmen nüjiang 楊門女將 [Women generals of the Yang family]. Adapted by Fan Junhong and Lü Ruiming. *Beijing xiju* 北京戲劇 [Drama of Beijing] 7 (1960): 12–27. [Beijing opera script]

Yao Silian 姚思廉 (Tang). *Chen shu* 陳書 [Chen history]. 2 vols. Beijing: Zhonghua shuju, 1972.

Ye Changhai 葉長海. *Quxue yu xijuxue* 曲學與戲劇學 [Theory and criticism of music drama and theatre]. Shanghai: Xuelin chubanshe, 1999.

——. *Zhongguo xijuxue shigao* 中國戲劇學史稿 [History of Chinese dramatic theory and criticism]. Shanghai: Shanghai wenyi chubanshe, 1986.

Ye Dejun 葉德均. *Xiqu xiaoshuo congkao* 戲曲小説叢考 [Collected studies on music drama and fiction]. 2 vols. Beijing: Zhonghua shuju, 1979.

Ye Yuhua 葉玉華. "Shuo beiqu zaju xiyou nüxing yanchang" 説北曲雜劇系由女性演唱 [Northern music drama was sung by females]. 1954. *Yuan Ming Qing xiqu yanjiu lunwenji* 元明清戲曲研究論文集 [Anthology of studies on the music drama of Yuan, Ming and Qing]. Ed. Zuojia chubanshe bianjibu. Beijing: Zuojia chubanshe, 1957. 310–3.

Yi Hong 一泓. "Wen Ruhua: Zhongguo zuihou de 'nandan'" 溫如華：中國最後的'男旦' [Wen Ruhua: China's Last 'Male *Dan*']. *Beijing gongrenbao* 北京工人報 [Beijing Worker's Daily] June 3, 1999. Section "Dushifeng" 都市風 [City style]. 4.

Yi Ping 伊平. "Si yu busi zhijian: tan Wen Ruhua zai Jingju *Baimian langjun* zhong de changqiang tansuo" 似與不似之間：談溫如華 在京劇《白面郎君》中的唱腔探索 [Between verisimilitude and dis-verisimulitude: a discussion of the vocal experiment of Wen Ruhua in the Beijing opera *The Fair-faced Gentleman*]. *Xijubao* 戲劇報 [Drama journal] 332 (January 1985): 40–1.

Yoshikawa Kōjirō 吉川幸次郎. "Bai Ranhō no chi'i" 梅蘭芳の地位 [Mei Lanfang's status]. 1956. *Yoshikawa Kōjirō zenshū*. Vol. 16. Tokyo: Chikuma shobō, 1970. 589–90.

——. "Bai Ranhō so no ta" 梅蘭芳その他 [About Mei Lanfang]. 1956. *Yoshikawa Kōjirō zenshū*. Vol. 16. Tokyo: Chikuma shobō, 1970. 597–601.

——. "Kabuki to kyogeki" 歌舞伎と京劇 [Kabuki and Beijing opera]. 1955. *Yoshikawa Kōjirō zenshū*. Vol. 16. Tokyo: Chikuma shobō, 1970. 587–8.

——. "Kyogeki zakkan" 京劇雜感 [Miscellaneous thoughts on Beijing opera]. 1956. *Yoshikawa Kōjirō zenshū*. Vol. 16. Tokyo: Chikuma shobō, 1970. 595–6.

——. "Minamiza kangeki zekku" 南座觀劇絕句 [Poetic quatrains written after watching drama]. 1956. *Yoshikawa Kōjirō zenshū*. Vol. 16. Tokyo: Chikuma shobō, 1970. 591–4.

——. *Yoshikawa Kōjirō zenshū* 吉川幸次郎全集 [Complete works of Yoshikawa Kōjirō]. 20 vols. Tokyo: Chikuma shobō, 1970.

——. *Yuan zaju yanjiu* 元雜劇研究 [Study of Yuan drama]. 1958. Trans. Cheng Ch'ing-mao 鄭清茂. Taipei: Yiwen yinshuguan, 1960.

Yu Huai (Qing) 余懷. *Banqiao zaji* 板橋雜記 [Miscellaneous notes from a wooden bridge]. *Biji xiaoshuo daguan* 筆記小説大觀 [Grand collection of notation books and fiction]. Ser. 5, Vol. 9. Taipei: Xinxing shuju, 1974. 4991–5025.

Yu Siu-wah 余少華. *Le zai diancuo zhong: Xianggang yasu yinyue wenhua* 樂在顛錯中：香港雅俗音樂文化 [Out of chaos and coincidence: Hong Kong music culture]. Hong Kong: Oxford University Press, 2000.

Yu Zhen 于臻. *Wutai yingxiong: Pei Yanling de yanyi shijie* 舞台英雄：裴艷玲的演藝世界 [A hero on stage: Pei Yanling's world of performing art]. Hong Kong: Suye chubanshe, 1994.

Yu Zhenfei 余振飛. *Yu Zhenfei yishu lunji* 余振飛藝術論集 [Essays by Yu Zhenfei on the art of Kunju opera]. Shanghai: Shanghai wenyi chubanshe, 1985.

Yue Meiti 岳美緹. *Wo — yige gudan de nüxiaosheng* 我 — 一個孤單 的女小生 [I — a solitary female young-male-role actor]. Shanghai: Wenhui chubanshe, 1993.

Yung Sai-shing 容世誠. *Xiqu renleixue chutan: yishi, juchang yu shequn* 戲曲人類學初探：儀式、劇場與社群 [The anthropology of Chinese drama: ritual, theatre and community]. Taipei: Rye Field, 1997.

Zhang Cixi 張次溪, ed. *Qing dai yandu liyuan shiliao zhengxubian* 清 代燕都梨園史料正續編 [Historical materials on the theatre of the Qing imperial capital, parts 1 and 2]. 1934 and 1937. 2 vols. Beijing: Zhongguo xiju chubanshe, 1988.

Zhang Faying 張發穎. *Zhongguo xibanshi* 中國戲班史 [History of Chinese theatre troupes]. Shenyang: Shenyang chubanshe, 1991.

Zhang Yuanchang 張元長(Ming). *Meihua caotang qutan* 梅花草堂曲 談 [Chats on drama from the thatched cottage of peach blossom]. *Xinquyuan*. Vol. 2. Ed. Ren Zhongmin. Shanghai: Zhonghua shuju, 1940.

Zhang Xie zhuangyuan 張協狀元 [Zhang Xie the principal graduate]. *Yongle dadian xiwen sanzhong jiaozhu* 永樂大典戲文三種校注 [An annotation of three *xiwen* plays from the *Yongle Canon*]. Ed. Qian Nanyang. Beijing: Zhonghua shuju, 1979. 1–217.

Zhao Shanlin 趙山林. *Zhongguo xiqu guanzhongxue* 中國戲曲觀眾 學 [Study of the audience of Chinese music drama]. Shanghai: Huadong Normal University Press, 1990.

Zheng Chuanyin 鄭傳寅. *Chuantong wenhua yu gudian xiqu* 傳統文 化與古典戲曲[Traditional culture and classical music drama]. Hubei: Hubei jiaoyu chubanshe, 1990.

——. *Zhongguo xiqu wenhua gailun* 中國戲曲文化概論 [Introduction to the culture of Chinese music drama]. Hubei: Wuhan University Press, 1993.

Zheng Sili 鄭思禮. *Zhongguo xingwenhua: yige qian'nian bujie zhijie* 中國性文化：一個千年不解之結 [The sex culture of China: a thousand-year knot]. Beijing: Zhongguo duiwai fanyi chuban gongsi, 1994.

Zhong Xiang Zhuren 眾香主人 (pseud.) (Qing). *Zhong xiang guo* 眾香國 [Realm of the fragrant ladies]. 1806. *Qing dai yandu liyuan shiliao zhengxubian.* Ed. Zhang Cixi. Vol. 2. Beijing: Zhongguo xiju chubanshe, 1988. 1009–36.

Zhongguo da baike quanshu: xiqu, quyi 中國大百科全書：戲曲，曲藝 [The great Chinese encyclopedia: traditional music drama, folk musical art forms]. Shanghai: Zhongguo da baike quanshu chubanshe, 1983.

Zhongguo gudian xiqu lunzhu jicheng 中國古典戲曲論著集成 [The comprehensive collection of discourses on classical Chinese music drama]. 10 vols. Beijing: Zhongguo xiju chubanshe, 1959.

Zhongguo xiquzhi bianji weiyuanhui 中國戲曲誌編輯委員會, ed. *Zhongguo xiquzhi: Shanxi juan* 中國戲曲誌：山西卷 [Annals of Chinese music drama: Shanxi volume]. Beijing: Wenhua yishu chubanshe, 1990.

Zhongguo xiquzhi bianji weiyuanhui 中國戲曲誌編輯委員會, ed. *Zhongguo xiquzhi: Tianjin juan* 中國戲曲誌：天津卷 [Annals of Chinese music drama: Tianjin volume]. Beijing: Wenhua yishu chubanshe, 1990.

Zhou Chuanjia 周傳家. "Xikan Qiunü hua nandan—*Qiunü zhuan* guanhou" 喜看仇女話男旦 — 仇女傳觀後 [Watching *Story of Damsel Qiu* with delight and a discourse on the male *dan* — some after thoughts]. *Xiju dianying bao* 戲劇電影報 [Theatre and film journal] June 3, 1997.

Zhou Chuanying 周傳瑛. *Kunju shengya liushinian* 崑劇生涯六十年 [A sixty-year career in Kunju opera]. Transcribed and edited by Luo Di. Shanghai: Shanghai wenyi chubanshe, 1988.

Zhou Enlai 周恩來. "Yaozuo yige geming de wenyi gongzhuozhe" 要做一個革命的文藝工作者 [Striving to be a revolutionary worker in the arts]. 1963. *Zhou Enlai lun wenyi* 周恩來論文藝 [Zhou Enlai on literature and the arts]. Beijing: Renmin wenxue chubanshe, 1979. 149–75.

——. "Zai Jingju xiandaixi guanmo yanchu dahui zuotanhui shang de jianghua" 在京劇現代戲觀摩演出大會座談會上的講話 [Speech given at the seminar on the festival of Beijing opera on modern themes]. 1964. *Zhou Enlai lun wenyi* 周恩來論文藝 [Zhou Enlai on literature and the arts]. Beijing: Renmin wenxue chubanshe, 1979. 194–213.

Zhou Enlai tongzhi qingnian shiqi zai Tianjin de xiju huodong ziliao huibian 周恩來同志青年時期在天津的戲劇活動資料彙編 [A collection of information on comrade Zhou Enlai's theatre activities in Tianjin in his youthful years]. Tianjin: Zhou Enlai tongzhi qingnian shidai zai Tianjin geming huodong jinianguan and Tianjin shi wenhuaju xiju yanjiushi, 1981.

Zhou Guoxiong 周國雄. "Shanxi Hongdong Mingyingwangdian xiqu bihua xintan" 山西洪洞明應王殿戲曲壁畫新探 [A new investigation of the Yuan theatre mural in Shanxi Hongdong]. *Huanan shifan daxue xuebao (shehui kexue ban)* 華南師範大學學報 (社會科學版) [Journal of South China Normal University (Social Sciences Edition)] 3 (1985): 100–9.

Zhou Huabin 周華斌. "*Lan Ling Wang* jiamian yanjiu — jianshu gu gewuxi ji jiamian zhiyuan" 《蘭陵王》假面研究 — 兼述古歌舞戲及假面之源 [A study of the mask of *Prince Lan Ling* — with a discussion of the origin of ancient singing-dancing and masks]. *Zhonghua xiqu* 中華戲曲 [Chinese music drama] 15 (Aug. 1998): 98–134.

Zhou Hui 周暉 (Ming). *Zhoushi qupin* 周氏曲品 [Zhou's ranking of music drama]. *Xinquyuan*. Vol. 2. Ed. Ren Zhongmin. Shanghai: Zhonghua shuju, 1940.

Zhou Jingshu 周靜書, ed. *Liang Zhu wenhua daguan* 梁祝文化大觀 [Grand collection of Liang-Zhu culture]. 3 vols. Beijing: Zhonghua shuju, 1999.

Zhou Mi 周密 (1232–1298). *Wulin jiushi* 武林舊事 [Hangzhou that was]. *Zhi buzu zhai congshu* 知不足齋叢書 [Series from Studio of Knowing One's Limitations]. Vol. 16. Ed. Bao Tingbo (Qing). Taipei: Xingzhong shuju, 1964.

Zhou Miaozhong 周妙中. "Guanyu Yuan qu de sange wenti" 關于元曲的三個問題[Three questions concerning Yuan music drama]. *Wenxue yichan zengkan* 文學遺產增刊 [Literary heritage supplementary series]. Vol. 2. Beijing: Zuojia chubanshe, 1956. 214–23.

Zhou Yibai 周貽白. "Nan Song zaju de wutai renwu xingxiang" 南宋
雜劇的舞台人物形象 [Stage figures in the *zaju* drama of Southern
Song]. 1959. *Zhou Yibai xiju lunwen xuan* [Selections from the
drama criticisms of Zhou Yibai]. Hunan: Hunan renmin
chubanshe, 1982. 576–81.

———. "Yuan dai bihua zhong de Yuan ju yanchu xingshi" 元代壁畫中
的元劇演出形式 [The performance of Yuan drama as represented
in Yuan wall paintings]. 1959. *Zhou Yibai xiju lunwen xuan*
[Selections from the drama criticisms of Zhou Yibai]. Hunan:
Hunan renmin chubanshe, 1982. 589–96.

———. *Zhongguo xijushi* 中國戲劇史 [History of Chinese drama]. 3 vols.
Shanghai: Zhonghua shuju, 1953.

———. *Zhou Yibai xiju lunwen xuan* 周貽白戲劇論文選 [Selections from
the drama criticisms of Zhou Yibai]. Hunan: Hunan renmin
chubanshe, 1982.

Zhuang Yifu 莊一拂. *Gudian xiqu cunmu huikao* 古典戲曲存目匯考
[A comprehensive catalogue of existing traditional music drama
titles]. 3 vols. Shanghai: Shanghai guji chubanshe, 1982.

Zhuquan Jushi 珠泉居士 (pseud.) (Qing). *Xu banqiao zaji* 續板橋雜記
[Sequel to *Miscellaneous Notes from a Wooden Bridge*]. *Biji
xiaoshuo daguan* 筆記小說大觀 [Grand collection of notation
books and fiction]. Ser. 5, Vol 6. Taipei: Xinxing shuju, 1974.
5027–60.

"Zhuxiao yishujia Guan Jinpeng" 駐校藝術家關錦鵬 ("Stanley Kwan,
Artist-in-Residence"). Hong Kong: Hong Kong University of
Science & Technology Center for the Arts, 1996. [A Chinese-
English bilingual pamphlet.]

Western-Language Sources

Abbate, Carolyn. *Unsung Voices: Opera and Musical Narrative in the
Nineteenth Century*. Princeton: Princeton University Press, 1991.

Ackroyd, Peter. *Dressing Up: Transvestism and Drag: The History of
an Obsession*. New York: Simon & Schuster, 1979.

Ahmad, Aijaz. "Jameson's Rhetoric of Otherness and the 'National Allegory'." 1987. *In Theory: Classes, Nations, Literatures.* London: Verso, 1992. 95–122.

Allen, Joseph R. "Dressing and Undressing the Chinese Woman Warrior." *Positions* 4.2 (Fall 1996): 343–79.

Allen, Louise. *The Lesbian Idol: Martina, kd and the Consumption of Lesbian Masculinity.* London: Cassell, 1997.

Arnott, Peter D. *Public Performance in the Greek Theatre.* London: Routledge, 1989.

Aston, Elaine, and George Savona. *Theatre as Sign-System: A Semiotics of Text and Performance.* London: Routledge, 1991.

Austin, Gayle. *Feminist Theories for Dramatic Criticism.* Ann Arbor: University of Michigan Press, 1990.

Baker, Roger. "*Onnagata* and *Tan.*" *Drag: A History of Female Impersonation on the Stage.* London: Triton, 1968. 149–56.

Barbin, Herculine. *Herculine Barbin: Being the Recently Discovered Memoirs of a Nineteenth-Century French Hermaphrodite.* Introduced by Michel Foucault. Trans. Richard McDougall. New York: Pantheon Books, 1980.

Barish, Jonas. *The Antitheatrical Prejudice.* Berkeley: University of California Press, 1981.

Beeman, William O. "Mimesis and Travesty in Iranian Traditional Theatre." *Gender in Performance.* Ed. Laurence Senelick. Hanover, NH: University Press of New England, 1992. 14–25.

Bray, Alan. *Homosexuality in Renaissance England.* 1982. 2nd ed. London: Gay Men's Press, 1988.

Brecht, Bertolt. "Alienation Effects in Chinese Acting." *Brecht on Theatre.* Trans. and ed. John Willett. New York: Hill & Wang, 1964. 91–9.

Bronfen, Elisabeth. *Over Her Dead Body: Death, Femininity and the Aesthetic.* New York: Routledge, 1992.

Brŭsák, Karel. "Signs in the Chinese Theatre." 1939. *Semiotics of Art: Prague School Contributions.* Trans. K. Brŭsák. Eds. Ladislav Matejka and Irwin R. Titunik. Cambridge, Massachusetts: MIT Press, 1976. 59–73.

Bullough, Vern L. and Bonnie Bullough. *Cross Dressing, Sex, and Gender*. Philadelphia: University of Pennsylvania Press, 1993.

Butler, Judith. *Bodies That Matter: On the Discursive Limits of "Sex"*. New York: Routledge, 1993.

——. *Gender Trouble: Feminism and the Subversion of Identity*. New York: Routledge, 1990.

Case, Sue-Ellen. "Classic Drag: The Greek Creation of Female Parts." *Theatre Journal* 37.3 (October 1985): 317–27.

Chan, Sau Yan. *Improvisation in a Ritual Context: The Music of Cantonese Opera*. Hong Kong: Chinese University Press, 1991.

Cheng, Francois. *Chinese Poetic Writing*. Bloomington: Indiana University Press, 1982.

Chou, Hui-ling. "Striking Their Own Poses: The History of Cross-Dressing on the Chinese Stage." *The Drama Review* 41.2 (Summer 1997): 130–52.

Chou, Wah-shan. *Tongzhi: Politics of Same-Sex Eroticism in Chinese Societies*. New York: Haworth Press, 2000.

Chou, Ying-hsiung. "The Linguistic and Mythical Structure of *hsing* as a Combinational Model." *Chinese-Western Comparative Literature: Theory and Strategy*. Ed. John J. Deeney. Hong Kong: Chinese University Press, 1980. 51–78.

Chuang Tzu. *Chuang Tzu: Basic Writings*. Trans. Burton Watson. New York: Columbia University Press, 1964.

Clément, Catherine. *Opera, or the Undoing of Women*. 1979. Trans. Betsy Wing. Minneapolis: University of Minnesota Press, 1988.

Confucius. *Analects*. Trans. D. C. Lau. Harmondsworth: Penguin, 1979.

Cusack, Dymphna. *Chinese Women Speak*. Sydney: Angus & Robertson, 1958.

De Lauretis, Teresa. "Feminist Studies/Critical Studies: Issues, Terms, and Contexts." *Feminist Studies/Critical Studies*. Ed. Teresa de Lauretis. Bloomington: Indiana University Press, 1986. 1–19.

——. *Technologies of Gender: Essays on Theory, Film, and Fiction*. Bloomington: Indiana University Press, 1987.

Dekker, R. and L. van de Pol. *The Tradition of Female Transvestism in Early Modern Europe*. London: Macmillan, 1989.

Deleuze, Gilles, and Félix Guattari. *Anti-Oedipus: Captialism and Schizophrenia*. 1972. Trans. Robert Hurley, Mark Seem, and Helen R. Lane. Minneapolis: University of Minnesota Press, 1983.

Digani, Mario. *The Homoerotics of Early Modern Drama*. Cambridge: Cambridge University Press, 1997.

Dolan, Jill. *The Feminist Spectator as Critic*. Ann Arbor: University of Michigan Press, 1988.

Dollimore, Jonathan. *Sexual Dissidence: Augustine to Wilde, Freud to Foucault*. Oxford: Oxford University Press, 1991.

Dolby, William. *A History of Chinese Drama*. London: Elek, 1976.

Elam, Keir. *The Semiotics of Theatre and Drama*. London: Methuen, 1980.

Elvin, Mark. "Tales of Shen and Xin: Body-Person and Heart-Mind in China during the Last 150 Years." *Zone: Fragments for a History of the Human Body*. Part 2. Eds. Michel Feher, et al. New York: Urzone, 1989. 267–349.

Emigh, John, and Jamer Hunt. "Gender Bending in Balinese Performance." *Gender in Performance*. Ed. Laurence Senelick. Hanover, NH: University Press of New England, 1992. 195–222.

Feinberg, Leslie. *Transgender Warriors: Making History from Joan of Arc to Dennis Rodman*. Boston: Beacon Press, 1996.

Ferris, Lesley. *Acting Women: Images of Women in Theatre*. New York: New York University Press, 1989.

——, ed. *Crossing the Stage: Controversies on Cross-Dressing*. New York: Routledge, 1993.

——. "The Legacy of Goethe's Mimetic Stance." *Crossing the Stage*. New York: Routledge, 1993. 51–7.

Foucault, Michel. *The History of Sexuality: Volume 1: An Introduction*. 1976. Trans. Robert Hurley. New York: Vintage Books. 1990.

Furth, Charlotte. "Androgynous Men and Deficient Females: Biology and Gender Boundaries in Sixteenth-and Seventeenth-Century China." *Late Imperial China* 9.2 (Dec. 1988): 1–31.

——. *A Flourishing Yin: Gender in China's Medical History, 960–1665*. Berkeley: University of California Press, 1999.

Garber, Marjorie. *Vested Interests: Cross-dressing and Cultural Anxiety*. New York: Routledge, 1992.

Giles, Herbert A. *A History of Chinese Literature*. New York: D. Appleton & Co., 1901.

Gilligan, Carol. *In a Different Voice*. Cambridge: Harvard University Press, 1982.

Gilmartin, Christina, et al, eds. *Engendering China: Women, Culture, and the State*. Cambridge, MA: Harvard University Press, 1994.

——. "Gender in the Formation of a Communist Body Politic." *Modern China* 19.3 (July 1993): 299–329.

Godzich, Wlad. "The Future Possibility of Knowledge." Foreword to *Heterologies: Discourse on the Other*, by Michel de Certeau. Trans. Brian Massumi. Minneapolis: University of Minnesota Press, 1986. vii–xxi.

Goethe, Johann Wolfgang von. "Women's Parts Played by Men in the Roman Theatre." 1788. Trans. Isa Ragusa. *Crossing the Stage*. Ed. Lesley Ferris. New York: Routledge, 1993. 48–51.

Goldberg, Jonathan. *Sodometries: Renaissance Texts, Modern Sexualities*. Stanford: Stanford University Press, 1992.

Greenblatt, Stephen. *Renaissance Self-Fashioning: From More to Shakespeare*. Chicago: University of Chicago Press, 1980.

Harris, John Wesley. *Medieval Theatre in Context: An Introduction*. London: Routledge, 1992.

Herdt, Gilbert, ed. *Third Sex, Third Gender: Beyond Sexual Dimorphism in Culture and Society*. New York: Zone Books, 1994.

Hinsch, Bret. *Passions of the Cut Sleeve: The Homosexual Tradition in China*. Berkeley: University of California Press, 1990.

Hong Kingston, Maxine. *The Woman Warrior: Memoirs of a Girlhood Among Ghosts*. 1975. New York: Vintage Books, 1989.

Howard, Jean E. *The Stage and Social Struggle in Early Modern England*. London: Routledge, 1994.

Hsia, C. T. "The Military Romance: A Genre of Chinese Fiction." *Studies in Chinese Literary Genres*. Ed. Cyril Birch. Berkeley: University of California Press, 1974. 339–90.

Hsü, Tao-ching. *The Chinese Conception of the Theatre*. Seattle: University of Washington Press, 1985.

Hu, Chin-yuan. "Common Poetics? — The Reappraisal of Chinese-Brechtian Theatre." *Tamkang Review* 16.2 (Winter 1985): 193–206.

Humm, Maggie. *A Reader's Guide to Contemporary Feminist Literary Criticism*. New York: Harvester Wheatsheaf, 1994.

Hung, Chang-tai. *War and Popular Culture: Resistance in Modern China, 1937–1945*. Berkeley: University of California Press, 1994.

Hwang, David Henry. *M. Butterfly*. New York: Plume, 1989.

Innes, Sherrie. *Tough Girls: Women Warriors and Wonder Women in Popular Culture*. Philadelphia: University of Pennsylvania Press, 1998.

Irigaray, Luce. *Je, tu, nous: Toward a Culture of Difference*. 1990. Trans. Alison Martin. New York: Routlege, 1993.

——. *Speculum of the Other Woman*. 1974. Trans. Gillian C. Gill. Ithaca: Cornell University Press, 1985.

Jagose, Annamarie. *Queer Theory: An Introduction*. New York: New York University Press, 1996.

Jameson, Fredric. "Third-World Literature in the Era of Multinational Capitalism." *Social Text* 15 (Fall 1986): 65–88.

Jardine, Alice A. *Gynesis: Configurations of Woman and Modernity*. Ithaca: Cornell University Press, 1985.

Jardine, Lisa. *Still Harping on Daughters: Women and Drama in the Age of Shakespeare*. Brighton, Sussex: The Harvester Press, 1983.

Kahn, Madeleine. *Narrative Transvestism: Rhetoric and Gender in the Eighteen-Century English Novel*. Ithaca: Cornell University Press, 1991.

Kaulbach, Barbara M. "The Woman Warrior in Chinese Opera: An Image of Reality or Fiction?" Trans. Christian Rogowski. *Fu Jen Studies: Literature and Linguistics* 15 (1982): 69–82.

Kelly, Katherine E. "The Queen's Two Bodies: Shakespeare's Boy Actress in Breeches." *Theatre Journal* 42 (1990): 81–93.

Ko, Dorothy. *Teachers of the Inner Chambers: Women and Culture in Seventeenth-Century China*. Stanford: Stanford University Press, 1994.

Koestenbaum, Wayne. *The Queen's Throat: Opera, Homosexuality and the Mystery of Desire*. New York: Vintage Books, 1994.

Leung, K. C. *Hsü Wei as Dramatic Critic: An Annotated Translation of the Nan-tzu hsü-lu*. Eugene: Asian Studies Program, University of Oregon, 1987.

Levine, Laura. *Men in Women's Clothing: Anti-Theatricality and Effeminization 1579–1642.* Cambridge: Cambridge University Press, 1994.

Levy, Dore. *Ideal and Actual in The Story of the Stone.* New York: Columbia University Press, 1999.

Li Chi: Book of Rites. Trans. James Legge. 2 vols. New York: University Books Inc., 1967.

Liang, Mingyue. "Chinese Traditional Opera." *Music of the Billion: An Introduction to China Musical Culture.* New York: Heinrichshofen Edition, 1985. 230–67.

Li, Ziyun. "Women's Consciousness and Women's Writing." Trans. Zhu Hong. *Engendering China: Women, Culture, and the State.* Eds. Christina K. Gilmartin, et al. Cambridge, MA: Harvard University Press, 1994. 299–317.

Lilley, Rozanna. *Staging Hong Kong: Gender and Performance in Transition.* Honolulu: University of Hawaii Press, 1998.

Liu, Dalin. *Chinese Sex Artifacts Over 5000 Years.* Hong Kong: Ming Pao Publications, 2000. [A Chinese-English bilingual publication]

Liu, James J. Y. *The Art of Chinese Poetry.* Chicago: University of Chicago Press, 1962.

——. *Chinese Theories of Literature.* Chicago: University of Chicago Press, 1975.

——. *Language—Paradox—Poetics: A Chinese Perspective.* Ed. Richard John Lynn. Princeton: Princeton University Press, 1988.

Loomba, Ania. *Gender, Race, Renaissance Drama.* Delhi: Oxford University Press, 1992.

Lu, Tonglin, ed. *Gender and Sexuality in Twentieth-Century Chinese Literature and Society.* New York: State University of New York Press, 1993.

Mackerras, Colin, ed. *Chinese Theatre: From Its Origins to the Present Day.* Honolulu: University of Hawaii Press, 1983.

——. *The Performing Arts in Contemporary China.* London: Routledge & Kegan Paul, 1981.

——. *The Rise of the Peking Opera 1770–1870.* New York: Oxford University Press, 1972.

Mair, Victor H. "The Narrative Revolution in Chinese Literature: Ontological Presuppositions." *Chinese Literature: Essays, Articles, Reviews* 5 (1983): 1–27.

Malti-Douglas, Fedwa. *Woman's Body, Woman's Word: Gender and Discourse in Arabo-Islamic Writing*. Princeton: Princeton University Press, 1991.

McKendrick, Melveena. *Theatre in Spain: 1490–1700*. Cambridge: Cambridge University Press, 1989.

——. *Woman and Society in the Spanish Drama of the Golden Age: A Study of the* Mujer Varonil. London: Cambridge University Press, 1974.

Miller, D. A. *Place for Us: Essay on the Broadway Musical*. Cambridge, MA: Harvard University Press, 1998.

Miner, Earl. *Comparative Poetics: An Intercultural Essay on Theories of Literature*. Princeton: Princeton University Press, 1990.

Moi, Toril. *Sexual/Textual Politics: Feminist Literary Theory*. London: Methuen, 1985.

Muir, Lynette R. "Women on the Medieval Stage: The Evidence from France." *Medieval English Theatre* 7.2 (December 1985): 107–19.

——. "The Saint Play in Medieval France." *The Saint Play in Medieval Europe*. Ed. Clifford Davidson. Kalamazoo, MI: Medieval Institute Publications, Western Michigan University, 1986. 123–80.

Orgel, Stephen. *The Illusion of Power: Political Theater in the English Renaissance*. Berkeley: University of California Press, 1975.

——. "Nobody's Perfect: Or Why Did the English Stage Take Boys for Women?" *South Atlantic Quarterly* 88 (1989): 7–29.

——. "The Subtexts of *The Roaring Girl*." *Erotic Politics: Desire on the Renaissance Stage*. Ed. Susan Zimmerman. New York: Routledge, 1992. 12–26.

Parker, Andrew, and Eve Kosofsky Sedgwick, eds. *Performativity and Performance*. New York: Routledge, 1995.

Peacock, James L. "Ethnographic Notes on Sacred and Profane Performance." *By Means of Performance: Intercultural Studies of Theatre and Ritual*. Eds. Richard Schechner and Willa Appel. Cambridge: Cambridge University Press, 1990. 208–20.

Petroff, Elizabeth Alvilda. *Body and Soul: Essays on Medieval Women and Mysticism.* New York: Oxford University Press, 1994.

Pearson, Jacqueline. *The Prostituted Muse: Images of Women and Women Dramatists 1642–1737.* New York: St Martin's Press, 1988.

Phelan, Peggy. "Crisscrossing Cultures." *Crossing the Stage: Controversies on Cross-Dressing.* Ed. Lesley Ferris. New York: Routledge, 1993. 155–70.

Pian, Rulan Chao. "Aria Structural Patterns in the Peking Opera." *Chinese and Japanese Music-Dramas.* Eds. J. I. Crump and William P. Malm. Ann Arbor: University of Michigan Press, 1975. 65–89.

Puccini, Giacomo. *Madam Butterfly.* Trans. Charles Osborne. In Carner Mosco, *Madam Butterfly: A Guide to the Opera.* London: Berrie & Jenkins, 1979.

Riley, Jo. *Chinese Theatre and the Actor in Performance.* Cambridge: Cambridge University Press, 1997.

Robertson, Jennifer. *Takarazuka: Sexual Politics and Popular Culture in Modern Japan.* Berkeley: University of California Press, 1998.

Rose, M. B. "Women in Men's Clothing: Apparel and Social Stability in *The Roaring Girl.*" *English Literary Renaissance* 14.3 (Autumn 1984): 367–91.

Scott, A. C. Introduction. *Traditional Chinese Plays: Longing for Worldly Pleasures, Fifteen Strings of Cash.* Vol. 2. Ed. A. C. Scott. Madison: University of Wisconsin Press, 1969. 3–11.

——. *Mei Lan-fang: Leader of the Pear Garden.* Hong Kong: Hong Kong University Press, 1957.

Senelick, Laurence, ed. *Gender in Performance: The Presentation of Difference in the Performing.* Hanover, NH: University Press of New England, 1992.

Shakespeare. *The Norton Shakespeare.* Eds. Stephen Greenblatt et al. New York: W. W. Norton & Co., 1997.

Shapiro, Michael. *Gender in Play on the Shakespearean Stage: Boy Heroines and Female Pages.* Ann Arbor: University of Michigan Press, 1996.

Shen, Grant. "Acting in the Private Theatre of the Ming Dynasty." *Asian Theatre Journal* 15.1 (Spring 1998): 64–86.

Shepherd, Simon. *Amazons and Warrior Women*. New York: St. Martin's Press, 1981.

Shih, Chung-wen. *The Golden Age of Chinese Drama: Yüan Tsa-chü*. Princeton: Princeton University Press, 1976.

Smith, Bruce R. *Homosexual Desire in Shakespeare's England: A Cultural Poetics*. Chicago: University of Chicago Press, 1991.

Snow, Lois Wheeler. *China On Stage: An American Actress in The People's Republic of China*. New York: Random House, 1973.

Solomon, Alisa. "It's Never Too Late to Switch: Crossing Toward Power." *Crossing the Stage: Controversies on Cross-Dressing*. Ed. Lesley Ferris. New York: Routledge, 1993. 144–54.

——. *Re-dressing the Canon: Essays on Theater and Gender*. London: Routledge, 1997.

Song, Geng. "The Fragile Scholar: The Construction of Masculinity in Traditional Chinese Romances and its Cultural Constituents." Diss., University of Hong Kong, 2000.

Stallybrass, Peter. "Transvestism and the 'Body Beneath': Speculating on the Boy Actor." *Erotic Politics: Desire on the Renaissance Stage*. Ed. Susan Zimmerman. New York: Routledge, 1992. 64–83.

"Stanley Kwan, Artist-in-Residence." Hong Kong: Hong Kong University of Science & Technology Center for the Arts, 1996. [A Chinese-English bilingual pamphlet.]

Straub, Kristina. *Sexual Suspects: Eighteenth-Century Players and Sexal Ideology*. Princeton: Princeton University Press, 1992.

Ssu-Ma Ch'ien [Sima Qian]. *Records of the Grand Historian of China*. 2 vols. Trans. Burton Watson. New York: Columbia University Press, 1961.

T'ien, Ju-k'ang. *Male Anxiety and Female Chastity: A Comparative Study of Chinese Ethical Values in Ming-Ch'ing Times*. Leiden: Brill, 1987.

Traub, Valerie. *Desire and Anxiety: Circulations of Sexuality in Shakespearean Drama*. London: Routledge, 1992.

Trinh, T. Minh-ha. *Woman, Native, Other*. Bloomington: Indiana University Press, 1989.

Ts'ao, Hsüeh-chin [Cao Xueqin], *Dream of the Red Chamber*. Trans. Chi-chen Wang. New York: Twayne, 1958.

Van Gulik, Robert Hans. *Sexual Life in Ancient China: A Preliminary Survey of Chinese Sex and Society from ca. 1500 B.C. till 1644 A.D.* Leiden: E. J. Brill, 1961.

Vitiello, Giovanni. "Exemplary Sodomites: Male Homosexuality in Late Ming Fiction." Diss., University of California at Berkeley, 1994.

Volpp, Sophie. "Gender, Power and Spectacle in Late-Imperial Chinese Theater." *Gender Reversals and Gender Cultures: Anthropological and Historical Perspective.* Ed. Sabrina Petra Ramet. London: Routledge, 1996. 138–47.

Wadler, Joyce. "The Spy Who Fell in Love with a Shadow." *The New York Times Magazine* (August 15, 1993/Section 6): 30–38 passim.

Waley, Arthur. "The Green Bower Collection." 1957. *The Secret History of the Mongols and Other Pieces.* London: Geroge Allen & Unwin Ltd, 1963. 89–107.

Wang, Wenzhang, ed. *Two Hundredth Anniversary of Anhui Opera Coming to Beijing.* Beijing: Wenhua yishu chubanshe, 1991. [A Chinese-English bilingual publication.]

Webster, John. *The Duchess of Malfi.* 1623. Ed. Elizabeth M. Brennan. London: A & C Black, 1983.

Wiles, Timothy J. *The Theater Event: Modern Theories of Performance.* Chicago: University of Chicago Press, 1980.

Willett, John, ed. and trans. *Brecht on Theatre.* New York: Hill & Wang, 1964.

Wilson, John Harold. *All the King's Ladies: Actresses of the Restoration.* Chicago: University of Chicago Press, 1958.

Yung, Bell. *Cantonese Opera: Performance as Creative Process.* Cambridge: Cambridge University Press, 1989.

Zarrilli, Phillip. "What Does It Mean to 'Become the Character': Power, Presence, and Transcendence in Asian In-body Disciplines of Practice." *By Means of Performance: Intercultural Studies of Theatre and Ritual.* Eds. Richard Schechner and Willa Appel. Cambridge: Cambridge University Press, 1990. 131–48.

Zeitlin, Judith. "Dislocations in Gender." *Historian of the Strange: Pu Songling and the Chinese Classical Tale.* Stanford: Stanford University Press, 1993. 98–131.

Zung, Cecilia S. L. *Secrets of the Chinese Drama: A Complete Explanatory Guide to Actions and Symbols as Seen in the Performance of Chinese Dramas*. 1937. New York: Benjamin Blom, 1964.

Recorded Material and Films

I   *Performances Recorded on Video or Released on Videocassette, VCD and DVD*

Baimian langjun 白面郎君 [The fair-faced gentleman]. Beijing Jingjuyuan [Beijing Opera Company of the City of Beijing]. Written by Weng Ouhong 翁偶虹. Leading players: Wen Ruhua 溫如華, Qin Xueling秦雪玲. CCTV, 1995.

Bawang bieji 霸王別姬 [Hegemon king says farewell to the concubine]. Beijing beifang Kunqu juyuan [Beijing Northern Kunqu Opera Company]. Leading players: Yang Fengyi 楊鳳一, He Yongxiang 賀永祥. Private collection. Video recording of a performance in Beijing, 1987.

——. Beijing beifang Kunqu juyuan [Beijing Northern Kunqu Opera Company]. Leading players: Dong Yaoqin 董瑤琴, He Yongxiang 賀永祥. Released by Mei Kei Hong Video Production Co., Ltd, Hong Kong. Video recording of a performance in Beijing, c. 1980s.

Beifang Kunqu Juyuan lao yishujia wutai yishu 北方崑曲劇院老藝術家舞台藝術 [The art of the senior artists of the Northern Kunqu Opera Company]. DVD. Produced by the Northern Kunqu Opera Company. Released by Beijing Dongfang Audio and Video Corporation, 2002.

Hu Jia Zhuang 扈家庄 [Hu's manor]. Leading players: Wang Zhiquan 王芝泉. Released by Jingding yingye youxian gongsi [Jingding Film Co. Ltd], Hong Kong. Video recording of a performance at Sun Beam Theatre, Hong Kong, 1987.

Liang Zhu/Lover, The 梁祝. Written and produced by Raymond To Kwok-wai 杜國威. Premiered Dec. 18, 1998-Jan. 13, 1999 in Hong Kong. Video CD. Universe Laser & Video Co. Ltd.

Tiangang zhen 天罡陣 [The Big Dipper battle formation]. Beijing beifang Kunqu juyuan [Beijing Northern Kunqu Opera Company]. Leading player: Yang Fengyi 楊鳳一. Private collection. Video recording of a performance at Jixiang Theatre in Beijing, November 26, 1988.

——. Beijing beifang Kunqu juyuan [Beijing Northern Kunqu Opera Company]. Leading player: Yang Fengyi 楊鳳一. Released by Mei Kei Hong Video Production Co., Ltd, Hong Kong. Video recording of a performance in Bejing, c. 1984.

Yangmen nüjiang 楊門女將 [Women generals of the Yang family]. Zhongguo Jingju yuan [The China Beijing Opera Company]. Leading players: Yang Qiuling 楊秋玲 and Wang Jinghua 王晶華. Released by Zhongguo luyin luxiang chuban zongshe [The Head Office of China Audiovisual Publishing Company]. Video recording of a performance in Beijing, January 1, 1991 for the celebration of the bicentennial anniversary of the entry of Anhui opera troupes into Beijing.

II Films

Bawang bieji 霸王別姬 [Hegemon king says farewell to the concubine]. China 1955. Dir. Wu Zuguang 吳祖光. Beijing Film Studio. Leading players: Mei Lanfang 梅蘭芳, Liu Lianrong 劉連榮.

Bawang bieji 霸王別姬／*Farewell My Concubine*. Hong Kong/China 1993. Dir. Chen Kaige 陳凱歌. Tomson (HK) Films Co. Ltd. in association with China Film Co-production Corporation and Beijing Film Studio. Leading players: Leslie Cheung 張國榮, Zhang Fengyi 張豐毅.

Liang Shanbo yu Zhu Yingtai 梁山伯與祝英台 [Liang Shanbo and Zhu Yingtai]. China 1953. Dir. Sang Hu 桑弧 and Huang Sha 黃沙. Shanghai Film Co. Leading players: Yuan Xuefen 袁雪芬, Fan Ruijuan 范瑞娟.

——. Hong Kong 1963. Dir. Li Han-hsiang 李翰祥. Hong Kong Shaw Brothers Studio. Leading players: Ling Po 凌波, Le Ti 樂蒂.

Liang Zhu 梁祝／*Lovers, The*. Hong Kong 1994. Dir. Tsui Hark 徐克. Golden Harvest/Film Workshop. Leading players: Nicky Wu 吳奇隆, Charlie Young 楊采妮.

Liang Zhu henshi 梁祝恨史 [The regretful story of Liang and Zhu].
Hong Kong 1958. Dir. Li Tik 李鐵. Zhili Film Co. Leading players:
Fong Yim-fen 芳艷芬, Yam Kim-fai 任劍輝.

M. Butterfly. US 1993. Dir. David Cronenberg. Geffen Films. Leading
players: Jeremy Irons, John Lone.

Yangmen nüjiang 楊門女將 [Women generals of the Yang family]. China
1960. Dir. Cui Wei 崔嵬, Chen Huai'ai 陳懷皚. Beijing Film Studio.
Leading players: Yang Qiuling 楊秋玲, Wang Jinghua 王晶華.

*Yang ± Yin: Gender in Chinese Cinema/Nanshengnüxiang: Zhongguo
dianying zhi xingbie* 男生女相：中國電影之性別. UK 1996. Dir.
Stanley Kwan 關錦鵬. British Film Institute.

III *Television*

20/20 Edition on the Story of Bernard Boursicot and Shi Pei-pu.
Reported by Barbara Walters. Prod. Kate Wenner Eisner. ABC
1992.

GLOSSARY

Baimao nü 白毛女
banbian tian 半邊天
Bao'enyuan 報恩緣
baoliu jumu 保留劇目
beidou xi 北斗戲
Beijing beifang Kunqu juyuan 北京北方崑曲劇院
Beijing Jingjuyuan 北京京劇院
Beijing junqu zhanyou Jingjutuan 北京軍區戰友京劇團
biaoyan yishujia 表演藝術家
biji 筆記
buduan geminglun 不斷革命論
buhen 補恨

Cairenfu 才人福
caizi jiaren 才子佳人
Canlu gushi 殘簍故事
canjun xi 參軍戲
Cao Jin Xiu 曹錦秀
Cao Xueqing 曹雪芹
caoshu 草書
changjianyou 倡兼優

changxi de 唱戲的
changxiang 常想
changyu 常欲
Chen Zigao 陳子高
chou 丑
Chuanju 川劇
chuanke 串客
chuanqi 傳奇
chuanshen lun 傳神論
chuanzibei 傳字輩
Chundengmi 春燈謎
Chunqiu pei 春秋配
ci 詞
cuiqiang 吹腔

Daimian 代面
Damian 大面
dan 旦
dan mo shuangquan 旦末雙全
danben 旦本
danjiao 旦角
daoban 導板
daomadan 刀馬旦
dayitong 大一統
dazhangfu 大丈夫
dianjiang 點將
Ding Jizhi 丁繼之
dingxing 定性
Dou'e yuan 竇娥冤
Du Jinfang 杜近芳
duanxiu 斷袖

fang 放
"Fangyou" 訪友
Fanhuameng 繁華夢
fengjian lunti 封建論題

fentao 分桃
Fuhutao 伏虎韜
fujing 副淨
fumo 副末

gaige he qiangjiu 改革和搶救
gongguo ge 功過格
gongming 功名
goulian 勾臉
guniang 姑娘
guoju 國劇

Han Shichang 韓世昌
Han Zigao 韓子高
hangdang 行當
Hao Zhenji 郝振基
haofang 豪放
He Peizhu 何佩珠
henshin 變身
Heyuan ji 合元記
Hongdong 洪洞
Honglou meng 紅樓夢
Hongxin cike sizhong 紅心詞客四種
Hujia zhuang 扈家莊
Hu Sanniang 扈三娘
hua 化
Hua Mulan/Fa Mulan 花木蘭
huadan 花旦
Huang Chonggu 黃崇嘏
huapu 花譜
hu'er 胡兒
"Huiyan" 會宴

jia 假
jia ban 家班
jian 兼

Jianghuameng 江花夢
jiaofang 教坊
jichu 基礎
jiefu 節婦
Jinsuo ji 金鎖記
jing 淨
"Jingju *Qiunü zhuan* jianjie" 京劇仇女傳簡介
Jingxi 京戲
jingzhong baoguo 精忠報國
Jixiang xiyuan 吉祥戲院
juan 卷
junmei 俊美

kai fengqi zhixian 開風氣之先
kao 靠
kaoqi 靠旗
kong 空
Kunju 崑劇
Kunqu 崑曲

Lan Ling 蘭陵
Li Hongchun 李洪春
Li Sao 離騷
lidi chengtian 立地撐天
Liang Mengzhao 梁孟昭
"Liang Shanbei tanpeng" 梁山杯探朋
"Liang Shanbo ouchi" 梁山伯藕池
Liang Xiaoyu 梁小玉
liangxiang 亮相
Liao 遼
Liaodong yaofu 遼東妖婦
Liaozhai zhiyi 聊齋誌異
lienü 烈女
Lihuameng 梨花夢
Liu Jinding 劉金定
liyuan 梨園

Long Xie 龍燮
longyang 龍陽
Longzhouhui 龍舟會
Lu Xun 魯迅
lüeduo 掠奪

Ma Fengcai 馬鳳彩
mao'er xi 髦兒戲/貓兒戲
Mei Baojiu 梅葆玖
Mei Lanfang 梅蘭芳
Meng Lijun 孟麗君
Mengzhongyuan 夢中緣
Mingzhu 明珠
moben 末本
moni 末泥
"Mulan ci" 木蘭辭

nandan 男旦
nandiao 男調
nanfeng 南風
nan'nü xianghun 男女相混
nanse 男色
nanzihan 男子漢
niangniang 娘娘
Nü shasimen 女殺四門
nü tongxingai 女同性愛
nü wusheng 女武生
nükao 女靠
nüxi 女戲
nüyue 女樂

onnagata 女形
otokoyaku 男役

Pei Yanling 裴艷伶
piaoyou 票友
Pu Songling 蒲松齡

Qian Dai 錢岱
qiandan 乾旦
Qianjin xiao 千金笑
Qiankunquan 乾坤圈
qiao 蹺
qiba 起霸
Qin Hui 秦檜
Qing'er 青兒
qingse 情色
qu 曲
Qu Yuan 屈原
qupai 曲牌
Quanfu ji 全福記
quanguo zhuanye Jingjutuan zhong zuihou yiwei nandan yanyuan
全國專業京劇團中最後一位男旦演員

rankou 髯口
renxi bufen cixiong tongzai 人戲不分 雌雄同在
renyao 人妖
Ruan Dacheng 阮大鋮

sanqu 散曲
se 色
seqing 色情
seyi jujia 色藝俱佳
seyi shuangquan 色藝雙全
seyi youwei dongren 色藝猶為動人
seyi zhijing, zhengyan duomei 色藝之精，爭妍奪美
shangyuan 尚圓
Shaoxing xi 紹興戲
Shen Qifeng 沈起鳳
shen 神
sheng 生
shengdan bianju 生旦變局
shengdan xi 生旦戲
shengde baijing junqiao 生得白淨俊俏

shenghuo zhong de biantai 生活中的變態
shengren zhi pantu 聖人之叛徒
shengse shuangli 聲色雙麗
shi 實／詩
Shi ji zhuan 詩集傳
Shi Xiaomei 石小梅
Shiba luohan dou Wukong 十八羅漢鬥悟空
Shiba luohan shou dapeng 十八羅漢收大鵬
Shiji 史記
shou 收
shuai 帥
Shun Shi Xiu 順時秀
sijia geji 私家歌姬
sizen denai 自然でない
Sima Qian 司馬遷
Song Changrong 宋長榮
Soushen ji 搜神記

tanci 彈詞
Tayaonian 踏搖娘
tianzi guose 天姿國色
tianzu 天足
tongzhi 同志
Tongzhi tiaoge 通制條格
tuzi 兔子

Wang Fuzhi 王夫之
Wang Yian 王怡庵
Wang Yun 王筠／王惲
Wang Zhiquan 王芝泉
wanyue 婉約
Wen Ruhua 溫如華
Weng Ouhong 翁偶虹
wenxi 文戲
Wenxingbang 文星榜
wenwu xiaosheng jian qingyi 文武小生兼青衣

Wu Xiangzheng 吳祥珍
wuhua 物化
"Wushang" 誤傷
wusheng 武生

xiandi 賢弟
xianmei 賢妹
Xiang Gu Shi 香谷氏
Xiangsiyan 相思硯
Xiang Yu 項羽
Xianglin xian 祥麟現
xiaodan 小旦
xiaofan 小蕃
xiaosheng 小生
xiaoshuo 小説
xiayao 下腰
Xie Xucai 謝絮才
Xieduo 諧鐸
xiju 戲劇
xin geju 新歌劇
xing 興/形
xiongdi 兄弟
xionghun 雄渾
xiqu 戲曲
xiu 秀
Xiuru ji 繡襦記
xiu'se kanchan 秀色堪餐
xiwen 戲文
Xixiang ji 西廂記
xizi 戲子
xu 虛
Xu Lin 徐霖

Yang Fengyi 楊鳳一
Yang Xiaolou 楊小樓
Yang Yanzhao 楊延昭

Yang Yongxiu 楊用修
"Yangdu" 羊肚
yanse 顏色
yanyuan 演員
yao 妖
Yao Ziyi 姚子翼
"Yeyan" 夜宴
yi 藝
yifu zhong 義婦塚
Yinhua lu 因話錄
Yishi bao 益世報
Yizhongyuan 意中緣
You Meng 優孟
You Tong 优桐
Youyuan jingmeng 游園驚夢
Yu Ji 虞姬
Yu yuanyang 玉鴛鴦
yuan 圓
Yuan dianzhang 元典章
Yuan Xuefen 袁雪芬
yuanben 院本
yuanman zhimei 圓滿之美
Yue Fei 岳飛
Yue Meiti 岳美緹
yuehu 樂戶
Yueju 越劇
Yuzan ji 玉簪記

zaju 雜劇
Zhan Xianting 詹湘亭
Zhang Jian 張堅
Zhang Junqiu 張君秋
"Zeng Songshi xu" 增宋氏序
Zengshu ji 贈書記
Zhang Lingyi 張令儀
zhanqun 戰裙

Zhao Lin 趙麟
Zhao Rongchen 趙榮琛
zhen 真／陣
Zheng Tianshou 鄭天壽
zhengdan 正旦
zhengzhong 正宗
zhengming 正名
zhengmo 正末
zhennai nüzhong haojie, jiang qi shishou haohao yanmai, shoubing
真乃女中豪傑，將其屍首好好掩埋，收兵
zhezixi 折子戲
Zhongdu Xiu 忠都秀
Zhongguo xiqu xuexiao 中國戲曲學校
Zhou Fenglin 周鳳林
Zhou Gao 周杲
Zhu Erye 祝二爺
Zhu Lian Xiu 朱簾秀
Zhu Xi 朱熹
zhuanchang 專場
zhuangdan 裝旦
zhuangyuan 狀元
zhuanye nüling 專業女伶
"Zhuzhuang fangyou" 竹莊訪友
zican jinguo 自慚巾幗
zise 姿色

INDEX